THE BOOK
OF
SACRED STONES

THE BOOK OF SACRED STONES

*Fact and Fallacy
in the Crystal World*

BARBARA G. WALKER

Photography by Werner P. Brodde

1817

HARPER & ROW, PUBLISHERS, SAN FRANCISCO

New York, Grand Rapids, Philadelphia, St. Louis
London, Singapore, Sydney, Tokyo, Toronto

Grateful acknowledgment is made for permission to quote from *The Spiritual Value of Gem Stones* by Wally and Jenny Richardson and Leonora Huett, Devorss and Company, Publisher, Marina del Rey, California, 1980; from *The Crystal Connection* by Randall N. and Vicki V. Baer, Harper & Row, Inc., Publishers, New York, New York, 1984; and from Daya Sarai Chocron, *Healing with Crystals and Gemstones*, copyright 1986 by Daya Sarai Chocron (York Beach, ME: Samuel Weiser, Inc., 1986) Used by permission.

FIRST EDITION
Designed by Donald Hatch

Library of Congress Cataloging-in-Publication Data
Walker, Barbara G.
    The book of sacred stones: fact and fallacy in the crystal world
/by Barbara G. Walker: photography by Werner P. Brodde.
        p.   cm.
    Bibliography: p.
    Includes index.
    ISBN 0-06-250921-7
    1. Precious stones—Miscellanea.   2. Gems—Miscellanea.
3. Crystals—Miscellanea.   4. Occultism—Controversial literature.
I. Title.
BF1442.P74W35   1989
133.3'22—dc19   88-46010
                                                          CIP

89 90 91 92 93 HAD 10 9 8 7 6 5 4 3 2 1

Contents

Acknowledgments

For their gift of willing helpfulness, I thank my husband, Gordon N. Walker; my photographer, Werner P. Brodde; and all those who kindly lent mineral specimens for photographing: Helga Brodde, Joseph Cilen, Allan W. Eckert, Lisa Miller, Nick Rochester, John Rudowski, Phyllis and Bud Schiffer, Susan Schmitt, Donna Wilshire, and the Morris Museum of Arts and Sciences.

By the earth that is Her flesh,
By the air that is Her breath,
By the fire that is Her bright spirit,
By the living waters of Her womb,
And by the stones that are Her bones,
May the Peace of the Goddess be in your heart,
And a piece of the Goddess
Be with you always.

MODIFIED WITCH CHANT

PART ONE

A Survey of Crystal Mythology and Culture

Introduction

During the last decade or two, something has been happening that has few parallels in history. A branch of natural science—meaning, in the old sense, "knowledge of nature"—has been undergoing a progress reversal. That is, general information about the field has moved backward, from knowledge to ignorance, instead of the other way.

Most of our understanding of our world evolved gradually out of earlier errors. Chemistry evolved from alchemy. Astronomy evolved from astrology. Medicine evolved from magic. Zoology evolved from crude medieval bestiaries. Mineralogy evolved from primitive crystal mysticism: that is, ancient notions about the magical properties of stones. Gradually, real knowledge comes to replace earlier mistakes.

Rarely does it happen that a firmly established body of empirical knowledge is virtually ignored by a generation that seems bent on replacing it with superstitious error, and even believes its own fantasies to be a superior kind of knowledge, "higher" than the provable kind. This is happening now in the field of mineralogy.

Modern crystal mysticism deals with a subject about which much has been discovered. Yet practitioners pay almost no attention to those discoveries. Books of crystal mysticism proliferate, filled with misinformation. The composition, properties, even names of various minerals are misrepresented, misspelled, misstated, or simply absent because the writers have not cared to read about their subject.

Another notable occurrence of this sort took place around the beginning of the Christian era, when violently anti-intellectual forces in an advanced but effete society caused a rapid decline of education and a wave of crudely superstitious cults, the so-called mystery religions, which included Christianity itself. Emphasis on spirituality at the expense of rationality was a root cause of the Dark Ages. Into a limbo of forgetfulness went most of the ancients' hard-won expertise in engineering, building, navigation, medicine, and arts and crafts, and much miscellaneous knowledge of of the natural world. Schools were closed. Books and libraries were burned. The quest for empirical knowledge was condemned as devilish.

It took more than a thousand years for European civilization to begin to climb out of the pit of ignorance that was created in those dark times. Spiritual authorities did not help the ascent, but resisted it at every stage, even turning on some of the knowledge-seekers in frenzied hatred and burning them at the stake.

Today there are some early signs of a possible new wave of barbarism: the spread of illiteracy, religious fanaticism, irrational beliefs, inaccuracy, and indifference to proven facts. Modern crystal mysticism may be part of this trend. It is based on the very real human attraction to beautiful natural objects, but it also takes advantage of other human characteristics, such as the disinclination for disciplined learning.

It is the premise of this book that crystal mysticism can be a valid and rewarding study, potentially rich in appreciation of our Mother Earth; but not as it is being disseminated at present. The current level of crystal mystics' comprehension of their subject signifies a deplorably lazy attitude toward learning. Ignorance may feel comfortable, but in the long run it hurts. Much knowledge has been gained about minerals and crystals in the last two centuries or so. This knowledge should not be ignored or falsified. We can hardly expect to understand our Mother Earth by rejecting what has been discovered about her so far.

Therefore, this work is presented in the hope of shedding light into a growing cloud of darkness, and in the conviction that, to those who love Mother Earth, all stones are sacred stones.

For the Love of Stones

Nearly every morning, to begin my day, I enter the room where my collected mineral specimens occupy shelves and cabinets. My hand automatically goes out to pick up one or two of these objects. I never quite know which of them my hand will choose until the choice is made. I don't know the reason for a particular choice on a particular day. But, having chosen, I carry the object(s) to a chair by a window and settle down to meditate, preferably in a stream of sunlight that can illuminate the internal features of transparent stones.

The meditation begins with a process that I call making myself microscopic. As a mere particle, infinitely small, I enter the fantastic landscapes and structures that imagination can see within almost any transparent crystal that has internal cracks, veils, fracture planes, and refractive surfaces. I turn the stone slowly, finding a different scene with every new angle, a different perspective of color with every change of orientation to the light.

I walk on vast white plains of snow under a dark, starry sky. I see a great silver tower rising in the distance, beside a lake so mirror-bright that it might be glassy smooth ice or still water. Then I am in a dense forest of tall, straight tree trunks, reflecting themselves in a deep river. With another turn of the crystal I enter an enormous gateway between two frost-white marble pylons, so huge that they seem to reach the sky. Ahead lies a long ascending staircase, going up and up to an unknown destination lost in thick mist. Another turn of the crystal, and here is a stage backed by rippling, luminous curtains, where fantastically costumed figures are frozen in postures of a distorted dance.

Today I may have chosen an undistinguished-looking quartz point, which might appear to the casual observer as a six-sided chunk of flawed colorless glass. But the casual observer wouldn't know what brilliant colors are to be seen in that apparent transparency. As the sunlight strikes various fracture planes within, my stone blazes with rainbows. I see splendid iridescent scarves, butterfly wings, sheets of colored sequins, jeweled crowns. I walk among arches of green and gold flame, pillars draped with hot pink, strange pools colored a rich turquoise with banks of icy silver. I see drifts of sparkling stars, much like the glitter of sunlight on new-fallen snow. I see a thousand Christmas-tree lights. I enter a glowing golden castle and find an entire wall painted with colored light. Tilting the crystal ever so little in different directions, I can make the light change through a whole spectrum of gem colors: ruby, topaz, emerald, sapphire, amethyst.

This is an amazing world to be found in a simple stone, a chunk of silicon dioxide, one of the world's commonest minerals, the stuff of ordinary sand and of a large proportion of the earth's crust. Quartz is a member of that vast family of silicates that make up 80 percent of all rocks. It is hard, durable, inert. It can't be scratched by a steel blade. It can't dissolve in water, or even in most strong acids. It can't be magnetized. It can't conduct an electrical current and therefore functions as a good insulator. All the foregoing qualities will assume particular significance in subsequent discussion. Quartz does possess the property of piezoelectricity, but that is quite different from being an electrical conductor.

I know these things about my quartz crystal, but at the moment I think about it poetically rather than physically. I see it as a distillation of the beauty and mystery of my Mother Earth, an artwork created unseen in the darkness of her universal womb over hundreds of thousands of years. This object that I hold in my hand is probably older than the human race. It is like holding a piece of time. With infinite patience, its molecular layers were deposited eon after slow eon in Gaea's hot amniotic soup. Now I can turn it about in my fingers and find whole worlds of wonder in this child of her dark underworld.

How ephemeral seem all human creations, however beautiful, when compared to this simple stone. It is with something akin to reverence that I put it back on my shelf in the place that it occupies for this brief moment in time. I can't say where it has been or where it will be when I—and perhaps even my entire species—have passed into oblivion. But for the moment, it is here.

Every quartz crystal is as different from every other one as human faces and bodies are from one another. The same is true of all the other mineral specimens in my collection, or anyone's, for Nature never repeats herself. Each specimen shows me different scenes, colors, structures. Even those that have become familiar can surprise me with new images each day.

The nontransparent minerals too are full of images. Here, for example, is a heavy block of galena, sulfide of lead, the silver gray ore that provided the opaque crystals of the old-time crystal radio. Each time I pick up this piece, I see a different configuration of the walls, turrets, columns, stairways, windows, and towering constructions of mysterious machinery that seem to be carved in low relief all over its surface. Over here is a cluster of brown aragonite crystals: a miniature petrified forest, with mineralized logs tumbled about in every direction, flashing reflected points of sunlight on the wall. Here is an agate geode, showing me a wonderful Aladdin's cave in a richly colored desert landscape.

Spending a few moments each day with my mineral treasures is one of the ways I center myself and feel calmed. To those who love them, minerals are undeniably soothing. Granted, they don't return one's love, as do family members, friends, or pets. Yet one tends to invest them with something like personality, or at least uniqueness, and to respond to them *as if* they were sentient.

There is a sensual pleasure in handling them, just as there is a sensual pleasure in stroking the fur of a cat or dog. Thus, they seem to react to the sense of touch as well as to that of sight. Some people actually give them names and talk to them the way one talks to a pet. Somehow, the fact that they were created by Nature and not by humans seems to give them a kind of liveliness that mere artifacts cannot emulate.

Of course their supreme attractiveness to the majority of human beings has made those minerals we call gems the world's most wanted (and therefore most expensive) objects. Gems become artifacts, in a sense, being cut, polished, and mounted in ways that people believe enhance their beauty. Today, gemstones can even be artificially created, chemically and physically identical with the natural stones and less flawed. The lapidary's products have always been objects of desire. But in the recent wave of amateur mineral collectors and rock lovers like myself and thousands of others something new has been happening.

Indeed, this recent wave could be described as an inundation. After decades of ignoring mineralogy's subject matter, the general public has suddenly developed such eminently commercializable cravings for it that a whole new industry of rock shops and mineral shows has sprung up. Prices of raw minerals have gone through the roof, several times over. Many sources have been virtually mined out to keep up with the demand.

Gemstones are still as desirable as ever—more so, if anything—but almost equally desirable are many other minerals that would have gone unnoticed in the recent past. Dealers find it possible to sell for high prices such unglamorous rocks, such flawed and broken bits, as they would have discarded as worthless only fifteen or twenty years ago. The new mineral fanciers know less and want more than any group of people previously connected with the field. Even some dealers remain ignorant of the real nature of the materials they sell, having found that they can make a profit without troubling to learn anything about the abstruse and rather difficult subject of mineralogy. All they need to know is how far up the retail price can be pushed in any given year.

Nor has the demand brought about much improvement in the way minerals are extracted from their mother rock. Whole crystals have become rarities, in a market where broken, chipped specimens—blasted out of the matrix with dynamite and carelessly treated afterward—are still quite salable.

Clearly, there is a crystal craze in progress. Thousands of people are collecting crystals, for a variety of reasons. Some consider them easily resalable investments. Some delight in their aesthetic qualities. Some are fascinated by the science of mineralogy that deals with them. Some want to practice lapidary work as a hobby or a profession. Some view minerals as mystical, magical objects possessing sundry occult powers—a view found in nearly every human culture since prehistory. In fact, some of the very same beliefs held in antiquity about the mysterious powers of stones are still current in some circles today.

There is an amazingly broad spectrum of opinion about the proper study and use of crystal specimens, ranging from the strictly mineralogical to the strictly mystical. Usually, the followers of one school of thought don't want to know anything about the other. Crystal mystics commonly betray a grotesque ignorance of the very subject on which they claim expertise, that is, minerals—not to mention the basic principles of geology, chemistry, and physics as they apply to minerals. Conversely, professional mineralogists dismiss the claims of "crystal healers" that diseases can be cured by contact with certain stones as beneath contempt, too absurd to be noticed.

This present book seeks a middle ground where sound mineralogical study can enhance a sense of the beauty and mystery—even spirituality—of these eminently material objects. As Nature's artworks, stimulating to the imagination, attractive to the eye and hand, minerals have much to offer those who respond to them on an emotional level. Yet surely it insults their beauty and their venerable age to ignore the known facts about them, worse yet, to misrepresent those facts or distort them into foolishness. There is a need to demystify some of the more superstitious beliefs about minerals, while at the same time fully realizing their value as poetic metaphor and sacred symbol. Finding the middle ground may be a worthy goal for many who feel drawn toward the blossoms of Nature's underground rock gardens.

The modern crystal craze has some very disturbing aspects. Chief among these is the widespread dissemination of false information under the rubric of "higher truth" in countless books and pamphlets and in shops and lecture halls. Many self-styled experts do not even bother to learn the correct spelling of the minerals they discuss, let alone their real physical or chemical properties. To such irresponsible minds, any blurring or distortion of the truth seems unimportant. If they choose to contradict proven facts of mineralogy, geology, crystallography, or physiology, they feel that no harm is done. They say people are free to believe anything they want to believe, regardless of whether the belief can be scientifically justified or not. At other times, however, they are anxious to claim scientific validity for notions that are obvious nonsense.

There are no excuses for people who pretend to educate the public while actually misleading, that is, ignoring the true and proven while earnestly professing the untrue and impossible. Nature is a great teacher, but she instructs only those who come to her in honest humility, ready to labor at assimilating earlier lessons. Knowledge of nature does not come to the mentally lazy, who prefer subjective imagination to disciplined study.

Imagination is fine as metaphor, poetry, meditation, self-enrichment. Imagination is necessary. The world would be a dull place without it. But imagination is not the path to empirical knowing. The absurd mistakes of numerous crystal mystics offer ample evidence of this.

Our remote ancestors also made many absurd mistakes about mineralogical matters. They had, however, the excellent excuse that there was very little genuine knowledge at that time to point up the absurdities. They knew almost nothing about the chemical and physical properties of stones. They did not even know the real elements, those basic building blocks of all matter. Their simplistic "elements" earth, air, fire, and water could never have provided a true picture of Earth's composition. The complex crust of their planet was a great mystery to the ancients. What little they could observe, lacking today's sophisticated tests and techniques, gave them only pinpoints of knowledge. On such pinpoints they built mighty top-heavy structures of myth and imagination.

This is understandable. But it is discouraging to find many of these same ancient myths, with variations, seriously repeated today—in flagrant denial of all that has been painstakingly learned in the interim. There is a need to tie together the ancient myths and the modern ones, to trace the pathways of superstition through the centuries, and to discover the subconscious reasons behind them.

The true lover of Nature wants to know her truly.

I love my stones. I can make up stories about them endlessly. I can "feel" many kinds of responses to them. They can comfort and/or inspire me. They can influence my emotions. Having been so captivated by minerals, I am familiar with all manifestations of the hobbyist's obsession: mysterious sensations of affinity, the urge to carry about and handle certain pieces, the sound of the "spirit voices" that seem to speak inside one's head. I know the subtle warmth or tingling of the hands that approach a mineral's surface (actually, a reflection of the hands' own warmth, which can be sensed from almost anything). I know the pleasant spell cast by points of light moving within a transparent gem. I know the paths whereby intense concentration on a stone can lead one into the complex world of the unconscious. I know the awe inspired by the beauty and longevity of mineral forms.

Over and above all this, however, I know that the realities of the mineralogical realm are more wondrous than anything even the most creative human mind can invent. So I want to know even more: my minerals' origins, ages, proper names, chemical composition, physical attributes, habits of formation. Although these objects may help connect me with my inner self, I want the other connections also, those that bring me knowledge of the external world in which they exist, and have existed long before me, and will exist long after me.

Many who write about the "magic" of minerals waste their own and their readers' time by presenting imaginative fantasy in the guise of fact. It is irresponsible, to say the least, to "educate" the public into literal belief in nonsense. There is nothing wrong with fantasy per se, as long as it is understood to be mental play, not mental work. One can learn from play, too. But when some misguided souls undertake to misguide others into perceiving fantasies as real, then society as a whole succumbs to a creeping tide of ignorance.

In our society, women are particularly inclined to support almost any alternative approach to the mystic and the spiritual that may come along—not because women are more gullible than men, but because established patriarchal religion continues to deny women access to creative decision making on spiritual issues. The official morality is not women's morality. The official theology does not spring from the feminine spirit, but continues to deny the full importance or divinity of that spirit. Women who feel themselves drawn toward the spiritual side of their nature, then, crave new ways to apply their inner feelings to daily life. Without fully articulating their reasons, even to themselves, they find the rigid theologies of patriarchal gods incompatible. So they look elsewhere. Many women find some measure of spiritual authority—or at least, permission to develop a personal belief system—in various branches of occultism and shamanistic magic.

Therefore it is especially necessary for women to consider carefully the ideas presented by crystal mysticism and related subjects, keeping in mind that as women they might be particularly vulnerable to exploitation by irrational systems. Women not only need a skeptical attitude toward "revealed" religious patriarchy, they also need a skeptical attitude toward the more modern self-styled authorities who use female yearnings and spiritual needs to further their own fortune.

Women love beautiful things, so they are easily drawn to the beautiful bones of our Mother Earth, finding in stones much sensual satisfaction for both hand and eye. Such satisfaction is the true basis of crystal mysticism. The movement is fundamentally aesthetic rather than scientific; that is why so many colossally unscientific errors can be perpetrated within it, and repeated, and believed.

Yet there are many devoted crystal fanciers who feel ashamed of the irresponsible self-styled teachers, the callously exploitive publicizers, the crude and childish books that demean these lovely objects by telling silly lies about them. Mother Earth's sacred bones deserve better treatment. Her human children, also, deserve better information. Instead of contradicting the painfully acquired knowledge of the last two centuries or so, and retreating into Dark Ages of ignorance, crystal mysticism deserves to become worthy of acceptance by the educated as a legitimate mode of aesthetic appreciation and profound symbolic significance.

Stones are exquisite symbols of our Earth, which the ancients personified as the primal Mother Goddess who gave birth to all living things, and who was variously called Gaea, Terra, Ops, Demeter, Ceres, Hertha, Hawah, Eve, Mama, Maya, Hel, Hathor, Cybele, Prithivi, and hundreds of other names. In prepatriarchal times, humans perceived their own lives as essentially united with all other life forms and with Earth herself, as members of the same universal maternal clan. Such a philosophy fostered deeper respect for the land, its plants and animals, its rocks and soil, than did later philosophies that viewed all nature as "man's" inferior, soulless, exploitable possession.

Science now shows that the ancient "primitive" peoples had a better grasp of the reality than their more civilized successors. Earth's minerals are in fact the essential substances of all life forms. They are extracted from the rocks by water, wind, and weather, to become soil; extracted from the soil by plants, from the plants by herbivorous animals, and from such animals in turn by the flesh eaters, like ourselves. The vast diversity of living species on this planet is ultimately dependent on minerals, which enter into every nutrient substance that supports each life, from the smallest virus or bacterium to the greatest whale. We all are literally made of minerals. In a sense, then, we are indeed flesh of Mother Earth's flesh and bone of her bone.

Therefore, we have every reason to respect and revere Earth's mineral treasures, to contemplate their beauty in fitting awareness of their necessity to our very lives. In a way, our arbitrary division of all things into organic and inorganic is misleading, because there is continual intimate exchange between the two. Many minerals called inorganic are really essential parts of the existence of every organic form, drawing their elements from the same basic list. When we devote some time to deep esthetic appreciation of any crystalline mineral, we make an intellectual/ emotional connection with basic life substances. As all the cycles of creation were symbolized as Mother Earth by Her ancient worshipers, so all the complex interchanges of substance in geological and biological processes may be symbolized by mineral specimens that draw our attention. It is not a simplistic relationship that we can perceive, but a valid symbol of nature's infinite variety.

In this sense, the Chinese have long regarded rocks as foci of mystical contemplation. Chinese writings include some profound responses to this procedure. Kong Chuan's introduction to the catalog of Du Wan says:

> The purest essence of the energy of the heaven-earth world coalesces into rock. It emerges, bearing the soil. Its formations are wonderful and fantastic. Some with cavernous cliffs, revealing their interior; some with peaks and summits in sharp-edged layers. . . . The images of all things appearing in appropriate likenesses. Within the size of a fist can be assembled the beauty of a thousand cliffs. . . . The Sage [Confucius] once said, "The humane man loves mountains," and the love of stones has the same meaning. Thus longevity through quietude is achieved through this love.[1]

We may start by loving stones because they are beautiful. But what are they besides? What makes their beauty? What is their true nature? What worlds lie within them, waiting to be discovered?

1. Hay, 38.

What Is a Crystal?

What is the most familiar, common crystallized mineral on the face of the earth? Answer: ice. Water is a mineral, hydrogen oxide. Fortunately for the existence of life on this planet, water is one of the most widespread and stable of all mineral compounds. (Still, one misguided mystic calls it "unstable"!)[1]

Liquid, by definition, is noncrystalline. But when the temperature of liquid water falls below 32 degrees Fahrenheit, it crystallizes. Freezing is a synonym for crystallization.

The Greek name for ice is *krystallos*. Ancient Greeks gave this name to rock crystal (quartz) because they erroneously thought quartz was fossilized ice—that is, ice frozen so hard that it could never melt again. They were closer to the truth than they knew. Since crystallization is the same as freezing, all the earth's crystalline minerals are solidly frozen. The temperatures at which they pass from liquid to solid form may be hundreds or thousands of degrees higher than the freezing point of water, but the principle is the same.

The only other mineral that remains liquid through normal temperatures is mercury, which crystallizes at −38 degrees Fahrenheit. Polar explorers and other people in cold places find their mercury thermometers frozen and useless when temperatures fall below that point.

The word *crystal* means a mineral substance frozen into its solid state. Its molecules have arranged themselves in a comparatively rigid three-dimensional lattice. There is a characteristic lattice pattern for each different mineral. Nearly all the rocks and metals of the earth's crust are formed of such crystals.

Not all solid minerals are crystalline, however. A few have chilled from the liquid to the solid state too fast for crystals to form. This often happens in lava ejected from volcanoes to the earth's surface, where it cools rapidly. Such solids are defined as "glass." Obsidian is a common example of natural volcanic glass.

Glass is the opposite of crystal. In a glass, the molecules have no orderly lattice pattern. They are arranged at random, like the molecules of a liquid. Glass is actually a hardened liquid, or noncrystalline gel. Unlike crystalline material, glass has no specific freezing (or melting) point. As its temperature is raised, glass softens gradually over a wide range of degrees before liquefying altogether.

Thus, the common habit of referring to glassware as "crystal" is misleading. Whatever its composition, however nicely it may be cut or shaped, glass is not crystalline and never will be.

Quartz and other crystallized minerals feel colder to the touch than glass. The reason for this is that the crystal's orderly lattice pattern conducts heat away from the hand faster than the disorderly internal structure of glass can do it.

Natural crystals come in all sizes. Sometimes a single crystal can be many feet in length and can weigh tons. Sometimes a mineral can consist of microscopically small crystals that can't be seen by the naked eye. Such minerals give a false appearance of smooth, "glassy" texture. The various forms of chalcedony—agates, onyxes, jaspers, carnelians—are common examples of microcrystalline or cryptocrystalline minerals.

In general, rapid cooling of the mineral melt produces smaller crystals than slow cooling. Big crystals can take a long time to grow. It is thought that some of the larger quartz crystals are two hundred thousand to three hundred thousand years old. A magma intrusion, rising as liquid into the earth's crust from beneath, can take as long as a million years to solidify completely, that is, for all its component minerals to crystallize. Since each mineral has its own individual freezing point, the component minerals crystallize at different temperatures as the melt cools down.

Mineralogists recognize six basic crystal systems, which they call isometric, hexagonal, tetragonal, orthorhombic, monoclinic, and triclinic. These in turn are divided into thirty-two crystal classes based on the various axes of symmetry within the crystalline lattice. Still, minerals are not always easy to classify on the basis of superficial appearances. These can take many different forms in nature. The latter appearances are known as mineral "habits," meaning the forms that minerals can take in the course of their growth under normal conditions. According to their habits, the crystals of various minerals can form cubes, blades, needles, clothlike fibers (like asbestos), thin plates (like mica), or masses resembling kidneys, wheat sheaves, or bunches of grapes. Some minerals, such as tourmaline and beryl, form vertically striated columns. Others, such as marcasite, form serrated "coxcombs." Others make cottony puffs, threadlike tangles, or imitation roses. Often, the crystals of one mineral will grow around and enclose crystals of another that have formed earlier, thus creating what are called inclusions.

Many people use the word *crystalline* as a synonym for transparent, which tends to foster the false impression that crystalline minerals are only those that can be seen through. Nothing could be further from the truth. The majority of crystals in nature are opaque. Even gem material (like ruby, sapphire, diamond, emerald, garnet, for example) is more often opaque than transparent; this is why the transparent stones are regarded as rare and therefore expensive. Many minerals that are normally opaque will occasionally form transparent crystals. Sometimes these crystals can be used as gems, but only if they are hard enough.

It's really the quality of hardness, rather than transparency, that determines whether or not a mineral is a gem material. Minerals used as jewelry must be hard enough to take and hold a surface polish. A stone to be cut and faceted must be hard enough to retain the sharp edges of the facets; otherwise they soon become worn down and dull. Some minerals form beautiful transparent crystals that would make splendid jewelry, were it not that they are too soft to resist being damaged by every casual bump or knock—even by dirt or dust in the air. Dust particles can have edges sharp enough to abrade the polished surface.

A standard hardness scale is known to mineralogists as the Mohs scale. (Some crystal mystics—frequently weak spellers—make it "Moh's," or even "Mohr.")[2] Each mineral's relative hardness falls somewhere between 1 and 10 on this scale, according to which other minerals it can scratch or be scratched by. Talc, the softest mineral, has a grade of 1. Diamond, the hardest, has a grade of 10. Those in between are typified by (in ascending order) gypsum, calcite, fluorite, apatite, microcline, quartz, topaz, and corundum. It's preferable for jewelry stones to be at least as hard as quartz (number 7) or better. Softer stones are used for jewelry, but eventually they show signs of damage.

It is one of the marvels of the mineral world that two different crystalline forms of exactly the same mineral stand at both the top and the bottom of the Mohs hardness scale. The mineral is the element carbon. Diamond (hardness 10) is pure carbon. So is graphite (hardness 1), the soft black stuff popularly known as the "lead" in a lead pencil. Not only elemental carbon but many other minerals too are capable of assuming outward forms so different as to seem quite unrelated until their true chemical nature is revealed. Calcite alone has about three hundred crystal forms.

Like everything else created by Mother Nature, this mineral world looks comparatively simple until we begin to investigate its real character—which turns out to be enormously complex. The precise mechanisms of crystal formation are not yet fully understood. We do know, however, that all life on this earth is dependent on those mineral substances that make up the planet's crust and, in the process, sometimes produce those "flowers of the underworld" that have always delighted the human eye and stimulated the human imagination.

Unfortunately, imagination often overpowers common sense. One of the more imaginative ideas about crystals, which commands widespread if undeserved credence today, is the idea that they radiate a subtle, imperceptible energy, just as a fire radiates perceptible energy in the forms of heat and light. Some stones, such as large quartz crystals, are commonly called "generators" because they are supposed to be putting out a radiant energy that can be transmitted to other materials.

Only people ignorant of the basic laws of physics could believe this. One of nature's rules is that energy is produced by breaking down existing forms of matter. Fire gives off its heat and light energy by burning something—that is, by destroying the former substance of the fuel. Our local star, the sun—from which earth's energies ultimately derive—radiates enormous quantities of energy by consuming its own substance in a perpetual nuclear holocaust.

Here on earth, the minerals that really do give off some kind of energy are the radioactive ones. They break down their own substance, which is thereby converted into a different, more inert mineral. A quartz crystal, however, is not radioactive. Like other forms of silica, it is physically stable and chemically inert. It does not deplete its own substance. It just sits there. Quartz's hardness, durability, and resistance to chemical breakdown are direct consequences of this self-contained inertia.

Uninformed quartz enthusiasts point to the piezoelectric property of the mineral as proof of its energy-producing potential. This is one of those apples-and-oranges comparisons that sound rational but are not. Piezoelectricity does not mean that a mineral is producing electric current out of itself, all on its own. Piezoelectricity refers to the ability of some minerals (quartz among them) to develop a tiny static charge when the crystal lattice is momentarily deformed by mechanical pressure. Conversely, an external electric current can cause mechanical pulsation in the crystal. The frequency of this pulsation can be precisely controlled by the crystal's orientation. For example, a minutely thin plate of synthetic quartz (preferred for its superior uniformity over natural quartz) can be cut to the right angle to maintain any given frequency in an oscillator, watch, or other frequency-stabilizing mechanism. But the crystal is not a battery, capable of producing its own electricity. Energy must be supplied from outside. When there is no energy supply, the crystal lattice assumes its normal nonreactive condition.

Quartz will not even allow an electric current to pass through it. Like glass, quartz is a nonconductor and therefore a good insulator. Neither will quartz allow itself to be magnetized, nor will it respond to a magnetic field. Crystal mystics who frequently and fondly refer to the alleged electromagnetic properties of quartz are simply babbling a word they like the sound of. Electromagnetism is alien to the entire family of silicate minerals.

Pyroelectricity is another term poorly understood and much misrepresented by crystal mystics. This term refers to a mineral's propensity to develop a static charge when heated. Tourmaline is a good example of a pyroelectric mineral. But neither pyroelectricity nor piezoelectricity mean the same as generating or transmitting an electric current. Conductors, such as metals, pass electric current via loose electrons that actually flow through the material. The majority of minerals have no such loose electrons and therefore do not conduct electric current.

Another fact that mystics seldom understand is that many minerals are in series, inconsistent in their composition. Different specimens contain different proportions of their elemental components. For example, a sulfate having nine times as much strontium as barium might be called celestite, and a sulfate having nine times as much barium as strontium might be called barite; but there are also all possible proportions in between. At the midpoint of the series, the mineral is really neither the one nor the other but a balance of both. Mother Nature resists tidy classification. Yet a crystal mystic will cheerfully assign different properties to the same mineral under different names, or to different members of a series, without realizing that they may differ only in degree.

Mystics love to imagine that the alleged energies and forces given off by minerals are so subtle as to be perceptible only to acutely sensitive persons like themselves, so they alone are capable of describing mineral properties. One of their favorite notions is that these exquisitely subtle mineral energies can penetrate human flesh as easily as X rays, and "align" or "balance" the internal structures of the human body in imitation of the crystal lattice. This is said to heal the sick (by a mechanism not perceptible to scientific or medical verification) through "vibrations," a confused reference to the natural oscillations of atomic or molecular particles. Yet the same "vibrations" occur not just in rocks and minerals but in every form of matter: plastic, rubber, nylon, tooth enamel, rose petals, insect chitin (exoskeleton material), tree sap, wood, coal, bacteria, or industrial waste.

Moreover, living cells bear no resemblance to mineral structures, and are not physically affected by proximity to them, except in the case of radioactive minerals—the only ones that can be said to give off energy in any real sense. And their effect on animal tissues is not generally beneficial.

Another of the mystics' favorite errors is the notion that crystals have "high-frequency" vibrations or "high rates" of vibration; that is, more vibratory movement than other solid objects. This is false. A crystalline lattice occurs because the component molecules or ions are stacked together as tightly as possible, which means that the movement of particles within the lattice is maximally restricted. To freeze into a crystalline form, particles lose energy and indulge in less random motion. They move less, not more. The solidity and relative inertia of most mineral compounds are produced by the rigidity of their structures, which allows the component particles less movement than in a liquid or a gas.

"Crystal healings" work sometimes: not through imaginary vibrations but through the power of the mind, assuming that the patient is convinced of the possibility of healing and that the condition is amenable to mental manipulation. Holy water, Bibles, crucifixes, saints' bones, sharks' teeth, lucky stones, medals, and a thousand other amulets and talismans have worked the same way over many centuries.

It is not necessary to subscribe to any superstitious belief, however, to feel strongly drawn to minerals. Quite aside from any crude magic that may be attributed to them, nature's inorganic flowers are fascinating in themselves. Inventions of the self-styled Higher Consciousness or New Age mind turn out to be childish indeed by comparison with the realities of crystal structures, habits, qualities, chemical nature, and histories of formation.

The earth's crust is the underlying support of our whole living biosphere, both metaphorically and literally. Organic life first evolved out of inorganic constituents, the minerals. Earth is indeed our ultimate mother—not just her food-producing soil, but her very rocks, from which soil is created. No civilization would be possible without the inorganic resources that Earth provides. With good reason we recognize the earliest attempts at civilization occurring in an Age of Stone.

Virtually all stones are crystalline. When you pick up any common rock, you hold a complex aggregate of crystal forms in which the microscope can discern miraculous worlds of shape and color. When you stand on an ordinary beach, you are surrounded by millions of tons of crystalline quartz, identical in its essential nature to the psychic's quartz crystal ball or the mystic's "generator." One grain of sand is composed of the same arrangements of atoms as the most gigantic crystal of the same substance. Comparative size as perceived by human eyes is meaningless on the atomic level. Whether a single crystal is forty or fifty feet long, or too small to be seen by any unaided human eye, it is still the same material having all the same attributes.

It has long been an Oriental custom to treasure ordinary rocks for their aesthetic qualities and the spiritual insights that they suggest. Chinese gardens have usually included some interesting boulders for contemplation. Even indoor plant arrangements could be considered incomplete without some stone formation as an essential design element.

In combination with serious study of mineralogical realities, aesthetic-spiritual approaches to the mineral world can greatly enhance our appreciation of this precious planet, Spaceship Earth, the only home we will ever have. The true value of crystal mysticism lies in increased awareness of the mineral elements that make up our living environment, including the internal environment of our own bodies. Rocks, plants, insects, fishes, bacteria, and all other living things are made out of the same assortment of elements. Crystals are extremely rare in living tissues, whereas they are the usual forms in the inorganic world. Apparently ignorant of this, some crystal mystics now talk of "crystalline" components in human blood, lymph, or hormones.[3] In reality, biochemical reactions in human cells do not normally involve any crystallization. Crystallized deposits are pathological, like kidney stones or the uric acid salt crystals that cause gout.

Some crystal mystics are even confused about the distinction between crystals and cut glass, which is often misleadingly called lead crystal.[4] Others, equally confused, think the word *crystal* applies only to quartz, or they call "noncrystalline" such cryptocrystalline minerals as the chalcedonies, in which the crystals are too small to be seen without a microscope but are certainly present.[5]

There is also much disagreement about the alleged mystical properties of various minerals and about whether they are or are not changed by the artificial cuttings and polishings of jewelry manufacture. Crystal mystics are especially fuzzy on the subject of synthesized gemstones, whose very existence threatens many favorite mystical theories.

To eliminate some of the confusion, jewelry stones and other minerals may be divided into four groups: (1) imitations, (2) synthetics, (3) cut natural material, and (4) uncut natural material.

Imitations. Into the category of imitations fall many types of costume jewelry "stones" with the superficial appearance of precious gems. The most common material for these is cut or molded glass, which jewelers call *paste*. Also used are plastics, resins, ceramics, and cheap natural stones dyed to resemble something else. Throughout history, jewels have been doctored up in a thousand ways to fool the unwary into paying the price of a more expensive product.

Imitations are not always frauds, however. They may be sold without any misrepresentation as inexpensive make-believe. Now considered legitimate, too, are doublet or triplet stones. The former are constructed of an upper crown of precious material, cemented onto a base of something cheaper, like quartz or glass. The latter resemble a three-layer sandwich: a very thin slice of precious material between a transparent cap and base. These are no longer considered fraudulent, because (in theory, at least) the buyer is told how the gem is created. This rule also applies to frankly synthetic products made to imitate diamonds, such as cubic zirconia, lithium niobate, strontium titanate, and titanium dioxide. Sometimes a very naive buyer might be conned into paying diamond prices for such material, but as a rule it is sold simply for what it is.

Synthetics. After the invention of the Verneuil flame fusion furnace about 1900, it became possible to synthesize corundum and spinel. Later methods produced synthetic beryl, quartz, garnet, and other minerals. These are chemically and physically identical to their natural counterparts, having the same hardness, specific gravity, and composition.

Synthetic rubies, sapphires, and quartz are preferred for use in watches and electronic equipment because they are more perfect than natural stones, with fewer flaws, inclusions, and structural variations. For the same reasons, synthetic stones make better (and much cheaper) jewelry. Still, people prefer to pay high prices for natural stones because of a seemingly ineradicable false belief that *synthetic* is synonymous with *imitation*. Crystal mystics have the same belief, and usually treat synthetics with disdain.

Cut natural material. Natural stones, cut into facets or polished as cabochons (unfaceted gems), have been jewelers' stock in trade for centuries. Ruby, emerald, sapphire, diamond, garnet, topaz, aquamarine, and amethyst gems were created for the adornment of the wealthy. Today many other stones of inferior hardness are cut, not as jewelry, for which purpose they are unsuitable, but as display pieces for collections.

Some crystal mystics maintain that, because cutting and polishing do not alter a stone's crystal structure, it does not matter if the stone is so treated for mounting in jewelry. Others are horrified by the saws and grinding wheels, which, they claim, traumatize and ruin the mineral. A cut stone is sometimes likened to the old patriarchal ideal of a beautiful woman: painted, powdered, curled, corseted, contrived, mutilated in subtle ways, uncomfortably dolled up and taught artificial, robotlike "pretty" behavior. The natural stone, like the natural woman, is called the real one. Yet, strangely, few mystics want anything to do with natural stones that are not naturally pretty. Their works deal largely with conventional gem minerals and those that form interesting crystals.

Uncut natural material. Some minerals form such interesting crystals that the idea of altering them is deplored by more than crystal mystics. Professional mineralogists and crystallographers also love the natural shapes of stones and wish they could be more carefully preserved. "To a crystallographer a clear and sharply developed crystal bounded by brilliant natural faces is of much more interest than one that has been cut and provided with artificial facets. In the latter state it shows no more than a sparkling bit of cut glass. The whole thing has an air of artificiality and is therefore to a student of nature objectionable. Whenever possible he strives to rescue a specially interesting or unique crystal from this mutilation."[6]

It is true that from a visual/aesthetic viewpoint, natural crystals have much more to look at than a cut gem, which is usually too transparent and too symmetrical to exercise the imagination. To some people, even the sliding lights and flashing colors of such minerals as moonstone, cat's eye, and opal are more interesting in a rough piece of matrix than in a gold or silver setting. And the collector with limited funds knows uncut minerals offer a much wider range of material, for much less money, than cut gemstones. Most of the money spent on jewelry is really buying lapidary labor.

There may be a middle ground between the lapidary and natural-rock schools of thought, however. Natural stones can be tumble-polished: rolled, for weeks at a time, with progressively finer grades of grit in an electrically rotated drum. As streams roll and smooth pebbles, the tumbler smoothes the stones' outer surfaces so they become shiny and silky to the touch, retaining most of their original shape. Tumble-polished stones can become pendants or other jewelry items and still keep a natural look. The technique is comparatively inexpensive and gives handsome results with many different kinds of stones.

What is a crystal? Mineralogists and crystallographers have one definition, on which they agree. Crystal mystics have quite another definition—or rather, definitions, because they are many, and no two agree. Some of the mystical writers do not even agree with themselves. Their efforts to express their notion(s) of what constitutes a crystal present some of the most fascinating examples of word salad ever seen in print. Here is a selection:

> We can visualize the crystal as a vast network of spirals that receives energy, processes it along orderly pathways, and then transmits the collective oscillations outward in precise vibratory patterns. . . . Perhaps one day crystals will be encoded with holographic sequences of interdimensional realities and, when projected around the participants, will actually facilitate a direct transfer of consciousness to these dimensional planes.[7]

Whatever "holographic sequences of interdimensional realities" might be, they seem to be associated with the wearing of a "Spiral Crystal Crown" consisting of quartz crystals on a silver band fitted around the head, with "sterling silver coils" around and upward to a point four or five inches above the top middle of the head:

> This crown is excellent for dynamizing the entire brain-mind field as a whole and is expecially [sic] well suited for catalyzing the reprogramming process of star-seed and celestial-seed and accessing intergalactic spectrum vehicles. . . . The function of crystalline matrices is to replicate the causal

abstract geometrics of the Universal Mind, thus serving to provide a stable matrix of interdimensional continuity and ordered energetic interactions. The highest aspects of physical-plane crystal form energetics is [sic] as geometry-specific multidimensional access linkages and as numerological tools of defined energetic parameters. . . . The sole difference between any given element [sic] in the Periodic Chart of the Elements is its angle of crystallization into matter, reflective of its originating abstract axis code-patterns within the causal domains of Light.[8]

This source also defines the "effects" of quartz crystals' six faces as "endless mathematical formulas, geometric finalization, focusing micro-modulated coherence, resonant amplification, precursive processing, and columnar standing wave formation."[9] Any comprehensible elucidation of these "effects," in real English, may be left to the reader's imagination.

Another self-styled authority on crystals calls them orgone focalizers, whatever that may mean, and also an interface between amplification of thought forms and an unknown kind of energy attributed to the mythical orgones.[10] In some unexplained manner, this interface is said to create "ethereal forms," a term that accompanies orgones and orgone energies in the realm of the nonexistent. Such terms may often impress those who do not know that the words' referents do not exist.

The same author declares that all minerals are composed of only eight elements—aluminum, calcium, iron, magnesium, oxygen, potassium, silicon, and sodium—unaccountably ignoring the other ninety-five elements. He thinks porphyry is a single mineral, whereas porphyry is a general term for three different kinds of rock, each containing about fifteen different minerals.[11] He thinks the natural glass fulgurite, formed by lightning strikes in sand, is either man-made or from outer space, misspells it *fulganite*, and claims that it was used in Lemuria to separate human beings into male and female sexes—which implies that human beings were previously androgynous. He advises using only extrater-restrial "fulganite," but does not explain how extraterrestrial material is to be distinguished from the ordinary kind.[12]

Most of the properties of minerals are either unknown to, or completely misunderstood by, crystal mystics of this stripe. For example, it is postulated that crystals interact in bizarre ways with both human beings and sounds:

> In the act of a human energy system interacting with a quartz crystal especially, the crystal's energies establish a resonant rapport with the

biocrystalline matrices and stimulate not only an energetic amplification in the biocrystals but also greater states of vibrational coherency and actual changes in the biocrystalline lattice structures on the auric and microscopic levels (that is, recrystallization of bond angles, lattice-code reorientations, and the like). . . .

At specific indexed sonic frequency thresholds, intensely focused sonic input induces a state of hypercoherency within the crystal matrix. Normal molecular and lattice coherency orientations undergo a quantum matrix transposition to a higher level of energetic order in which the magneto-gravitic profile induces a major dimensional threshold level breakthrough.[13]

Certainly no one could accuse this author of hypercoherency—if there were such a thing. As for "biocrystalline matrices" and "biocrystalline lattice structures," the meaning of these terms will remain forever mysterious, especially to biologists. This kind of talk is depressingly typical of New Age crystal mystics, who use the language of science as young preliterate children use alphabet soup. They seldom understand that scientific words do have specific meanings, which cancel each other out when the words are haphazardly strung together and produce gibberish. Yet people will read this kind of apparent gibberish and imagine that they have been somehow enlightened, although they may not have comprehended a word of it. Words thus converted into nonsense is a common phenomenon in mystical circles. "All groups that promise ultimate truths and revelations require a private code. The public cannot tolerate religions, philosophies, and the like, which speak in languages readily understood."[14]

One of the oldest false notions about crystals still extant is the notion that they emanate their own light. Sometimes this is an intentional metaphor for spiritual illumination. At other times it is taken literally.[15] The idea arose far back in antiquity, among people who thought that light reflected or refracted from gemstones was generated from within the stones. The ancient Hindus supposed that light was provided in the underworld by huge gems, acting as minor suns. The Greeks had similar beliefs. The Talmud claims that the light in Noah's ark was provided by precious stones.[16] In Europe's Middle Ages it was said that an enormous ruby atop the temple of the Holy Grail gave off light like a beacon, leading the Grail knights home at night.

Of course, gems do not produce light. Flashes given back by reflection and refraction contain not one photon more than is put into the stone by ambient light. Fluorescent minerals that glow in the dark require the input of ultraviolet light. Phosphorescent minerals retain a glow for a while after the radiation source is removed, but the light is not their own; it is only a slow release of the excitation caused by earlier input. No mineral behaves on its own like a light bulb. Not even the most fanatical crystal mystic could expect to use a crystal as a flashlight. Nevertheless, it is often claimed that crystals somehow "store" light, despite the fact that no crystal has ever been seen doing so.[17]

It is even claimed that certain crystals are "laser wands" able to project "a laser beam of extremely intense light" all on their own. The author of this effusion seems not to have the least idea of what a laser beam is, or how it works, yet appears to be certain that these laser wand crystals were used long ago in "the healing temples of Lemuria" and have been preserved by "the beings of inner earth" (whoever they may be). At present, the laser wands are being "relocated" into the matrix rocks of South American mines, so they can be rediscovered.[18] Geologists might welcome further information about this bizarre phenomenon, but no such information is forthcoming; the scientific community will have to remain unaware of this particular miracle.

Some people extrapolate from glow-in-the-dark watch and clock dials, popularly called "radium" dials, to a belief that all radioactive minerals emit visible light. Actually, radioactive minerals do not glow. Their radiation is invisible. "Radium" watch dials are created by using small amounts of radium in combination with a phosphorescent mineral such as zinc sulfide. The radium does not glow, but it emits invisible gamma rays that excite the phosphorescence of the other mineral. The two do not occur together in nature.

Ever anthropomorphic, mystics also talk about humanlike "sentience and intelligence" in stones.[19] One says all stones are alive, "entities pulsating, radiating, vibrating at different rates. They create strong energy fields which enable us to be charged with their energies."[20] One author says, "The crystal is one of the new life forms upon the planet,"[21] apparently ignorant even of the basic fact that minerals crystallized, forming our planet's crust, long before there were *any* life forms on it. Another describes crystals as "inanimate objects, the lowest forms of life,"[22] apparently ignorant of the meaning of *inanimate,* which is "nonliving." Others again regard the entities supposedly dwelling in crystals as higher rather than lower forms relative to the position of human beings on some imagined scale of intelligence. Such entities are often called *devas,* from the old Sanskrit word for "gods," or sometimes angels or fairies. One writer says that you should regard the crystal creature as "your younger brother or sister."[23] It does seem incongruous, however, to regard as a younger sibling a being whose age would have to be at least several hundred thousand years.

The idea of spirits within stones is as old as the human race, however. Even the Old Testament God once dwelt in a stone, called a *beth-el,* or "house of God," corresponding to the Greek *baetyl.* A stone small enough to be carried or worn was viewed as a portable *beth-el:* the little house of a personal deity; hence the stone talisman or gem amulet, dear to every breed of humans from the beginning. Madame de Barrera said in 1860, "The more jewels, the more guardian spirits."[24] A modern crystal mystic says the same, claiming that one is more strongly charged with cosmic forces by wearing many precious stones.[25] By this not uncommon reasoning, those wealthy folk who go about ostentatiously dripping with diamonds, rubies, and emeralds must be in some way more cosmic than the rest of us.

So anthropomorphic is the view of one self-styled authority that he even declares crystals to possess "a body heat of 72.4 degrees F., which they endeavor to maintain. . . . A crystal of several thousand pounds could easily warm a room or two." Nevertheless, it is admitted that a house heated by nothing but crystals will always remain "a bit uncomfortable," that is, cold.[26] The notion that a crystal can serve as a heat source would seem silly enough on the face of it to require no refutation, but evidently no idea is too silly to be elevated to the status of fact in the mystics' weird world.

Equally silly is the notion that a crystal can serve as a primary source of electrical energy, or as some writers say, "electromagnetism," another word whose meaning they do not seem to understand. Crystals exist in equilibrium, neither giving off nor taking in such energies; they are not storage batteries. Misunderstanding of the piezoelectric effect characteristic of some minerals (but by no means all) has suggested a number of fuzzy and unwarranted verbal connections having nothing to do with scientific realities. The fact that synthetic quartz crystals are used to control vibrational frequencies in electronic transmitters, amplifiers, receivers, and so on does not mean that the crystals do the whole job. They are only "a small part of the mechanism . . . In no sense is the crystal actually doing the transmitting."[27] Yet the mystics continue to say things like, "The clear, pure crystal is essentially used for the absorbtion [*sic*] of energy to be utilized for power . . . for electricity, for generators, and so on."[28] One source asserts, for no apparent reason, that crystals belonging specifically to the monoclinic system "have a pulsating action. They are able to pulsate with the Universe and to be of a nature which expands and contracts."[29] Naturally, this statement is not supported by any observational evidence, for the good reason that it has never been observed. The long dead but currently popular "Atlantean" mystic Edgar Cayce did not even require a so-called generator crystal to be crystalline; he declared that the great central generator crystal of Atlantis—able to provide electrical power to an entire country—was made of nothing but cut glass.[30]

One of the strangest current notions about crystals came from the terminology of computer science, the reference to a "memory bank." Many mystics talk ecstatically about the vast amounts of historical and scientific information stored in the memory bank of the "crystalline mind." Certain crystals are called "record keepers" and are credited with a truly wonderful ability to pour all their stored knowledge directly into the brain of a person who touches them. "A single, large memory crystal is capable of more memory storage than the largest library on earth today. . . . The Library of Congress of the United States has only about a quarter as much information stored as has one large memory crystal."[31] The best part is that the student need not go to all the trouble of reading, studying, taking notes, or laboriously committing anything to memory in the usual tiresome and time-consuming ways. All this toil will be unnecessary in the magical crystal-based future, when you can "go to your library, move through the shelves of crystals until you find the area of knowledge you wish to absorb, and merely by holding the crystal, learn."[32] Indeed, the lazy student's dream comes true at last in the utopia envisioned by crystal mysticism.

Not only instant learning but many other marvelous effects are predicted for the coming Crystal Age—although these effects are usually described in vague terms. It is said that great cleansing and purifying of all human beings will take place in our time, brought about by crystals acting as catalysts.[33] One is left to wonder just what kind of purification this might be, or why it was not brought about long ago, because crystals and stones have always been as much a part of our planet as they are now. As a rule, mystical ideas about what either is taking place or will take place at some indefinite future time, because of the presence of crystals on this planet, are couched in terms so opaque as to convey absolutely nothing to the inquiring mind. For example:

> Crystals will acquire certain vibrational resonancies that imbalance their expressions as they respond to the healing needs of your planet with their ability to oscillate in phase with a given frequency that they would mend and resolve into a coherent and actively harmonic resonancy. . . . The coding of spiralling lattices is taking place on a network dimensionally extended into the so-called etheric realms of subtler vibration . . . a filamental extension of this latticework takes place at all times into other dimensions, and thus records the oscillations and vibratory transferences of languages of light and sound. . . . Roughly speaking, the same principals [sic] that govern holographic generation are at work with the generating of the wholistic extensions of information within crystals and within all dimensions of our physical creation as well.[34]

Whatever that may mean, it is clearly another product of the verbal-baroque style affected by many crystal mystics in which featherweight spelling and grammar vainly struggle to support heavyweight words preposterously crowded together. And as an ultimate absurdity, it is even postulated that human beings themselves may become more like crystals as they "evolve" toward some future state of omniscience. "The crystal grows from the imput [sic] of energy, as your mind grows from the imput [sic] of knowledge. . . . Every time you receive a spiritual imput, [sic] the purity of your crystalline structure increases and is enhanced." Apparently the effect is beneficial: "As a result of the crystallization process the physical ageing of your bodies will be slowed down considerably, providing you with extended years of prime health and often lengthing [sic] your physical life span."[35]

Several decades ago, certain classic science fiction stories were based on the premise of silicon-based life forms able to occupy planets that lacked the air, water, soil, and warmth required by the carbon-based life forms of our own earth. Evidently the premise filtered down eventually into crystal mysticism, although silicon-based life is not really possible, so far as we know. Crystal mystics may envision themselves gradually petrifying, but for the rest of us such a fate seems unlikely. In any event, would it be fun to live eternally as a rock?

From the viewpoint of New Age writings, it seems as important to deal with the question of what a crystal is *not* as to explain (however sketchily) what it is. One may safely say that a crystal is not a fairy, an angel, or a god. It is not a battery or a light source. It is not organic. It is not alive, as life is biologically defined. As intelligence is understood to be the functioning of a brain, it is certainly not intelligent. It is not a radio receiver or transmitter, an electrical generator, a space ship, or an apport from "another dimension" (undefined). It does not produce energy out of itself, unless it is radioactive. It is not magnetic, unless it is a compound of iron, nickel, or cobalt. It is not a medicine or a machine. It is not a laser or a library. It is not a magic wand, a magic carpet, or a gift from outer space. It is a thing of the earth, perhaps a thing of beauty and a joy forever; but the crystal mystics' perceptions of it are, one and all, subjective.

Subjectivity per se is nothing dreadful. Subjectivity greatly enhances our appreciation of most things, including minerals. The mystics' mistake lies in confusing the subjective with the objective. To talk of stones giving off "vibrations" is a gross misuse of a scientific term, and a distortion of its specific meaning. It would be more correct to say that for some of us, stones give off *associations*. Their colors, textures, weights, temperatures, sizes, shapes—and also our prior knowledge about them—arouse many associations on a deep emotional/esthetic level, especially then the mind is prepared to "feel" something about the stone. Given the same preparation, similar associations can seem to arise from any external object whatsoever. In essence, we perceive what we expect to perceive.

Crystals happen to be particularly appealing objects. They are naturally beautiful and/or interesting. Their origin is mysterious—at least it was mysterious, until the recent development of such sciences as geology and mineralogy began to shed some light on it. Still, there are many facts yet to be discovered, and many lay persons almost entirely unaware of the facts that have been discovered so far.

Moreover, we often place a high monetary value on certain stones. Money means a lot to some people. Modern culture has trained them in complex positive responses to the very idea of costliness. They will be automatically impressed by anything that is said to be worth a lot of money, no matter how arbitrary the value scale. Nature has no such value scales; but to understand New Age thinking in general, one must pay attention to this uniquely human viewpoint.

1. Stein, 8. 2. Stein, 170; Gurudas, 54. 3. Gurudas, 92. 4. Harold, 38. 5. Stein, 172. 6. Spencer, 90. 7. Baer & Baer, *W. L.,* 55, 137. 8. Baer & Baer, *C. C.,* 177, 181. 9. Ibid., 184. 10. Gurudas, 1, 10. 11. Ibid., 142, 174. 12. Ibid., 106. 13. Baer & Baer, *C. C.,* 46, 112. 14. Flammonde, 217. 15. Baer & Baer, *C. C.,* 141–143. 16. Fernie, 87. 17. Bonewitz, 164. 18. Raphaell, *C. H.,* 143, 148. 19. Baer & Baer, *W. L.,* 130. 20. Chocron, 45. 21. Bryant, 23. 22. Raphaell, *C. E.,* 1. 23. Harold, 89. 24. Fernie, 282. 25. Chocron, 51. 26. Rea, 306. 27. Bonewitz, 102, 165. 28. Alper 1, 1/26–1. 29. Richardson & Huett, 22. 30. Robinson, 68. 31. Rea, 295. 32. Alper 2, 7. 33. Chocron, 100. 34. Rea, 136, 277. 35. Alper 1, 3/16–2; 2, 8.

The New Age

Much of New Age spirituality is a marketing phenomenon. Almost everything associated with it is for sale:
distinctive music, art, literature, fashions, foods, herbs, crystals, classes,
workshops, oracles, amulets, charms, and the services of every kind of
guru, seer, medium, astrologer, spiritual adviser, therapist, or holistic
healer. Crystal mysticism is but one tentacle of the marketing octopus.

New Age magazines advertise magic jewelry, crystal pendulums and
dowsing rods, courses in "magnet therapy," Male and Female Polarity
Balancing Crystal Kits, video lectures by Ascended Masters of the Great
White Brotherhood, elixirs and potions for every human ill, books
containing the "lost teachings of Jesus," books containing the lost
history of the human race, books containing foolproof methods for
obtaining perfect health, wealth, happiness, eternal youth, and control of
others, and books not written by human beings. Whatever the believer
wishes to believe in, it is available for a price.

Many New Age beliefs associated with minerals and crystals are
actually Dark Age beliefs, dating back to the early medieval period or
even earlier. Some can be traced to ancient Greece, India, Egypt, or
Babylon. The childlike quality of New Age writing is reminiscent of a
simpler world, when the cosmos seemed more or less comprehensible to
the average human mind and its gods could be cajoled by direct human
entreaty.

The cosmos seems more complex now. Comprehension of even a
tiny portion of the whole requires years of arduous scientific training. To
some degree the New Age represents an antirational desire to com-

prehend without the disciplines of learning; hence the ambivalent New Age attitude that decries science yet appeals to "scientific" confirmation of its convictions.

Believers are told that they "must continually seek to expand their mental horizons," though not by studying the real world that they live in. This world is an illusion. "The major task which currently confronts mankind" is to "develop awareness of the Fourth Dimension—otherwise termed 'the Spiritual Plane'—and to relate to it in much the same manner as we currently do to the illusionary three dimensions of matter." This redefined fourth dimension (which was more generally called *time*) is to be understood particularly through the help of two Ascended Masters. One is that old reprobate the Comte de St. Germain; the other is called simply the Tibetan Master.[1] With such an agenda for "mankind's" major task, the really difficult problems—environmental pollution, overpopulation, overproduction, waste, inflation, crime, disease, war, and other human evils—can be comfortably ignored.

Having been informed by science that the distinctions between matter and energy tend to blur on the atomic level, and that atoms and molecules are in constant vibratory motion, New Age thinkers have leaped to an unwarranted conclusion that such vibrations can be perceived by subtle human senses, and even controlled by human gestures. Such accessible vibrations cannot be discovered or measured by any of the methods used for other kinds of vibrations. They are not transmitted through the atmosphere or any other form of matter that carries perceptible vibrations. To solve the logical dilemma that this theory obviously implies, a very ancient idea has been resurrected from the dust of centuries: the idea of ether.

The word *ether* was invented by the early Greeks to describe what they envisioned as a fifth element, even lighter, brighter, more volatile and rarefied than the fire element. Ether was the divine substance of stars, souls, and angelic spirits inhabiting the upper heavens. Bodies of this "ethereal" more-than-light substance would be given to blessed ones after their earthly death.

This idea permeated the Gnostic sects around the beginning of the Christian era, and also entered into canonical Christian theology. It was also theorized and believed that any living person may have an "astral" (starry) body made of ether, which could leave its material dwelling from time to time and wander about as the soul wanders forth during dreams.

The idea that ether was the substance of spirits and of heaven persisted all the way up to the late nineteenth century, when physicists were beginning to wonder about the nature of light "waves." They wondered how light could travel through space if space is empty. A wave must travel through some sort of medium, and it was already known that the medium of air was limited to a relatively thin shell around the earth. What medium lay outside the atmosphere to conduct the light of distant stars to earthly eyes? To the thinking of that time, the medium was ether: an attenuated gas filling all of space.

Today scientists know that space is a vacuum and that light can indeed travel through it; there is no such substance as ether. But this information has not quite percolated down to New Age thought, which still believes in ether as an all-pervading spirit-stuff that forms light-bodies, as in the ancient Greek concept. It is stated that space is not a vacuum but a mass of "ethereal fluidium."[2] This assertion would surely surprise NASA, which has been dealing with the extraterrestrial vacuum for several decades now. Apparently some mystics are far behind on current events.

At the same time that ether is supposed to fill empty space, it also fills the space around each human being as an external "astral" body, which may be called an aura, an ethereal body, an energy-layer double, or by several other terms, which are arbitrarily defined in different ways by different authors. One even envisions a complex set of external human bodies composed of "layers of energy" and possessing as many as forty-nine different levels![3] New Age folk often worry inordinately about the state of these ethereal entities. "In the ancient civilizations, the cleansing of one's Etheric Form of the effects of negative or destructive thought patterns was considered to be of primary importance."[4] These ancient civilizations were presumably those New Age favorites, Atlantis and Lemuria (of which, more later), because the extant writings of the oldest known civilizations mention no such concern.

The attraction that human beings feel for crystals and gemstones is often said to arise from ethereal existences. One mystic writes, "The mineral kingdom is attuned to the etheric forces."[5] Another says a person is drawn to a particular mineral specimen because "the indwelling elemental, recognizing your personal note of sound in the higher ethers, attracts your attention by projecting its own special sound in those same ethers."[6] The mineral's indwelling elemental is the *deva* or fairy, which lives in the "ethereal dimension." As proof of the existence of these creatures, one author cites *The Coming of the Fairies* by Arthur Conon [*sic*]

Doyle, "with its interesting photos of nature spirits."[7] Long ago, these spirits were shown to be paper cutouts from children's fairytale books, propped up on some bushes and mistily photographed.[8]

Once the notion of communication between human beings and etheric spirits of the minerals has been postulated and accepted, there is no limit to the varieties of interaction that can be attributed to them. "The 'mind' of crystals is similar to the human mind in terms of their holographic and electromagnetic manner of functioning . . . so it is that the human mind can effectively program the internal dynamics of the crystal mind." There is even a new version of the Greeks' angelic star-dwelling ether-beings, updated in pseudoscientific jargon: "What is sometimes known as the New Age is nothing less than a quantum dimensional transformation of consciousness into the fourth-dimensional Light-body. This culminating 'creative moment' will be brought about by crystal-based Light-technologies."[9] The implication seems to be that there are many New Age people walking around with minds made of light instead of ordinary brain tissue, and that crystals are involved in the change.

Like the unscientific ancients, the newer mystics sometimes imply that gemstones were placed in terrestrial rocks by heavenly (outer-space) entities, as "seeds" of intelligent spirit. "The star seed consists of these Light-body Intelligence networks whose primary evolutionary domains are the advanced cosmic, intergalactic species of greater spiritual advancement. The celestial seed originates from beyond the intergalactic energy-matter Light-spectrums—the celestial realms of pure energy emissions—inclusive of the domains of higher angelic orders and a spectrum of levels of mastership."[10]

Constant use of terms like *higher* and *lower* indicates that the New Age world tends to be intensely hierarchical and thus opposed to a basic tenet of feminism, although feminist spirituality is often classified as a New Age movement. One author mentions a "hierarchy of light" similar to the angelic hierarchies once described by such writers as Pseudo-Dionysius the Areopagite, "a complexly differentiated branching network of Light flowing from the highest level of abstract causal dimensions to the most densified [*sic*] of lower octave planes." It seems that Earth's evolutionary development depends on "certain highly trained, spiritually authorized individuals" (like the author himself, of course) to "utilize their consciousness to gain access to energy-code patterns from other dimensions." What happens then is that people's "blood crystals" (whatever they are) are infused by the "Christ body of Light," resulting in freedom from "the binding forces of the earth plane."[11]

If this sounds like some of the patriarchal-hierarchical ideas of early Christianity, in which the male principle was viewed as bright, airy, fiery, and wholly superior to the dense, dark, passive, earthy female principle—it is. Not even the language has been very much changed. The same source claims that a quartz crystal (possibly because of its phallic shape) is a "transmission center of pure White Light, the manifestation of the universal Father Principle." This makes it eminently Christian: "The White Light is the Divine Radiance of the Father of the Cosmos—the Logos. It is the Light of Christ-Consciousness, of Supreme Power, Purity, Perfection."[12] No impure, imperfect, fleshly female realities are wanted.

Another writer adopts the old Hindu custom of dividing stones into male and female varieties, with male versions characterized as somehow superior. "The crystals which attract the greatest attention are the 'positive' or 'masculine' variety, for they possess great clarity. Indeed, such crystals often emit the most intense energies. . . . The feminine varieties of quartz are often rather ugly, being cloudy or opaque."[13]

The energies supposedly emitted by crystals will transform human illness into health, according to much New Age thinking. The modernized explanations for this improbable phenomenon are richly varied, and often ingenious. For example:

> In healing, the interconnection of an imbalanced energy pattern with its more causal higher plane blueprint of perfection would induce the imbalanced patterns to be aligned with balanced codes, and healing would thereby occur. . . . Disease occurs when the underlying intelligence of the bio-energetic system . . . is impeded by imbalanced energy patterns, thereby creating a state of dissonance and subsequent disorder . . . . The role of a healing facilitator is to neutralize discordant interference with homeostasis and to accentuate the preexisting blueprint of perfection.[14]

> Gemstones also draw the body physical up to higher spiritual levels by working with the body's own natural evolution toward a crystalline dynamics [sic]. Understanding this came as through careful Lemurian studies of the integration of gemstones with the body's own cell salts and the parts of the body physical that contain crystalline and quartz-like properties. [We are not told which parts these are.] Vibrational remedies push toxicity out of the physical body into the subtle bodies and aura. Then they enter the ethers where they are cleansed.[15]

Crystal transforms pain into well-being by transferring and transforming negative energies and repairing the aura L-field.[16]

Unlikely theories about gemstone healing are by no means strictly modern. They have been around forever. The physician William Fernie wrote at considerable length on the subject in 1907, stating his opinion that the warmth of volcanic fires, or the sunlight of past eons, might be stored underground in the form of gemstones to exert a beneficent influence in later ages. "The Diamond, by its adamantine brilliancy, representing, as it does, the sublimated sunshine of many tropical aeons, may be found to supply renovated strength and vigor . . . the Turquoise, by its phosphates, may confer fresh brain-powers . . . Garnets likewise . . . by their oxides of iron, and Magnesium, can prove of admirable help to bloodless wearers."[17]

Three centuries earlier, the Honorable Robert Boyle had supposed that "invisible Corpuscles may pass from Amulets or from other external remedies, into the Blood, and Humours, and there produce great changes." And one century earlier, Professor Karl Baron von Reichenbach had elucidated the central idea of New Age healing: "Every Crystal exerts a specific action on animal nerves," in the form of a kind of luminosity emitted from the terminations of crystals—even from crystallized sugar candy—that affects "sensitive persons." The professor's term for this emanation was "odic force," which is still bandied about today.[18]

One of the oldest ideas behind gemstone healing is that of sympathetic magic: the principle of "like affects like," which probably prevailed in the Stone Age. The idea is particularly applicable to both ancient and modern interpretations of the colors of stones. It is said—and has always been said—that red stones affect the blood, and so may cure blood-connected ills such as leukemia, menstrual difficulties, AIDS, iron deficiency, hemorrhage, and so on.[19] Orange stones are "warming," like fire, therefore good for chills, agues, arthritis, frostbite. White stones help secretion of breast milk and semen, strengthen the teeth, reduce inflammations. Green stones reduce stress, high blood pressure, headaches, or eye troubles, according to the old superstition that looking at green is beneficial for the eyes. Black stones affect the bowels and "black" emotional disorders such as nightmares, depression, and insomnia. Yellow stones affect jaundice, exhaustion, and bladder and kidney troubles.

Of course, this is only a cursory list. There are innumerable others, both old and new. They all overlap so profusely that any given disease can be found curable by any given stone, somewhere, by some "authority." Some of the old gemstone recipes combined various colors in an effort to create a broad-spectrum panacea. The famous "Five Precious Fragments" consisted of mixed powders of ruby, topaz, emerald, gold, and silver leaf with several herbs. A similar mix was much used in Languedoc, said an eighteenth-century writer, "where you meet with but few persons not having a pot thereof."[20] Similar combinations were used recently by "a noted spiritual scientist" in India, one Benoytosh Bhattacharya, who healed people by holding their photographs in front of a silver disc set with various gems spun around by an electric motor. The patient's presence was not required. The "vibrations" affected only the photograph, and then the patient, through the immemorial medium of sympathetic magic.[21]

One of the most prevalent modern instances of sympathetic magic operating at several removes is the gemstone elixir fraud, which has been popular for centuries nearly everywhere in the world. From ancient times, physicians have administered powdered gems as medicine to patients wealthy enough to afford it. On behalf of poorer people, it was usually discovered that water in which a gem has rested for a while was almost as remedial as the gem itself. During the last century the Rajah of Matara in Borneo was said to possess a healing diamond of such power that water in which it had been immersed would cure every disease.[22] Nowadays the healing privilege has been extended to every precious stone and many common ones, so that bottles of water are sold under the name of "gem elixirs" in New Age shops and earnestly prescribed by New Age books. Some even say the water containing a gemstone can be "magnetized."[23] (Water is not magnetizable.)

The verbiage set forth to support the validity of gem elixirs is really quite remarkable. They are called "tinctures of liquid consciousness," "an evolutionary force," "a system of organized vibrational essences." They can cure by proximity alone. For instance, acupuncture treatments are "enhanced" by a gem elixir bottle in the same room; the bottle need not even be opened.[24]

It is said that gem elixirs are somehow "resonant" with individual vertebrae, having "empathy with the construct of each vertebra," thus affecting the sympathetic nervous system.[25] Presumably this should refer to spinal ganglia rather than to vertebrae, because the latter are not part of the sympathetic nervous system. It is said also that the efficacy of gem elixirs will be validated by scientific studies at some indefinite future time, perhaps to forestall skeptics who seek reliable data now. One may imagine, however, the public outcry against any ordinary commercial drug or medicine permitted on the market *before* efficacy is proved! A New Age healer seems largely unacquainted with the simplest principles of science, even describing halite (common salt) as only somewhat soluble in water, and advising that halite elixir (salt water) should be strained.[26] It would be interesting to see this instructor trying to alter the saltiness of salt water by straining it.

When gem elixirs make patients feel better, it is most likely due to the perennial placebo effect, which the Syrian physician Qusta ibn-Luqa well understood all the way back in the tenth century: "The state of mind affects the state of the body. Sometimes belief in the curative value of a prophylactic is enough."[27] We don't yet know how to create the placebo effect deliberately, without the intervention of a self-deluding credulity. Perhaps this knowledge will come in the future.

Another currently popular crystal healing technique is stroking, for which minerals are commercially shaped into "stroking wands," with one pointed and one rounded end. This too has ancient precedents. Similar wands made of metal were patented in 1796 by Dr. Elisha Perkins, who called them Metallic Tractors and claimed to cure all diseases by stroking the patient with them.[28]

The New Age vibration theory of healing has precedents too. One of the early popularizers of this theory was Dr. Albert Abrams, whom the *Journal of the American Medical Association* called "the dean of twentieth-century charlatans."[29] In his 1916 book *New Concepts of Diagnosis and Treatment*, Abrams said that every disease has its own rate of vibration, creating a "disharmony of electronic oscillations." He invented a machine called the Oscilloclast, which diagnosed each mail-order patient's disease from a spot of blood on a paper card. This was inserted into the machine, which then projected toward the patient (at whatever distance) the proper healing vibrations. "Though the diagnosis took but a moment, the cure could call for any number of treatments and run into money." Upton Sinclair became an eloquent convert to Abrams's following, which achieved such notoriety that the AMA investigated. When Abrams was sent samples of blood from sheep and other animals, he returned diagnoses of all sorts of human ills: genito-urinary tuberculosis, hereditary syphilis, cancer. Discredited, he died in 1924.[30]

His idea lived on, however, in the Micro-Dynameter of F. C. Ellis, who described his machine in 1930 as a simple instrument able to diagnose and treat every disease. Ellis's follower in the 1940s was "Dr." Ruth B. Drown, with her Radio Therapeutic Instrument, a box with two wires and two electrodes. Patients could mail Mrs. Drown a drop of blood on blotting paper for complete diagnosis and treatment by "radio wave."[31] Each treatment cost fifty dollars.

Like Abrams before her, Mrs. Drown declared that everything in the universe has its own vibratory rate: each organ, each gland, each disease. Her machine tuned into the body's "electromagnetic force." It was supposed to direct "the total body energy of a patient through the machine back to the diseased part at the same vibratory rate that had been discovered during diagnosis. . . . This steps up the vibrations in that particular area. Through the process of metabolism constantly going on in the body, the new cells which form will come in at the higher or normal rate and the diseased cells will automatically fall away."[32]

In 1952, one of Mrs. Drown's patients caused a scandal by dying under her treatment of a cancer that could have been easily eradicated by conventional therapy. Mrs. Drown was investigated, but continued to practice for ten years more, until she was indicted on a charge of grand theft. She died before her case came to trial.

Ruth Drown's spirit lives on in the New Age concept of radionics, "a healing method used since the beginning of this century, a machine is used to diagnose and prescribe for the individual. The vibrations from the correct gemstones . . . are then electromagnetically transferred to the medicating vehicle, which can be water or milk-sugar pills. The remedy may be taken either orally or by absorption through the skin. Alternatively, it may be sent electromagnetically via the ether to the patient."[33] This, in a book published in 1988, begins to sound weirdly familiar.

Long-range mail-order diagnosis and prescription were, of course, the stock in trade of "sleeping prophet" Edgar Cayce, whose quaint writings still enjoy brisk sales in New Age circles. Cayce was not the clever sort of charlatan. In 1889, when he was twelve years old, he was still in the third grade at school. His father once said, "He was dull. No doubt about it." Young Edgar was accustomed to taking naps on books "to absorb their contents."[34] He was clever enough, however, to disclaim responsibility for his prescriptions, declaring himself only a channel for other, spiritual entities whose recommendations came through him while he slept. Many of his "cures" involved minerals and gemstones, though he was usually confused about their names, properties, and chemical composition. He said, "Vibratory forces arising from certain stones and metals collaborate with similar forces originating within individuals to permit them to attune to the Creative Forces of the universe."[35]

In a typical Cayce-style endorsement, one Ken Carley is quoted as an enthusiastic supporter of Cayce's pronouncements about stones. Ken Carley calls himself a commercial gem and mineral dealer and a lapidary in business for many years. It is odd that he seems unfamiliar with the gemstones mentioned, "some of them with really strange names," he says. Mentioning a green stone with "bright specks of copper all through it," he calls this mineral both Epidote and Copper. Shattuckite is misspelled ("shattakite") and clumsily described as "a massive opaque silicified form of azurite and malachite." Bornite is also misspelled ("burnite") and said to be no longer available because it came from a single mine in Montana, now closed.[36] Actually, bornite is of common occurrence and is a major copper ore. Edgar Cayce himself knew almost nothing about the metals and stones that he urged on his followers. Denying the unfounded claim of some crystal mystics that the lost capstone of Egypt's Great Pyramid was made of quartz, Cayce declared instead that it was "an alloy of copper, brass, and gold," apparently believing that brass is a pure metal.[37]

Not only Egyptian pyramids, mystical healing, and Creative Forces of the universe but also the lore and legends of outer space figure prominently among New Age believers—most of whom, after all, grew up in the space age on a diet of science-fiction entertainment. Typically unable to separate fact from remembered fantasy, many such believers envision space beings communicating with humans, sending crystals to earth, meddling in terrestrial affairs, and otherwise playing the traditional role of *deus ex machina*. According to one source, the entire family of beryls (beryllium aluminum silicates)—which includes emerald, aquamarine, morganite, goshenite, heliodor, or golden beryl—came from outer space and did not grow from earth substances at all.[38] Another source says that all the world's black-hued crystals are "apports" from elsewhere, none of them having originated on earth.[39] Still another source pretends to know about an undiscovered planet, and even knows its name ("Noele"), though no one else on earth will perceive this planet until "the close of the twentieth century."[40]

Mysterious secret knowledge has always been the occultist's stock in trade. To prevent investigation, it is invariably claimed that undefined but dreadful catastrophes will ensue if such knowledge is injudiciously revealed. For example, a New Age lecturer referred to an "energy pyramid" of great power in the state of Arizona. Asked to give its exact location, he declared that "mankind" is not ready to be told this, and disclosure would cause "chaos and havoc." The same lecturer stated that spaceships have crashed on the earth and have been "secured in secret" by present governments. These ships were piloted by large intelligent crystals.[41]

New Age writers do not expect to be called upon to prove any of their claims. They feel that a mere unsupported statement is good enough; any reader who finds this inadequate is asked to "release without being judgmental" whatever is found not to ring true.[42] In other words, the burden of proof rests with the audience, and the false is not to be "judged" false—a curiously self-serving ethic. But one of the early founders of the New Age movement, that cynically deliberate spellbinder G. I. Gurdjieff, once said in an uncharacteristically revealing paragraph: "The fact of the matter is that in occult literature much that has been said is superfluous and untrue. . . . They have not given you knowledge. . . . Judge everything from the point of view of your common sense. Become the possessor of your own sound ideas and don't accept anything on faith."[43]

A significant contribution to New Age thinking that the followers of Edgar Cayce especially accepted on faith was the Atlantis mythos, burgeoning at present, and treated by many New Age writers as if it were real history instead of a hypothesis long since proved absurd. Having read several of the earlier books on Atlantis that were popular in his day, Cayce became convinced that his sleeping self could communicate with the folk of that allegedly drowned world, just as many an entranced New Ager might communicate with preternaturally intelligent entities on other planets. Many of Cayce's disquisitions dealt with the appearance, customs, and technology of Atlantis. This material is still avidly read, and is mistaken for truth by many who have never been taught real history. Even now, the actual origins of the Atlantis mythos remain unknown to most people. To provide some small remedy for this, there follows a survey of the birth and growth of an entire subdivision of occult literature.

1. Harold, 22, 117. 2. Gurudas, 2. 3. Stein, 4–6. 4. Harold, 109. 5. Parkinson, 17. 6. Harold, 32. 7. Gurudas, 9–10. 8. Randi, chap. 2. 9. Baer & Baer, *W. L.*, 67, 108. 10. Baer & Baer, *C. C.*, 42. 11. *Ibid.*, 140, 147, 352. 12. Baer & Baer, *W. L.*, 25. 13. Harold, 33–34. 14. Baer & Baer, *C. C.*, 101–102, 331. 15. Gurudas, 5, 8. 16. Stein, 143. 17. Fernie, 18–19. 18. *Ibid.*, 52, 219. 19. Stein, 177. 20. Fernie, 3, 25. 21. Baer & Baer, *W. L.*, 118. 22. Fernie, 71. 23. Stein, 174. 24. Gurudas, 18–19, 43. 25. *Ibid.*, 52. 26. *Ibid.*, 25, 36. 27. Anderson, 111. 28. Holbrook, 35. 29. Flammonde, 51. 30. Holbrook, 130–133. 31. Flammonde, 53. 32. Young, 239–257. 33. Parkinson, 15. 34. Flammonde, 62, 64. 35. *Scientific Properties*, 4. 36. *Ibid.*, 48, 72. 37. Robinson, 91. 38. Lorusso & Glick, 37. 39. Alper 1, 3/9–2. 40. Richardson et al., 110. 41. Alper 2, 5, 72. 42. Raphaell, *C. E.*, preface. 43. Webb, 500.

The Real History of Atlantis

There is only one primary source for all the complex mythology of Atlantis, which thus becomes an upside-down pyramid constructed on a single pinpoint of reference. That pinpoint is Plato. About 335 B.C., Plato's *Timaeus* and *Kritias* first mentioned the fabled continent beyond the Pillars of Hercules (Gibraltar).

Plato's account was hearsay of hearsay. He claimed that Socrates had heard the tale from Kritias, who heard it at third hand from his great-grandfather Dropides, who heard it from his relative, the half-legendary Athenian lawgiver Solon, who heard it from a priest of Isis in Egypt, a hundred and fifty years before Socrates. The Egyptian priest claimed that there was a great Athenian empire nine thousand years previous to his own time, that is, about 9600 B.C., when there was actually no Athens at all. The priest said that this Athenian power came into conflict with the empire of Atlantis, which was founded by the sea god Poseidon on a continent in the western ocean.

Of course, neither Plato nor any of this string of other informants mentioned such modern inventions as generator crystals, flying machines, marvels of telepathic communication and astral travel, or any other currently popular Atlantean concept. These embellishments were added by creative imaginations of the nineteenth and twentieth centuries.

Perhaps the name of Atlantis was suggested to Plato by his reading of Thucydides, who did mention an earthquake-born tidal wave that destroyed an Athenian fort on the small island of Atalanta (named for the heroic huntress of Greek myth) and "wrecked one of two ships which had been drawn up on the shore." Strabo said that the island of Atalanta had been split in two, so a ship canal could be put through the gulf. By the time of Philo the Jew (first century A.D.), "the island of Atalantes" had grown to dimensions "greater than Africa and Asia," and was entirely submerged in one day and night by an extraordinary earthquake and flood.[1]

Few early writers took the story seriously, however. Christian authorities tended to interpret the conflict between Athens and Atlantis as an allegory of the encounter between good and evil. By the sixth century, however, the geographer-monk Kosmas Indicopleustes presented the story as a garbled Greek version of the biblical tale of Noah. Belief in a once-real Atlantis was suspended for a thousand years and began to form again only after discovery of the New World.

In 1553, the Spanish historian Francisco López de Gómara suggested that Plato's Atlantis was America. This idea was largely adopted by Sir Francis Bacon in his work *The New Atlantis* (1624), by Buffon in the eighteenth century, and by Alexander von Humboldt in the nineteenth. But America was by no means the only candidate. In 1675 a multivolume book by the Swedish scholar Olof Rudbeck strove to demonstrate that Atlantis was Sweden, which therefore served as the source of all civilization. Others since "proved" Atlantis to have been Spain, Britain, Palestine, Africa, Arabia, Mexico, Ceylon, and many other places, including even the arctic regions.

The progress of Atlantis toward its present position in occultism was next furthered by Diego de Landa, the Spanish bishop of Yucatan in the sixteenth century. De Landa confiscated and burned all the Mayan books he could seize, calling them works of the devil, but later he devised a means of translating the surviving few with a "Mayan alphabet" that he created by forcing the natives to invent hieroglyphic equivalents for Latin letters. He began his researches with the durable notion that American Indians were the lost ten tribes of Israel. This notion was adopted by William Penn and later New England Puritans. It also figured prominently in the Mormon mythology of Joseph Smith.

An erratic French abbé, Charles Étienne Brasseur (1814–1874), used de Landa's synthetic Mayan alphabet to mistranslate one of the few remaining Mayan codexes. He theorized that two letters, M and U, represented the name of the sunken Atlantic continent. His compatriot Augustus Le Plongeon (1826–1908) lived in Yucatan, dug about in the Mayan ruins, and published *Queen Moo and the Egyptian Sphinx,* a romantic fantasy about the queen of Atlantis (or Mu), who escaped the deluge, went to Egypt, built the Sphinx, and became the Goddess Isis. Le Plongeon was influenced not only by Brasseur but also by Madame Blavatsky's *The Secret Doctrine* and by the pseudoscientific cult of pyramidology founded by the eccentric Scotsman Charles Piazzi Smyth.

The earliest and perhaps greatest American popularizer of the "historical" Atlantis was Ignatius T. T. Donnelly, a Minnesota congressman who wrote *Atlantis: The Antediluvian World* (1882). Donnelly was the first to argue that an Atlantic-ocean Atlantis was the source of all civilizations. He also tried to prove in other books that Shakespeare's plays were written by Francis Bacon, and that the Pleistocene Ice Age was caused by earth's collision with a comet. Most of the "evidence" adduced by Donnelly was simply wrong. He claimed—erroneously— that Egyptian civilization appeared suddenly out of nowhere, without Neolithic precedents; that Hannibal used gunpowder; that the Assyrians had pineapples; that cotton plants of the same species grew in both hemispheres; and many other bits of nonsense, which his enthusiastic readers seldom bothered to check.

In the 1880s, Helena Blavatsky based *The Secret Doctrine* largely on Donnelly's work, with parts plagiarized without credit from Wilson's translation of the Vishnu Purana and from the Rig Veda's Hymn of Creation. Madame Blavatsky claimed that her writings were based on a certain *Book of Dzyan,* written in the dead "Senzar" language of Atlantis, that her mahatmas had shown to her during her trances and allowed her to translate. Later Theosophists added many details similarly derived from revelations of "astral clairvoyance," which has recently been rechristened "channeling." W. Scott-Elliot learned by this means about the various Root Races, some egg-shaped, some made of invisible either, some jellylike, some fifteen-foot-tall, egg-laying, hermaphroditic Lemurians who were instructed by "Lords of the Flame" from the planet Venus. There were various subraces called Rmoahals, Tlavatlis, Toltecs, Turanians (proto-Aztecs), Semites, and Akkadians, all of whom occupied Atlantis. They raised wheat (which was originally brought from another planet), invented the banana, and wrote on sheets of metal (rather like Joseph Smith's apocryphal golden plates). They powered their aircraft with the mentally directed *vril* force, which was originally invented by the novelist Bulwer-Lytton in his utopian fantasy novel *The Coming Race* (1871).

Further material for Atlantis buffs was provided in 1912 by a hoax perpetrated by Paul Schliemann, grandson of the great archaeologist Heinrich Schliemann. In an article published with great fanfare in the *New York American,* Schliemann announced the opening of his famous grandfather's legacy, some sealed papers and an ancient vase containing artifacts "from the King Cronos of Atlantis." Quoting freely from Donnelly and Le Plongeon, Schliemann claimed that this material confirmed the inundation of Mu-Atlantis and promised to reveal all in a subsequent book, which never appeared—nor were the alleged artifacts ever seen. Wilhelm Dorpfeld, collaborator of the elder Schliemann, testified that his colleague had never shown any interest in the Atlantis myth and that the article was a fake. Nevertheless, Atlantis enthusiasts still quote Paul Schliemann and even confuse him with his eminent grandfather.

Fourteen years later, James Churchward in his old age published *The Lost Continent of Mu.* Denying previous writers' assertions that Mu was a synonym for Atlantis, Churchward made Mu a huge continent in the Pacific Ocean, supporting a population of 64 million. His information was based on "Muvian tablets" that he claimed to have seen, and translated by the power of intuition, in either Mexico or India, or perhaps it was Tibet. Atlantis, he said, was a Muvian colony. The Muvians also went to Asia and established the Uighur Empire twenty thousand years ago. (The real Uighur Empire existed from the tenth to twelfth centuries A.D.). Churchward envisioned the Atlantean continent afloat on something like pontoons, "great gas-filled chambers" underneath its earth. When these chambers collapsed, the continent sank. Geologically, of course, no such thing is possible.

More details were added to the growing mythos by Rudolf Steiner's *Lemuria and Atlantis,* dealing with both sunken continents at once. The Atlanteans, he said, could heal wounds instantly, tame animals, grow crops, and control the "life force" by magic words. More wonders were piled on top of these by other occultists like Manly P. Hall and Edgar Cayce. Such people did no research, but simply "knew" the magical minutiae of Atlantean and/or Lemurian life. In other words, they made it up.

Lewis Spence tried the semireasonable approach in various books:

The Problem of Atlantis, Atlantis in America, The History of Atlantis, and
The Problem of Lemuria, the Sunken Continent of the Pacific. Spence
claimed that the Cro-Magnon people were survivors of the Atlantean
cataclysm, as were the Mayans, who lived on yet another sunken
continent (they were by now proliferating like rabbits), Antillia, a
western Atlantis that sank later, to fill the gap of many millennia between
the fall of the mother continent and the establishment of Central
American civilization. Spence's arguments on geological, anthropologi-
cal, or linguistic grounds were, however, quite untenable.

"Scientific" evidence for the Atlantis mythos has always proved too
unscientific to be taken seriously. Typical was the proposal of the French
geologist Pierre Termier that the glassy tachylite recovered from the
Atlantic ocean floor two miles down must have erupted originally from
above-ground volcanoes, because only in air could this lava material cool
quickly enough to form noncrystalline glass. Later it was demonstrated
that such material forms just as well under water as in air. Nevertheless, Atlantists still quote Termier's erroneous theory to "prove" their
myth.[2]

Even if a mid-Atlantic land could have been submerged by an
earthquake larger than any in recorded history, it would have had to be
low, flat, and never more than a few feet above sea level. Plato's Atlantis
was "mountainous." Moreover, any large flooded land would remain
close to the surface as a shoal area. Even Plato sensibly assumed that the
subsidence of Atlantis would have left an impassable barrier of mud
shoals just beyond the Pillars of Hercules, so the sea in that area would
be no longer navigable. No such shoals exist. The only submerged high
ground is the mid-Atlantic ridge, where submarine volcanoes are slowly
growing. Intensive explorations by several scientific expeditions have
shown no sign of sunken cities there. On the contrary: the depth of
Atlantic sea-bottom sediment shows that there have been no significant
geological changes for about seventy million years, a period more than
twenty times longer than the existence of any human beings on this
earth, let alone civilization, which began only a mere seven or eight
thousand years ago.

The only reasonable evidence for a possible factual basis for Plato's
utopian fable comes from recent archaeological investigations on the
island of Thera (Santorin) in the eastern Mediterranean. Much of this
island did in fact fall into the sea in the fifteenth century B.C., having
blown itself apart in a volcanic explosion more violent than the famous

eruption of Krakatoa in 1883. When Thera blew up, great waves drowned the coastal cities of nearby Crete while the rest of Crete's land mass was smothered by volcanic ash. The eruption may have caused tsunamis giving rise to deluge myths all around the shores of the eastern Mediterranean. It is thought that the catastrophe marked the death of Minoan culture, which would have been remembered in early Greek myths. A sizable Minoan city has been discovered on the island of Thera itself, buried under tons of volcanic debris.

Not in the least deterred by the total lack of real evidence, however, Atlantis buffs go on exuberantly inventing and reinventing this vanished culture(s) by blandly matter-of-fact descriptions that present the myth as genuine history. Edmund Harold explains how Atlanteans lit their homes and cities and powered their "airships, submarines and pleasure craft" with energy flowing forth from gigantic quartz crystals. They even used such crystals to adjust the mental attitudes of criminals and convert them into useful citizens, for "the pulsating electromagnetic energy released by each crystal in turn brought about startling transformations within those who were subjected to it."[3] The fact that quartz crystals exude no such electromagnetic energy does not even slow down the onward momentum of myth building.

One writer declares that crystals were used in Atlantis for "genetic coding" and in Lemuria to develop extrasensory perception. The average life span in Lemuria was several thousand years. Lemurians' pineal glands were three times the size of human pineal glands now. We are told that because Egyptian priests were directly descended from Atlanteans, examination of their mummified remains will show pineal glands of extraordinary size. Of course, examination of Egyptian mummies can confirm nothing of the sort, because Egyptian mummies have no pineal glands, all soft tissues having been removed from their skull cavities. Although Lemurians became Atlanteans and subsequently Egyptian priests, they also became the fairies and elves, or nature spirits, for whom a recently popularized term is *devas* (from the Sanskrit word for gods). These ex-Lemurians live in "an ethereal dimension faster than the speed of light," which seems to imply that they must be going somewhere.[4]

Innumerable modern "teachers" make offhand references to Atlantis as if it were as much a part of history as Greece or Babylon. "Numerology existed in Atlantis, and likely earlier in Lemuria," says one.[5] Others have multiplied the mythical prehistoric civilizations far beyond poor modest sunken Atlantis. There were not only the "well-known cultures" of Atlantis and Lemuria, but also those of the Cyclopeans, Poseidans, Anti-Atlanteans, Uramorans, and Oraxians, who "existed in the area of Siberia approximately 150,000 years ago. . . . The entire culture existed under a magnetic dome of energy created through a crystal-based force field. Around the perimeter were placed several thousand crystals that served as grounding points for the magnetic dome. The power to these crystals was generated from a central core of crystals and conducted to the perimeter crystals through a system of copper rods."[6]

Needless to say, there is no shred of hard evidence for such details anywhere on earth, but this does not stop the Atlantis fanciers, who receive their information from elsewhere. Such information is "channeled" from long-dead Egyptian priests, or "ascended masters," or entities from another plane of existence, all of these being euphemisms for plain everyday imagination. As one of the most popular settings for decades of fantasy and science fiction stories, Atlantis is above all the realm of the imagination, where anything one cares to say about it immediately comes true.[7]

A strange paradox may be noticed among the recipients of "information" from such mythological sources. On the one hand, practitioners display an amazing degree of hubris in their assumption that any idea that enters their heads must be—or must have been—true, no matter how improbable it may be. On the other hand, they have an equally amazing mistrust of their own creative powers. They seem unable to believe in their own minds' ability to envision fantasy or invent fiction. Such diversions must be attributed to alien intelligences or spirit guides. Perhaps the main problem of Atlantis/Lemuria/Mu/Orax enthusiasts is that they don't understand mental play—not even their own.

It is often assumed that contributors to the Atlantis myth must have been Atlanteans themselves in a previous life (and always upper-class, in-group, spiritually "advanced" Atlanteans, at that); otherwise, they could not know so much about it. Edgar Cayce claimed that he was an Atlantean, and so was every prominent leader "in any country or clime."[8] The idea proved popular, since ordinary humans are usually disinclined to believe that other ordinary humans like themselves can exceed them in intelligence.

According to Cayce's pseudomemory, early Atlanteans fabricated balloons out of elephant hide (!) "for the moving of building materials." Later on, they developed lasers, airships, submarines, telephones, elevators, telescopes, explosives, photography, radio, television, electricity, and giant "generator" quartz crystals to power everything. Despite our own civilizations' demonstration that such developments spread all over the world in less than a century, Atlantean technology existed for thousands of years without moving beyond its borders. Moreover, despite frequent waves of migration from Atlantis to other continents— America, India, Egypt, the Iberian peninsula, the Caucasus—the enlightened ones never took any of their technology with them. Within a short time, Atlantean colonists were back down to the level of oxcarts and river rafts.[9]

The history, geography, chronology, arts, and culture of Atlantis (and its by now numerous sister utopias) vary considerably from one informant to another. The spirit guides don't seem to collaborate—or read each other's books. To choose one of the more recent outpourings of this material: typical Atlantis mythology occurs in the works of Frank Alper, who affects the titles of both Reverend and Doctor, as well as the "spiritual name" Christos. His Atlantis is sometimes a city, sometimes a continent, and sometimes even a planet "within this galaxie [*sic*]," which was destroyed many millions of years ago. "The planet served as a form of experimentary [*sic*] laboratory. They [*sic*] also assisted in problems that arose in other areas of the galaxie [*sic*]."[10]

In a series of lectures in 1981, Alper began his history with the Pacific continent of Lemuria, which existed for a hundred thousand years and was connected by tunnels, "deep beneath the earth's crust," to Atlantis, which he placed on the east coast of the United States. There is still "a large network of tunnels," according to Alper, connecting all the continents with each other. Some of these tunnels have been recently rediscovered—by whom, he does not say. Four miles from the "Horth" [*sic*] Pole, a tunnel descends into the bowels of the earth, where dwell Atlantean "Uramoran" beings, millions of years old. They are "crystaline" [*sic*] in form and "do not injest [*sic*] food, such as you do." There is also an anti-Atlantis presently situated seven hundred miles below the earth's surface "in the vivinity [*sic*] of the South Pole." When asked by a listener how tunnels could exist in the molten magma under the earth's crust, Alper's spirit guide quickly cut off communication.[11]

The Lemurians and Atlanteans were at war with each other for fifty thousand years. Both continents sank into the ocean in 85,000 B.C. Survivors of the cataclysm carried on business as usual, living in "huge caverns beneath the sea that were free from water." The elders were able to travel frequently to the surface. In 77,777 B.C., spaceships arrived from "universes far beyond this universe," bearing "highly evolved" scientific equipment and "many types of vegitations [sic] and foods" to help rebuild Atlantis on the sea bottom. Eventually, Atlantis will rise again from the waves. It will be a natural Garden of Eden, "with elves playing their flutes" and also with ultramodern "cities of giant structures of crystal and glass, of highly sophisticated [sic] computerized equipment."[12] Edgar Cayce (died 1945) also predicted that Atlantis would arise from the ocean off the east coast of the United States in 1968 or 1969.[13]

Alper declares that the fall of Atlantis was brought about by excessive scientific curiosity—specifically, experiments in which men interbred with animals to produce the half-human creatures of classical mythology, such as satyrs, centaurs, sphinxes, horned gods, serpent men, sea monsters, the animal-masked deities of Egypt, and the man-headed bulls and lions of Babylon. Alper forgot that in another "channeling" he declared that there were no animals in Atlantis. Cheerily ignoring the biological impossibility of interspecies breeding, Alper asserts that all these mythological creatures were real. Atlantean scientists who created them sinned against the natural order of things by devising "experiments of their own, to utilize their power and abilities to explore unknown and forbidden areas, to challenge the unknown"—in other words, by doing exactly what scientists are supposed to do. Yet no fault is found with other Atlantean meddlings with nature, such as methods whereby "certain specie [sic] of infectous [sic] plants that were contagious were returned to pure energy form to eliminate the threat of infection." In the future Atlantis, similar dissolution will be imposed on disobedient people. "Lack of proper use shall automatically disslove [sic] them," he says in a rather apt if unintentional stumble.[14]

The idea that human sins bring about earthquakes, subsidence of lands, and other natural disasters was also part of Edgar Cayce's worldview. He said "the sin of man" is even responsible for sunspots![15]

Atlantis was definitely not democratic. On the contrary, it was rigidly hierarchical. Citizens declared their social status by the number of knots on their belts. But Alper contradicted himself on this: once he said there were "from one to nine" knots; another time he said "from zero to seven" knots; a third time he said there were as many as twelve knots.[16] In any event, it was a society founded on slave labor performed by the lowest caste, strong but stupid brutes good for nothing but toil.

It was also a sexist society. Its double standard imposed sexual fidelity on a wife but allowed her husband complete freedom. "When a man wished to unite with a woman that was not his to unite with, he would do so, under the following system of release. He felt that he was a child of God, and if, as a child of God, he loved another child of God, then why was he not permitted to achieve a blending of the vibrations to enhance his love." Yet the woman who illicitly achieved a blending of her vibrations was sentenced to hard labor among the slaves in the fields. Perhaps under pressure from irate female devotees, Alper's spirit guide later recanted and declared that Atlantis had no monogamy, polygamy, slavery, servitude, or double standards. Nevertheless, "The majority of those serving in a 'work' capacity in the Temple were in a female expression"—which is Alper's odd way of saying that the workers were women, a system surely not unfamiliar among ourselves.[17]

According to these almost invariably male enthusiasts, everything Atlantean was Father-oriented. Even witnessing the birth of a child is described by Alper as "sitting in awe of the miracle of the Father"! There is no Goddess. There is only God. The goal of humanity is "*man*'s struggle to become one with the *Father*" (italics mine). "As the soul evolves, it's [*sic*] frequencies of energies keep increasing enabling it to tune into levels of truth closer and closer to the Father. . . . This form of evolution and growth . . . is to be dearly strived for." Alper lays a heavy responsibility on his hearers: "You are here to fill the needs of God."[18]

There is a lot of talk about love as the basis for Atlantean culture, but the human foundation of love is effectively undercut by taking babies away from their mothers to be raised in collective nurseries. According to Alper, children were given no toys, only spiritual instructions. Girls were forbidden by law to become pregnant before they married at the age of sixteen. Naively enough, Alper seems to think such laws were never broken. "There were no such events as 'unwed mothers.'"[19] Can one classify an unwed mother as an event?

Pregnant women were sealed up in crystal-walled cubicles for twenty-four hours while their fetuses were programmed by crystal power for their role in life after birth. The cubicles surrounded the Healing Temple grid, made of "a metallic alloy, alien to this planet," that consisted of a mixture of silver, copper, and ground quartz (none of which are alien to this planet), supported by a "pedastel" [*sic*]. The same cubicles were used for healing "when an individual became seriously inflicted [*sic*] with an ailment." Death, apparently, was rare, occurring mostly from excessive astral projection, which severed "the silver chord [*sic*]." Nevertheless, the people described as direct descendants of Atlanteans, namely the "Souix [*sic*] and Mohawk" Indians, seem to live no longer than anyone else. Alper disagrees with other "authorities" who affirm the Atlantean origin of the Mayan people. They "were not from Atlantis, but migrated directly here from other worlds."[20]

One may well wonder why such a delirious mess of undigested science fiction, millennialism, utopianism, quackery, and semiliterate English exerts such widespread appeal and is accepted by thousands as genuine history. One answer, of course, is that genuine history and especially prehistory are seldom adequately taught in modern schools. But perhaps a more telling answer is that though Atlantis is no more historical than the biblical Garden of Eden, it exerts an archetypal appeal very like that of Eden. It postulates a primordial paradise—an idea possibly rooted in universal lost memories of intrauterine life—from which a Fall precipitated humanity into a less perfect, less comfortable world. Deluge myths have been generally associated with the birth trauma. Myths of great and wise ancestors (like the biblical giants) are associated with hidden infantile memories of large and seemingly omnipotent adults.

Atlantis differs from Eden in one important respect. As a product of our own intensely technological culture, which grew out of the mind-set of the Industrial Revolution, Atlantis is an abundantly *technological* Eden. Its fabled wisdom is not scriptural fiction but science fiction. Although the New Age expresses disillusionment about technology per se, it still clothes in the trappings of popularized, misinterpreted, misunderstood science that archetypal need to believe in a primal perfection. So the Atlanteans, Lemurians, Oraxians, and so on were scientific wizards destroyed by their own hubris—a fate that many fear, with considerable reason, for our own civilization. Atlanteans are really ourselves, viewed through the distorted mirrors of a children's funhouse by people who fear reality and cannot recognize fantasy.

The Atlantis archetype has all the elements common to myths of every age and culture: moral precept and warning, the drama of catastrophe, the aura but not the discipline of hard knowledge, the ever-present, ever-repeated Fall from paradise, another version of the Deluge, and that fine old comforter of the common man, the story of past intellectual greatness that built its towers too high, encroached on realms set aside for the gods, and suffered destruction.

Then, too, there is the superlatively attractive hint that such intellectual greatness can be retrieved, through communication from friendly ancestral spirits, by one's *self;* and of course this time the fatal hubris will be avoided. One can become infinitely wise without even trying. The long, grinding disciplines of learning can be bypassed. One can have one's cake and eat it without the trouble of having to bake it. "Don't use your mind to explain or rationalize," one mystic advises reassuringly.[21] Visions need not be subjected to the burden of proof. Whatever is stated often enough, however ridiculous it may be, can become true.

One Atlantis-related belief that seems enormously attractive in a world ever plagued by physical and emotional distress is the belief that Atlantean pseudoscience could and can give people renewed health and emotional stability. The key word most used in New Age mysticism is *healing.* This idea, more than any other, endears all mystics to their followers. It is the universal promise that worked for Stone Age magicians, tribal shamans, classical priestesses of Asclepius, Hygeia, and Panacea, early Christians and Gnostics with their miracle cures, witches and wisewomen with their folklore charms, and every smooth-talking charlatan who ever came along with another method of selling hope to the sick. New Age "healing" frequently claims to have originated in Atlantis, home of those marvelous crystals that could do everything, including behave like electrical generators—something no crystal known to modern science has ever been seen doing. How these notions came about and what their implications are merit investigation in some detail.

1. de Camp, 236, 313. 2. de Camp, 170–171. 3. Harold, 2–3. 4. Gurudas, 5–9. 5. Parkinson, 34. 6. Baer & Baer, *W. L.,* 6–10. 7. de Camp, ch. 11. 8. Robinson, 64. 9. Robinson, 53, 58, 85. 10. Alper 2, 13. 11. Alper 1, 1/19–2, 2/2–2, 8/3–5; 2, 79–80. 12. Alper 1, 1/19–2, 1/26–2,5; 2, 64. 13. Robinson, 63. 14. Alper 1, 8/31–2; 2, 49, 56, 66, 74. 15. Robinson, 172. 16. Alper 1, 1/19–2, 4/24–5; 2, 76. 17. Alper 1, 8/3–1,2; 8/31–2, 1/19–5. 18. Alper 1, 2/2–5, 8/24–2; 2, 59. 19. Alper 1, 8/31–2,3; 2, 36. 20. Alper 1, 1/19–4, 3/9–5,6; 4/24–6. 21. Chocron, 29.

Healing

If modern mystical literature is to be believed, almost any known disease can be cured simply by the application of crystals to the outside of the body—or even just by resting in the same room with some crystals. A fairly typical list of the conditions curable by such means includes the following: multiple sclerosis, diabetes, leukemia, breast cancer, hepatitis, emphysema, mental depression, "toxification," ulcers, colitis, spinal disorders, neuromuscular problems, Parkinsonism, bronchitis, heart disease, narcolepsy, arthritis, sprains, underactive pituitary, gum problems, sinus conditions, high blood pressure, hearing problems, hypoglycemia, obesity, broken bones, burns, inflammation of the sciatic nerve, spinal cord damage, herpes, venereal disease, chemical dependency, lupus, bone growths, allergies, epilepsy, hyperactivity, migraines, lymph disorders, mental retardation, cerebral palsy, muscular dystrophy, skin growths, strep throat, and diseases of the thyroid, adrenals, spleen, liver, prostate, genitals, transmandibular joint, and eyes—plus "general forms of cancer."[1]

The desperation of sick people has always provided a blood scent for those human sharks who, throughout history, have managed to trade ephemeral hope for a patient's hard cash. Some of the sharks are cynical con artists; these tend to be the most successful. Others are half sincere, convincing themselves that at least some of their clients receive some benefit in the form of an improved outlook. Still others are entirely self-deluded and believe their own nonsense. These last are the most dangerous. They often advise against any recourse to traditional medicine until it is too late. They often compound the discouragement of a failed "cure" by cruelly blaming the victim: they claim that the patient subconsciously resisted the cure because of some perverse need to hold onto the disease.

One such healer even writes that a patient's death during treatment can be cheerfully accepted as "a blessed event. That soul has completed its task, and there is a great and joyous welcoming committee greeting it in the primary reality."[2] The cure that fails is not at fault. The patient is at fault for having insufficient faith. "These energies must be accepted by the individual. He must believe that he, or she can be healed, and they must no longer have a need for the disease."[3] Such a creative way of avoiding malpractice suits apparently has not yet occurred to the medical profession!

In view of the peculiar rationales offered by crystal healers, however, anyone with a modicum of physiological knowledge could hardly accord them any faith, or even credence. It is claimed, for example, that all stones emit sounds that have great potential for healing.[4] When did anyone ever hear a sound emitted by a stone, or when did any sound cure a disease? It is claimed that crystals cure bursitis by "brealing [sic] down the calcification deposits that occur in various joints," although bursitis has nothing to do with calcification.[5] It is claimed that double terminated quartz crystals placed under each eye can reverse the aging process.[6] It is claimed that crystals affect a second, "causal" heart that is located on the right side of the chest.[7] This world-shaking discovery that each of us has two hearts has been somehow overlooked in centuries of anatomy studies. It is claimed that diseases can be eliminated by sitting inside a circle of quartz crystals that (though completely nonmagnetic) create "a particular type of magnetic field," which in turn can "repolarize the organs inside the physical body, to eliminate disease, and to correct the aberations [sic] in the magnetic field around every organ in the body."[8] The magnetism theory of medicine died with Franz Mesmer in 1815, but this fact has not yet been assimilated by crystal mystics.

Bacteria, viruses, environmental toxins, parasites, genetic defects, the inevitable deteriorations of old age, and similar disease producers are not, however, widely recognized in the mystics' world. The general theory is that all illness is caused by wrong acts and attitudes, anxieties, fears, and unresolved conflicts. Physical "imbalance and disharmony" result from conflict between the personality and the soul; but by understanding this, we are told, we may cure our own diseases.[9] Such may well be the case with emotional illnesses, but most physical illnesses are not to be so simplistically dealt with. As far as crystal healers are concerned, stones can do it all. "As the healing essence of quartz crystals vibrate [sic] the soul of humanity, vast hoizons [sic] of hope and joy appear."[10] Stones' extraordinary (though undiscovered) vibrations can energize, heal, uplift, and "attune" the human spirit.[11] Stones cure all the usual undefined problems dear to the crystal mystic: imbalances, blockages, karmic debts, stress, spaciness, negativity, impurity, toxicity, disharmony, conditions of being off center or ungrounded, and the like. These things are safe enough to say, since no one knows what they really mean anyway. But it is similarly claimed that stones cure many other conditions, such as toothache, tumors, hemorrhoids, cystitis, cancer, AIDS, bladder infections, sexual dysfunction, asthma, colic, depression, irregular menses, osteoporosis, polio, convulsions, gout, tuberculosis, calcium deficiencies, and even aging and death![12]

Mystical theories about the causes of disease are nothing if not colorful. One healer insists that people have the ability to "metabolize the orgone supply from the surrounding atmosphere," and if this ability fails, then one needs "predigested energy from others."[13] Another asserts that "beams of white light" enter into the center of every cell, nerve, and tissue of the body, and that healing with stones of various colors depends on "certain molecular reactions that take place in the organs through the medium of the rays."[14] Magnetic energies, another declares, are used "in the area of altering the cellular structure of the body. This enables man to communicate better with their space brothers and to eventually enable them to have their energies transported from one place to another."[15] Facts—orgones do not exist; light does not enter the interior of a living body; and magnetism does not affect the structures of cells—carry no weight with inventors of such theories.

One mystical healer laments the intransigence of medical doctors who refuse to work with those gifted individuals who can instantly diagnose any illness by gazing at the patient's aura, that is, "people able to see the inner processes of the body by simply looking." The writer herself has X-ray vision, like a human CAT scanner, and can even see into the body *microscopically;* no germs or other microorganisms can hide from her all-seeing eye. Nay, more: she does not even require a view of the patient's physical body; she can perform these feats of diagnosis by telephone! "I have a scanner inside my head," she says modestly. She can also "roll back time" and discover the original cause of the illness.[16] How is it possible that doctors have resisted the help of this diagnostic prodigy?

Another healer firmly believes in prevention, which means buying as much jewelry as one can afford and wearing it constantly to ward off evil influences. This is not an extravagance, because spending money on preventive jewelry in the present is preferable to paying doctors' bills in the future.[17] On the other hand, healers of a different school of thought object to the wearing of jewelry. "Stress to the heart is the most likely result of continuous use of crystals as pendants."[18] One goes so far as to define the wearing of shaped and polished crystals as "blasphemy toward the mineral kingdom."[19]

The treatment of stones that have themselves been used as treatment is another subject of considerable controversy among healers. Nearly all regard such stones as dangerously charged with "negative energy" after they have been in contact with a patient. One source states flatly that after a crystal has been used to heal, it must be buried in the earth immediately and abandoned. "Once a healing crystal has been buried after being used on the body, leave it there. Never touch it again."[20] Of course, this is fairly drastic and could run into money, as new crystals would have to be bought constantly to replace those in their graves. Another adviser is easier on the pocketbook, recommending that the crystal be buried only for a short time, either in a flowerpot or under a popsicle stick to show its position in the ground. Alternatively, it can be buried in a cup of dried herbs, passed under running water, or simply blown upon with the breath—all quite simple and inexpensive.[21]

Many like to recommend sea salt, either dry or in a brine solution, for "cleansing" (not cleaning) crystals after use. Ordinary table salt won't do. The sea salt also can be used only once and must be discarded afterward, because "it is a semi-toxic substance after it has been used in this way."[22] Exact recipes are given for "cleansing" brine solutions, such as two pints of warm water, two tablespoons sea salt, two tablespoons cider vinegar. Imperfections in a quartz crystal are removed, it is said, "by the reaction of the salt crystals upon its structure."[23] This would surprise a mineralogist, who knows perfectly well that the structure of quartz is entirely impervious to salt; brine and vinegar can have no more effect on quartz than on glass, which is similarly nonreactive.

Of course, the negative energies supposedly removed by all this careful treatment are mythical in any case, so it doesn't much matter how the proprietor of the crystals decides to purify them. Short of a crystal carrying real germs on its surface after touching someone with an infectious disease, there is little danger. The psychic contamination so greatly feared is a mental image only. It is most easily dealt with by not forming the mental image in the first place. Yet one healer, fearful of "vibrations and other imprints which need to be cleansed and purified," recommends leaving the stone under running water for six to eight hours.[24] In such a case, you had better know the mineral you are dealing with. Some minerals are water soluble and can be purified into total nonexistence by such treatment. Far less troublesome is another method of "cleansing" crystals by ringing Tibetan bells over them. The effectiveness of this is said to "range from 40% to 80%."[25] How these precise measurements were taken, and from what, remains altogether unexplained.

Other sore questions concern the composition of healing crystals: whether they must be natural uncut stones, or shaped and polished minerals like the "stroking wands" sold in psychic shops, or synthetic minerals, or even glass; and if the latter, should it be a naturally occurring glass like obsidian, or a man-made product? Some purists insist that only naturally formed crystalline substances will do; others accept anything. One writer says that ordinary glass balls will do for scrying (crystal gazing), or even a glass pie plate containing a little water, but the plate is still referred to as "crystal."[26] The problem of synthetic gems baffles many mystics. They know the synthetic stones are physically and chemically identical to nature's versions, and if anything, purer; but they don't like the *idea.* One source straddles the fence by saying, "The vibrations of the man-made stones are helpful, but are *not* as totally beneficial, much as an artificial vitamin is not as easily assimilated by the body as a natural vitamin is."[27] The choice of simile is unfortunate, because "artificial" or laboratory-created vitamins are identical to the natural vitamins in foods, and the body recognizes no difference between them.

Despite its many inconsistencies, patent absurdities, and obvious quackery, crystal healing has become popular for a number of reasons. One reason is that patients often feel slighted and neglected by busy medical doctors, who have little time or inclination to relate to them as whole people and may seem to be primarily interested in receiving prompt payment of unpleasantly high fees. Patients may turn to psychic healers for the appearance of attention, caring, and sympathy that such healers can provide. These emotional satisfactions can actually alleviate symptoms, especially if the complaint has an emotional basis.

Another advantage of crystal healers is that their "treatments" never cause pain. They may be ineffective, but they are not traumatic. Most people can feel comforted by sitting or lying down quietly for a while, perhaps with soft background music, while someone else speaks soothingly and places small bits of stone on or around their bodies. It seems a harmless, relaxing way to spend an hour or so, unless the healer is greedy enough to demand a fee of medical magnitude. Crystal healers generally charge as much as they think they can get away with, but not more than the patient can afford. The majority do not earn exorbitant amounts of money. Why, then, do they bother?

One self-styled authority sets forth the healer's psychological motivation with naive directness: healing with crystals is "learning to be God."[28] Physicians can feel this too, but only after arduous years of training. Crystal healers can attain such pseudogodhood after half an hour of training, or after reading one short, minimally demanding book. If they are psychologically adept at manipulating others, they need no other skills. Certainly the last thing which seems to be required of them is accurate knowledge of their tools, the minerals.

Most crystal healers are apparently ignorant of the principles of mineralogy, and seem to understand little about the crystalline structures whose wonders they tout. One writes, with lofty disdain for study, "It is not my aim to delve into the different substances that make up the stones."[29] Evidently, few have any notion of what the ionic lattice of any given mineral looks like, or what elements are included in its makeup. Some seem ignorant even of the very elements; they still believe in the mythical five postulated by the ancient Greeks: earth, water, air, fire, and ether.

In fact, it does not matter which specific substances the healers use in which ways. Of the dozens of crystal-healing books, no two entirely agree on technique. Malachite on the throat chakra? Tourmaline between the feet? Citrine or tigereye over the kidneys? Rose quartz or aventurine pieces in a triangle? Should the heart chakra stones be green, pink, or yellow? Which stone(s) should be placed on the third eye? There is no agreement. Each "authority" has different answers. If patients were not so impressed by all the nonsense about gemstones, the same effects could be obtained with chips of marble, ceramic bathroom tiles, bits of colored glass, nuts and bolts, or chunks of ordinary gravel—which is, after all, just as much a crystallized natural product as any gemstone is.

The question is sometimes asked, If crystal healing is just a game after all, why should anything more be expected of it? If crystal healing is basically harmless, gentle, and often emotionally satisfying, what can be wrong with it? Why should anyone object?

One objection arises from the fact that crystal healing is a placebo procedure masquerading as a genuine remedy. Although placebos frequently work, this is not sufficient reason to accept them as medicines, because there are too many occasions when they don't work. Real medicines, such as antibiotics, do not require faith on the part of the patient. They will do their job regardless of what the patient believes. Imagine a pharmaceutical company trying to market a medicine that would help only those consumers able to achieve just the right state of mind! Clearly, patients' belief is no proof of efficacy. It can even be a serious danger when an erroneous belief interferes with seeking more effective measures. Sad cases have been known of people in the early stages of severe illness perilously postponing real treatment because they clung to their faith in quackery.

It is also decidedly unethical to sell false claims for real money. The more expensive the healers' treatments or products, the more dishonest they appear. If one plays imaginative games with crystals in one's own living room with a few friends, it is pleasure and not business. But when buying and selling become involved, the buyer has the right to expect that what is sold will not be misrepresented.

One of the most flagrant examples of misrepresentation is the recent "gemstone essence" scam: crystal mystics sell tiny bottles of water supposedly charged with the "energies" of gemstones that have been immersed in it. Consumers evidently have too little grounding in basic science to realize that nothing passes into water from any insoluble mineral, so they will pay a fancy price for a little vial of "sapphire water" or "beryl water" that they could get at no cost, right from their own kitchen faucet. There is no sapphire or beryl physically or chemically combined with the H_2O. Water remains just water. The only human condition that it is likely to cure is thirst.

The insolubility of gemstones is readily apparent to anyone who knows that they are often found in the gravels of stream beds, having weathered out of the softer rock that once enclosed them and washed downstream with the rains and floods of many thousands of years. If these minerals could be dissolved by water, they would have long since disappeared.

Crystal healers put forth many theories purporting to prove how the human body is affected by proximity to minerals, but none of them really deserves the name of theory—let alone proof. For the most part, they are muddled word play. For instance, after stating that every mineral has its own unchanging vibration rate (which, however, has never been measured or proved), some mystics say that "using minerals to treat a human affliction on whatever level is to raise the frequency level or vibratory rate of the gem being utilized at this moment."[30] We are not told how the changeless rate of the mineral is changed to a higher rate. Another source claims that human "imbalances" are corrected by exposure to the steady, balanced vibrational energies within a crystal, yet the same source says that it works the other way: "Strong imbalanced thoughts and emotions are particularly prone to upsetting the energetic balance within a crystal."[31]

Crystal healers might inspire more confidence if they did not seem so abysmally ignorant of basic anatomy and physiology, not to mention other sciences, even at the grade-school level. A weird vision of the circulatory system appears in one "expert" notion of "the heart where the blood flows in, rather than where it is forced out through the lungs."[32] Another thinks the adrenal glands are located "near the solar plexus region," that ammonia is an acid, that arthritis is caused by "unhealthy thinking," and that the "molecular structure" of the body can be rearranged by visualizing a desirable state of health. Pseudoscientific babble produces numerous nonexplanations, such as "Chemical balance, between the ferric and oxygenic (i.e., magnetic) conditions of the blood, is necessary." Healing can be brought about, not only by minerals themselves, but even by looking at photographs of minerals; "you can actually receive the vibration as it has been caught by the camera."[33]

Sailing out into space without even a basic workable vocabulary, the healer cannot distinguish a solar system from a galaxy and believes that our outer planets—Uranus, Neptune, and Pluto—"entered our galaxy" in the years of their discovery, 1781, 1847, and 1930 respectively, instead of having been there all along.[34] In short, the crystal healers make so many misstatements of simple, well-known scientific facts that the intelligent reader can hardly be persuaded that they know what they are talking about.

It is illegal in most states for sellers of herbs to prescribe herbal "cures" or to make specific statements about which illnesses will be overcome by which products of the herbal apothecary. This is tantamount to practicing medicine without a license and can lead to prosecution. However, no such laws seem to restrain the crystal healers. They can and do make the wildest claims, of a sort that might put an herb shop out of business. Legislators apparently have not begun to realize that frauds are being perpetrated, similar to the ones during the patent-medicine frenzies that inspired consumer-protective laws around the turn of the century. Through the sale and use of seemingly innocent stones, many people are in effect practicing medicine without a license, raising false hopes in the chronically ill, and taking money on the pretense of selling services that are, in fact, illusory.

Therefore, even if no serious harm is done, people are being misled. Crystal healers tread a thin line between the role of counselor or adviser and that of con artist. Many of them step over to the unethical side of the line. To have good intentions is not sufficient excuse. To mean well is not enough. To offer a placebo disguised as a medicine is not honest. That which is good and rewarding about crystal mysticism should not be dependent on misrepresentation of any kind.

Another kind of moral responsibility rests on knowledgeable mineralogists and mineral dealers, many of whom observe the crystal healing phenomenon with bemused cynicism but do nothing to impede it because they find it hugely profitable. At a recent mineral show, one dealer was overheard saying to another, "The healy-feelies are the greatest thing that ever happened to my business. They bought all my quartz for thirty times what I paid for it." Another dealer told what he considered a funny story about mystics who came to his table with crystal pendulums and bought whatever made their pendulums swing. "One of the lady loonies said my crystals were the most active she ever saw. The real magic was that my table was standing in a breeze from the open door."

Dealers have learned the mystical buzzwords. They speak with apparent authority to their "healy-feely" customers about vibrations, chakras, bioelectricity, imbalances, record keepers, teacher crystals, elestials, third-eye stones, and all the rest. Most dealers are contemptuous of the crystal mystics' world of fantasy, but they know it's good for business. One dealer remarked with satisfaction that the mystics have "dragged up" the prices of all mineral specimens along with their favorite species. "Now I can get gem prices for pieces of junk that I would have thrown away before the healy-feelies came." Such dealers have a bottom-line philosophy that misinforming or misleading the public is OK as long as it leads to profit.

Still, there is another bottom line below and apart from the one labeled Money. Even if placebo healing works sometimes, is the sale of a placebo morally justifiable?

For centuries, people have been at least temporarily healed by anonymous rags, teeth, or pigs' bones masquerading as saints' relics, by cheap trinkets mass-produced by commercial religions, or by egomaniacal spellbinders claiming holy powers. Surely it insults Mother Earth to classify her beautiful creations with such trash.

It also insults the human mind to stuff it with so many fallacies that little room is left for facts. When misinformation about the world of nature become s a habitual mode of thinking, then entrenched errors can overwhelm even fundamental truths, and the way is open for another Dark Age of ignorance.

Probably there is a healing force within the human spirit, but we don't yet know how to tap it deliberately, without delusion. Study of this subject is a challenge for the future. Meanwhile, let us not confuse this force—whatever it is—with external objects. It does not dwell in external objects. It is part of the self. Popularized crystal lore too often converts spiritual needs into tools of exploitation, rather than developing the impulse toward enlightenment.

Let the buyer beware of those who are learning to be God.

1. Alper 2, 33. 2. Brennan, 279. 3. Alper 1, 3/2–1. 4. Chocron, 9. 5. Alper 1, 3/2–1. 6. Raphaell, *C. E.*, 58. 7. Rea, 195. 8. Alper 1, 1/26–3. 9. Chocron, 99. 10. Raphaell, *C. E.*, 51. 11. Chocron, 53. 12. Stein, 277–283. 13. Brennan, 104. 14. Chocron, 4. 15. Alper 1, 2/9–3. 16. Brennan, 152, 155, 161, 163, 167. 17. Chocron, 51–52. 18. Rea, 96. 19. Bryant, 16. 20. *Ibid.*, 40. 21. Stein, 151. 22. Rea, 12. 23. Harold, 45–46. 24. Chocron, 30. 25. Rea, 144. 26. Bryant, 60–61. 27. Richardson et al., 73. 28. Rea, 170. 29. Chocron, 29. 30. Lorusso & Glick, 12. 31. Baer & Baer, *C. C.*, 127. 32. Richardson & Huett, 43. 33. Bravo, 43, 100, 134, 158, 183, 189. 34. *Ibid.*, 33, 68, 174.

Crystal Meditation

Quiet, private contemplation of a crystal can be a true ceremony, as orderly and aesthetically satisfying as a Japanese tea ceremony. A little time spent alone with one of Earth's pretty bones can make one feel calm, centered, and soothed. It is an opportunity to encounter natural beauty, both in the external object and in the inner imaginative faculty that it stimulates.

Choose a time when there is nothing pressing to be done within the next hour or so and no interruptions will occur. Sit or recline comfortably, crystal in hand. If convenient, light some fragrant incense. Listen to peaceful music. Relax. Hold the crystal gently in both hands until its surface no longer feels chilly. Then begin to turn it about, very slowly, pausing at each position to study the play of light on both surface and internal features. Sometimes a mere millimeter's change will present a very different set of forms.

Any mineral will do for a meditation session. Opaque objects can serve as well as transparent ones. Even an ordinary stone can be used. However, the most popular material is clear or semiclear quartz. A natural quartz crystal, a crystal cluster, or a polished piece of quartz can show ribbons and streaks of rainbow colors when the principal light source is behind you, illuminating the near sides of its inner cracks and refraction planes. Internal "veiling" (drifts of tiny gas bubbles) can sometimes light up with rainbow-colored sparks, especially under sunlight. Colored varieties of quartz, such as amethyst, citrine, smoky quartz, and rose quartz, also show rainbow flashes at times, so will transparent crystals of other common minerals, such as fluorite, calcite, and beryl.

When the light source is in front of you (that is, behind the crystal), you may see brilliant rainbow colors along the side faces of a natural hexagonal quartz crystal. The angle of vision is so crucial to this effect that, as a rule, it can be seen by only one eye at a time. Check this by holding the crystal steady when you have found the right angle; then close first one eye and then the other. The bright glow of rainbow colors will be seen by one eye, but the same area of the crystal will appear dulled or dark to the other eye.

In addition to various rainbow effects, crystals can show illusions of landscapes, clouds, stars, caves, towers, statues, buildings, faces, and figures. Send your mind's eye in amongst them. Imagine yourself smaller than a speck of dust, passing through the transparent parts of the crystal as if through air. View the shapes around you as if they were solid, or as if they were enormous—miles in extent, perhaps. It is possible to become so immersed in such in-crystal sightseeing tours as to quite lose track of the passage of time.

Visual effects will vary, also, according to the quality and direction of the light and the reflected background color of walls, floors, or other ambient surfaces that can be seen in the crystal. For such reasons, the same crystal can show new, unexpected scenes each time it is viewed. The trick of crystal meditation is to be open to whatever seems to appear, never to force an image or to have a preconceived notion of what should be there. Even a crystal that has become familiar through many sessions can still surprise you.

Some people enjoy meditating in a dim or dark room with a single bright spotlight focused on the crystal. A pencil-thin beam of high-intensity light can produce remarkable results. Laser light gives particularly interesting patterns. The interior refraction planes of transparent crystals—especially those with many cracks—can scatter laser light in fascinating ways.

An excellent way to use laser light is to project the beam through a crystal onto a blank wall in an otherwise dark room. Some crystals can scatter the laser beam into marvelous curtains, fans, and rivers of fiery light, flashing and changing shape with every hair's-breadth turn of the crystal, sometimes lighting up the entire wall. No two crystals produce the same patterns, nor do any two positions of the same crystal. A faceted stone, such as a brilliant-cut diamond, can split a laser beam into a galaxy of starry light sparks that seem to fill the whole room.

Direct sunlight is an excellent illumination for crystals, which behave like any other prism in breaking up the white light of the sun into component spectral colors. Such colors are the famous "rainbow veils of Maya" that Hindu mystics called the essence of the living, perceptible world of nature. This doctrine of the rainbow veils was based on observations that nearly all of us have already made in our childhood: that is, many surfaces viewed under bright sunlight will seem to be made of an infinity of tiny rainbow-colored sparks. This iridescence is readily seen on leaves, insect chitin, and human skin and hair, as well as inorganic substances like rocks or sand.

Oriental mystics reasoned from such observations that the Goddess Maya, maker of the material universe, used rainbow light as her principal building material to create all things visible to the eye. Her name means "magical appearances" or "illusion," because the sages taught that the real universe lay behind Maya's rainbow veils, which served to clothe and disguise the true essence of things. The idea that final revelation dwells somehow beyond or underneath the veil of a supreme Goddess is also prevalent in ancient Egyptian, Greek, and Mesopotamian mythology. Maya was one of the many names of the Virgin form of the Triple Goddess Kali—the same Virgin who gave birth through many cycles of incarnation to the Savior, entitled Buddha or "Enlightened One": one who was able to see beyond the veil. In the West, a similar "Enlightened One" was Hermes, whose Virgin Mother was named Maia.

One of the favorite fancies of crystal meditators is that the crystal does provide a glimpse beyond the veil, thus symbolizing a kind of door or gateway into some aspects of nature that are normally concealed. This may well be taken as another interesting route into hidden realms of the unconscious, which can become accessible also through trance, dream, creative inspiration, or sudden insight. In fact, crystal meditation partakes a little bit of all of these. Sometimes the visions thus provided will represent clues to the solving of problems in ordinary daily life when the mind makes the connection between the two. This is the basis of the kind of esoteric enlightenment that some people call the result of "crystal gazing."

To further enhance your appreciation of your mineral specimens, try observing them under magnification. A good reading glass or other magnifier can show you details that the naked eye cannot see. A jeweler's loupe, which magnifies about ten times, can put you into a whole new landscape of crystalline cliffs, caves, and colors; can bring you into a far more intimate relationship with your stone; and can show you previously unsuspected inclusions and other interesting features. In fact, jewelry owners are often astonished by the many flaws and imperfections that the loupe can show in their apparently perfect, "eye-clean" faceted gems. The truth is that there are virtually no utterly flawless gems, of any reasonable size, in existence.

Remember that magnification requires brighter light. Stones viewed through a loupe will appear dark unless placed in a strong, direct light. Bright sunlight is always usable. For cloudy-day or nighttime viewing, use a high intensity lamp.

Mineralogists are keenly aware of the great beauty to be found in the realm of the very small, beneath the capacity of the unaided human eye to see. Therefore, some mineralogists and gemologists like to specialize in micromounts, which are tiny crystals prepared especially for viewing through a microscope. Micromounts generally show more perfect crystal forms than larger specimens. If you attend a mineral sale or demonstration where microscopes are set up to view micromount displays, by all means seize the opportunity. To spend some time at the microscope is to engage in a particularly rewarding kind of crystal meditation.

Another aspect of a crystal meditation can put you in touch with the cycles of the earth, the idea of time, and knowledge of the natural world through learning. It is not enough for the true seeker just to hold and contemplate a little piece of Mother Earth. Contemplation should be enhanced by reading, so that after one has looked it up, one knows as much as possible about the particular mineral in hand and can make a mental list of its characteristics. What is its chemical formula? Crystal class? Hardness? Specific gravity? Probable age? How and where did it form? Is this specimen typical of the mineral in general? Is it somehow aberrant? If so, how? Does it have inclusions of other minerals? If so, what are they?

It is both humbling and inspiring to envision the tremendous stretches of time covered by the slow formation of Earth's crystals. Consider the enormous heat and pressure deep underground, where intrusions of molten magma ("Mother blood") rose up into crustal rocks and began to cool, slowly, slowly, while various minerals within the superhot soup began to form their characteristic crystals. What point—early, late, or intermediate in the cooling process—marked the birth of your crystal? How long might it have taken to grow to its present size?

Such questions must be answered by guesswork, but it should be educated guesswork. Find a book that will give you some real answers. Then, as you meditate on your stone, picture its formation in the bowels of the earth, its slow growth in the darkness, its metamorphosis, if any, or if it is a sedimentary rock, the eons of accumulation that created it. Did it grow in a pegmatite (coarse-textured rock formation), a geode, a limestone cavern, a lava tube? Did it erode out of its mother rock and travel to another place? Did it blow suddenly out of a volcanic womb? Think: if this stone could talk to you, what might it tell about its own history?

Try to picture that history. Take yourself back to a time when there were no human beings on earth; or beyond that, to a time when there were no land animals; or even beyond that, to a time when there was no life at all and earth's crust was still half molten. Try to see the vast stretches of geologic time. Put yourself in the extrahuman time frame of a rock. Consider the origins of things. Expand your mind, to return to the little everyday world refreshed.

This kind of meditation can take you out of yourself and make a connection with the ages. Personal troubles seem less significant in this grand context. Life in general seems the more precious for its brevity and its intricate relation to the whole. To meditate on any natural object—a leaf, a flower, a running stream—is soothing and uplifting in the symbolism it suggests. To meditate on a stone is particularly calming because of its obvious suggestions of vast time spans, patient development, and quiet, impassive endurance of mighty forces and pressures. Try to imagine the orderly arrangement of ions in the stone's crystalline lattice, as well as the natural jogs and displacements of that order that have given this specimen its unique character. Nature has never made two human beings, two plants, or two crystals exactly alike. Consider the magnitude of that diversity.

When a crystal is small enough to fit easily into a pocket or purse, you can carry it around with you for a while. Touch it every now and then. Think of it as a companion, traveling with you, silent and discreet, awaiting a moment of leisure when you can give it some more attention. In time, it can acquire a personality, something like a pet—in your mind, that is, where it counts. Your crystal can feel *to you* like an intimate friend, able to communicate hidden truths.

Here is the age-old essence of crystal gazing, scrying, or communing with the "spirits" in stones. Stones do communicate hidden truths, because the unconscious mind is always hidden, and meditation on a stone is one way of reaching those concealed depths. The profound stillness of a crystal can help the conscious part of your mind to be still, so that unconscious material can come forth. At the same time, the inner liveliness of a crystal can evoke the rich, creative fantasy world that lies in the unconscious, waiting to be tapped.

In a sense, then, your crystal is you. This is why some people develop such intensely personal feelings about stones. Like a favorite book, painting, or piece of music, a crystal can lead you into your inner fantasy world, where you feel naturally at home. The images that it evokes are your own images, projected just as you might project them into the random shapes of clouds, trees, flames, or moving waters.

This also explains why many crystal fanciers feel more drawn to natural uncut stones than to faceted gems or shaped artifacts. The cut stone may be brilliant, but it has lost its spontaneity and also, therefore, the spontaneous responses of the viewer. Its surface patterns are artificially organized and rigidly geometrical. It is like the human cosmologist's mathematical model, imposed on a natural universe that probably does not match the model. Cut stones have a new, artificial symmetry imposed on them. Their beauty is the art of the lapidary, not the art of nature. The pattern is reproduceable. A natural, uncut crystal, however, is a unique entity that will never be copied exactly.

This helps to explain the intensely anthropomorphic responses of many collectors to the natural specimens in their collections. Owners often feel that each specimen has its special personality. The recent fad for "pet rocks" was another expression of this same human tendency to anthropomorphize the inanimate, as were all primitive beliefs about communicating with the spirits in stones.

Some people may talk to their crystals as they would talk to a pet, not for conversation but for an ordering of their own thoughts. Some like to pick up, hold, stroke, and fondle their crystals, which can have the same soothing effect on the handler as the fondling of prayer beads or worry beads; constantly manipulating a hard object seems a natural occupation for the restless human hand.

Like any possession invested with personal meaning by its possessor, a stone can be the object of quite genuine love. There are people who love antiques, or artworks, or music, or clothes, or cars, or tools, or family mementos. There are people who love stones. Crystal mystics frequently allude to such love by insisting that stones need to be "cherished," treated with affection, and kept close to one's body. Of course, a stone has no needs of the human kind, but very probably its human owner needs to treat it so.

Thus one can play personalization games with crystals just as a child might play with dolls. Even in the clear knowledge that they are not living things, one can give them gender, temperament, mood, memory. One can exercise the imagination by talking to them as if they had ears to hear: "Ah, Cerussite, how heavy you are today! Are you putting on weight? Pyrite, you needn't look so shiny smug. You aren't real gold, you know. Jasper darling, you will have to stand up better than that. See Calcite, how proudly she stands now. Do you need a touch of the grindstone at your foot? What's this, Citrine, another chip? Have you had it long? Come, Zircon, you can go with me today, because it's your kind of day, dark and cloudy. Moldavite, I promise you will go with me tomorrow. Don't sulk, Gypsum, you had your turn last week. Besides, you know you're delicate and shouldn't spend too much time away from your shelf."

To those who consciously or unconsciously personalize stones, there is more than simple acquisitiveness involved in the acquisition of them. Such a collector may purchase a crystal because "it spoke to me," or "as soon as I picked it up, I knew I had to take it home." Feelings of affinity can be very powerful. Something about the shapes, colors, or other qualities of certain stones may touch deep-buried memories or desires.

Deep contemplation of any aspect of nature is a holy communion— holier than any man-made flour cake identified by words with the body of a dead god. That was Buddha's meaning when he silently offered his followers a single flower as the ultimate sermon. Nevertheless, flowers, sunsets, running waters, summer days, and other natural things of beauty are ephemeral. Of all nature's products, a stone comes closest to John Keats's ideal thing of beauty that is a joy forever. Compared to the brief "flower" of a human life, the stone is for all practical purposes existent forever. It can be changed, but it cannot be obliterated.

An inscription by the Chinese sage Ni Yuanlu (1594–1644) says:

"When a stone is small it is eminent and, when large, it is full of grandeur. . . . Quiescent substance and severe bones: fantastic form and upright body. It achieves the *Dao* and is at rest; the extent of its longevity is not recorded."[1]

1. Hay, 97.

The Biblical Gems

Through the centuries, both Christian and Jewish scholars have pondered interminably over the biblical list of twelve gems on the breastplate of the high priest (Exodus 28:17–20; 39:10–13). The list has been interpreted in many ways: as a secret revelation of the stones' occult powers, as a symbolic allusion to the twelve tribes, as a prophecy of the twelve apostles, as a calendar of holy days, or as a representation of the zodiac. In the ancient Near East, certain stones were commonly associated with zodiacal figures. Inattentive readers of the Bible often wrongly assumed that the same series of twelve gems reappeared in the apocalyptic vision of the Heavenly City (Revelation 21:19–20), the former being taken as an oracular prediction of the latter. Actually, the list of Revelation is quite different from the Exodus assortment.

To further confuse the issue, ancient sources themselves failed to agree on the arrangement or materials of the famous breastplate. Hebrew, Greek, and Latin versions of the Bible differed from one another. Various English translations also differ. Josephus's *Jewish Wars,* written in Hebrew, carried a different list from the one given in the same author's *Jewish Antiquities,* written in Greek.

The accompanying chart compares a few of these disparate lists, showing that they differ from one another as well as from the gems of the Heavenly City in Revelation. In the column for the King James Bible, the first name is the standard one; others are cited as glosses or occur in other translations, such as the Revised Version.

One problem is that no one knows exactly what minerals the original Hebrew words referred to. The ancients generally were careless about such terminology, making one word do for several different minerals that might look roughly similar, or else inventing multiple words for different colors or types of the same mineral; moreover, the words did not always apply to the same minerals that they describe today. A few of the difficulties become clear when the original terminology is discussed in detail.

Hebrew Scriptures	Greek Septuagint	Latin Vulgate	Josephus: Jewish Wars	Jewish Antiquities	King James Bible	Revelation's Heavenly City
1. Odem	Sardion	Sard	Sard	Sardonyx	Sardius, ruby or carnelian	Jaspis (jasper)
2. Pitdah	Topazion	Topaz	Topaz	Topaz	Topaz, or peridot	Sapfeiros (sapphire) or lapis lazuli
3. Bareketh	Smaragdos	Emerald	Emerald	Emerald	Carbuncle, or emerald	Chalkedon (chalcedony)
4. Nofek	Anthrax	Carbuncle	Carbuncle	Anthrax, or carbuncle	Emerald, or carbuncle	Smaragdos (emerald)
5. Sappir	Sapfeiros	Sapphire	Jasper	Jasper	Sapphire, or lapis lazuli	Sardonyx
6. Yahalom	Jaspis	Jasper	Sapphire	Sapphire	Diamond, onyx, jasper, or sardonyx	Sardius (sard)

7. Leshem	Ligyrion	Ligure	Agate	Ligure	Ligure, jacinth, sapphire, or amber	Chrysolithos (chrysolite, peridot)
8. Shebo	Achates	Agate	Amethyst	Amethyst	Agate	Beryllos (beryl)
9. Achlama	Amethystos	Amethyst	Ligure	Agate	Amethyst	Topazion (topaz)
10. Tarshish	Chrysolithos	Chrysolite (peridot)	Onyx	Chrysolite	Chrysolite, beryl, topaz, or chalcedony	Chrysoprasos (chrysoprase)
11. Shoham	Beryllion	Onyx	Beryl	Onyx	Onyx or beryl	Hyakinthos (jacinth) or sapphire
12. Yashpeh	Onychion	Beryl	Chrysolite	Beryl	Jasper or onyx	Amethystos (amethyst)

1. *Odem.* Like the Egyptian *chenem,* this meant simply "a red stone" and was indiscriminately applied to red jasper, red feldspar, and carnelian. Josephus called this stone sardonyx, but in the *Jewish Wars* he agreed with Epiphanius in translating *sardius* as "carnelian," or "the flesh-colored stone."

2. *Pitdah.* This was the ancients' *topazius,* which probably meant not topaz but peridot (chrysolite); Pliny said *topazius* meant a greenish stone. Nevertheless, the *pitdah* may have been yellowish. Sir Flinders Petrie identified it as the yellow serpentine used in Egypt.

3. *Bareketh* was the same as *smaragdus,* which meant "emerald," but also referred to other green stones, such as amazonite (microcline) and serpentine.

4. *Nofek* was rendered either *anthrax* or *carbunculus,* the latter another general term for red-colored gems such as garnet, ruby, or carnelian bloodstone, but the King James or Authorized Version translates *nofek* as "emerald."

5. *Sappir.* Though rendered "sapphire," this stone was almost certainly lapis lazuli. Both Pliny and Theophrastus said *sapphirus* was a blue stone with golden spots, which can only describe lapis lazuli with its usual dots of golden pyrite. Lapis lazuli was worn on the breast of a high priest or chief justice in Egypt, where it represented the Goddess Maat, Mother of Truth.

6. *Yahalom* meant "to smite" by derivation, which is hardly enlightening as to the nature of the stone. Some scholars supposed that green jasper was meant (because the Septuagint said *jaspis*); others guessed at jade or sapphire. The modern rendering "diamond" is based on no better foundation than the notion that diamond is harder than other stones and therefore able to "smite" (scratch) them.

7. *Leshem.* Older sources translate this as *ligurion,* which used to mean amber, but was later applied to some varieties of jacinth. About A.D. 400, Epiphanius proposed to call this stone *hyacinthus,* a word applied indifferently to jacinth or sapphire. A similar Egyptian word, *neshem,* meant a brown agate.

8. *Shebo* seems to have meant a banded agate, though Josephus called it amethyst.

9. *Achlama* meant amethyst according to most sources, but it was also rendered "ligure" or "agate."

10. *Tarshish* simply means a stone from Tartessus, in Spain. It must have traveled a long way, but none of the ancient sources seems to have

known what it was. The Authorized Version calls it "beryl." Other versions have onyx or chrysolite (peridot). Topaz and yellow jasper have been suggested also.

11. *Shoham*. Although the Septuagint says this was beryl, other versions of the Bible call it onyx. Later scholars have proposed that it meant malachite, which bore the same name as beryl in Egypt.

12. *Yashpeh* apparently meant the ancients' *jaspis* or jasper, though none of the early Bible translations rendered it so. *Yashpu* was the Assyrian word for jasper. Sometimes, green jasper was substituted for the highly esteemed green jade (nephrite).

From the foregoing, it can be seen that no one can know what gems the Jewish high priest wore on his breastplate—or even whether the breastplate existed at all, in view of the biblical writers' known propensity to plagiarize other people's scriptures and adapt pagan religious customs to the worship of their own god. Gem-studded breastplates were standard wear for Mesopotamian priest-kings and Egyptian prelates. An Assyrian text offers another description of such an ornament:

> The splendid stones! The splendid stones! The stones of abundance and of joy, made resplendent for the flesh of the gods. The *hulalini* stone, the *sinyarru* stone, the *hulalu* stone, the *sandu* stone, the *uknu* stone, the *dushu* stone, the precious stone *elmeshu*, perfect in celestial beauty; the stone of which the *pinyu* is set in gold, placed upon the shining breast of the king as an ornament. Azagsud, high priest of Bel, make them shine, make them sparkle![1]

Bel was the same god who caused the Flood, according to texts written before the biblical Noah version and from which the Noah version was copied. So many of this god's attributes were taken over by Yahweh that it would be hardly surprising to find Yahweh's priests dressing like the priests of Bel.

As for Revelation's gem-encrusted Heavenly City: this too was an idea common everywhere in the ancient world. The Puranas describe Krishna/Vishnu's holy city Devaraka as "ornamented with gems," having emerald pillars, ruby and diamond cupolas, sapphire crossroads, and "highways blazing with gems." Similarly, the royal city Kusavati nestled in seven ramparts made of gold, silver, beryl, crystal, agate, coral, and a rainbow collection of jewels. Its very trees bore jeweled fruit. In the West, Lucian's *Vera Historica* described a jewel-city in the Isles of the Blessed, with emerald walls and temples made of beryl, in which the altars were huge single crystals of amethyst.[2] Most Moslem heavens were made of precious stones.[3]

About the eighth or ninth century, Christian writers began to assign the twelve stones of the Heavenly City to the twelve apostles after the manner of some of the ancient heavens, which were divided into sectors ruled by angels or saints. A list composed in the latter part of the tenth century, and fraudulently attributed to a fifth-century bishop of Caesarea, gave: Peter = jasper, Paul = sapphire, Andrew = chalcedony, John = emerald, James = sardonyx, Philip = sardius, Bartholomew = chrysolite, Thomas = beryl, Matthew = topaz, Thaddeus = chrysoprase, Simon Zelotes = jacinth, and Matthias = amethyst. The order of the apostles' names, however, differs in different books of the New testament, so there were several contradictory lists. Another widely disseminated list gave: Peter = jasper, Andrew = sapphire, James = chalcedony, John = emerald, Philip = sardonyx, Matthew = amethyst, Thomas = beryl, Thaddeus = chrysoprase, James the Less = topaz, Simon = hyacinth (jacinth), Matthias = chrysolite, and Bartholomew = carnelian.[4]

While Christians were mineralizing the apostles, Jews did the same with the names of various angels or archangels. One list gave: Malchediel = ruby, Asmodel = topaz, Ambriel = carbuncle (garnet), Muriel = emerald, Herchel = sapphire, Humatiel = diamond, Zuriel = jacinth, Barbiel = agate, Adnachiel = amethyst, Humiel = beryl, Gabriel = onyx, and Barchiel = jasper. Such lists were based on the ancient pagan custom of assigning gems to zodiacal signs and to the spirits that were supposed to govern each of the twelve astrological months. From the same traditions arose the practice of assigning "birthstones" to the months or to signs of the zodiac. Here too, lists vary.

Romans had zodiacal gem lists in the classical period. The idea of the list was preserved throughout the Christian centuries by Christians' enthusiasm for astrology, which persisted despite the early church's condemnation of astrological study as a devilish art. Birthstones and birth signs continued their relationships, although many substitutions were made through misunderstandings, copying errors, or changes of taste. The old pagan spirits of the zodiacal stones persisted too, secretly invoked by many in their original guise even after they had been converted into archangels or apostles. Eventually, jewelers' associations made up "official" lists of birthstones for the benefit of their customers and the increased profits of their own businesses. With so many varying sources and traditions, both old and new, birthstone and birth-sign lists have never been truly standardized. The following is a composite list of stones that have been frequently associated with specific times of year—including the repetition and overlapping that evolved from numerous revisions.

January: garnet, rose quartz
Aquarius (January 21–February 18): garnet, turquoise, hawkeye
February: amethyst, onyx
Pisces (February 19–March 20): amethyst
March: aquamarine, red jasper, bloodstone
Aries (March 21–April 20): red jasper, carnelian, bloodstone
April: diamond, rock crystal, sapphire
Taurus (April 21–May 20): Rose quartz, orange carnelian, sapphire
May: emerald, chrysoprase
Gemini (May 21–June 20): Citrine, agate, tigereye
June: Pearl, moonstone, agate
Cancer (June 21–July 20): emerald, chrysoprase, green aventurine
July: ruby, carnelian, onyx, turquoise
Leo (July 21–August 22): citrine, rock crystal, onyx
August: peridot, aventurine, sardonyx
Virgo (August 23–September 22): yellow agate, citrine, carnelian
September: sapphire, lapis lazuli, chrysolite (peridot)
Libra (September 23–October 22): smoky quartz, orange citrine, chrysolite
October: opal, tourmaline, beryl
Scorpio (October 23–November 22): red carnelian, sard, aquamarine
November: topaz, tigereye
Sagittarius (November 23–December 21): chalcedony, blue quartz, topaz
December: turquoise, zircon, ruby
Capricorn (December 22–January 20): onyx, cat's eye, ruby

A rather charming old-fashioned rhyme popular in the nineteenth century listed the "Lucky Birth Stones" for women as follows:

> By her in January born
> No gem save Garnets should be worn;
> They will ensure her constancy,
> True friendship, and fidelity.

The February-born shall find
Sincerity, and peace of mind,
Freedom from passion and from care,
If they the Amethyst will wear.

Who in this world of ours, her eyes
In March first opens, shall be wise.
In days of peril, firm and brave,
And wear a Bloodstone to her grave.

She who from April dates her years,
Diamonds shall wear, lest bitter tears
For vain repentance flow; this stone,
Emblem for innocence is known.

Who first beholds the light of day
In spring's sweet flowery month of May,
And wears an Emerald all her life,
Shall be a loved, and happy wife.

Who comes with summer to this earth,
And owes to June her hour of birth.
With ring of Agate on her hand,
Can health, wealth, and long life command.

The glowing Ruby shall adorn
Those who in warm July are born;
Then will they be exempt and free
From love's doubt, and anxiety.

Wear Sardonyx, or for thee
No conjugal felicity;
The August-born without this stone,
'Tis said, must live unloved, and lone.

A maiden born when autumn leaves
Are rustling in September's breeze,
A Sapphire on her brow should bind;
'Twill cure diseases of the mind.

October's child is born for woe,
And life's vicissitudes must know;
But lay an Opal on her breast,
And hope will lull those foes to rest.

Who first comes to this world below,
With drear November's fog, and snow,
Should prize the Topaz's amber hue,
Emblem of friends, and lovers true.

If cold December gives you birth,
The month of snow, and ice, and mirth,
Place on your hand a Turquoise blue;
Success will bless whate'er you do.[5]

Clearly, there is no agreement about gem lists of any kind: birthstones, the zodiac, the Bible, or any other source. But it is a human characteristic to love arranging things in lists. Pope Gregory the Great, taking his inspiration from the forged writings of Pseudo-Dionysius the Areopagite, once drew up a list of gems associated with the complete hierarchy of celestial beings. According to Gregory, the six-winged Seraphim (usually depicted with red skin) were represented by carnelian. Topaz stood for the Cherubim (shown as only a head between two wings). The Thrones, represented by fiery wheels with wings filled with eyes, were associated with jasper. Chrysolite (peridot?) stood for the Dominions, humanlike winged creatures dressed in white albs with green stoles. Sapphire was assigned to the Virtues, and beryl to the Powers. The Principalities (heavenly soldiers) were associated with onyx, the Archangels with ruby, the Angels with emerald.[6]

As for the meanings of various gems according to their positions in various lists—well, make up your own. Everyone else does.

1. Kunz, 230, 291–300. 2. *Ibid.,* 236–237. 3. Anderson, 130. 4. Wodiska, 234. 5. Fernie, 41–42. 6. Anderson, 141–142.

PART TWO

The Minerals

Introduction ❈ ❈ ❈

This section deals with individual gem materials and other minerals under their common names, listed alphabetically. Some minerals recur frequently in such a list, notably silicon dioxide, which may appear under many common names: agate, amethyst, aventurine, bloodstone, carnelian, chalcedony, chrysoprase, citrine, enhydros, Herkimer diamond, jasper, onyx, opal, quartz, rose quartz, sardonyx, smoky quartz, tigereye. Such names are of long standing and have been taken for different substances with different properties. On the other hand, the numerous varietal names of such stones as tourmaline or garnet are not separately listed, because they are largely unknown to the general public.

Since this work is not a mineralogical textbook, selection of listings is admittedly arbitrary and incomplete. Choices are based on historical significance, esoteric tradition, and the availability of specimens in current trade, including most minerals that the layperson is likely to see in a crystal shop or mineral show. Thus the reader may acquire enough acquaintance with these substances to know when they might be misrepresented and may be encouraged toward further learning from the many excellent textbooks now available. A secondary purpose of this selection is to point out some minerals not usually cited by New Age sources that might have as much aesthetic or spiritual quality to recommend them as the old standbys. The true lover of stones is always on the lookout for new sorts of stones to love. Some items—such as coral, amber, ivory, pearl—are not minerals at all by the strict definition, because their origin is organic. They are found together with minerals at shops and shows, however, and their age-old common use as gems long antedates today's strict definition of a mineral.

The Mohs Hardness Scale

The Mohs scale of mineral hardness was established on the basis of scratchability. Each listed mineral can leave a scratch on the next lower-numbered one, and can be scratched by the next higher-numbered one. Diamond is the only occupant of the number 10 slot. All other minerals are classified from 1 through 9.9 on the basis of their hardness.

10: Diamond
 9: Corundum (sapphire, ruby)
 8: Topaz
 7: Quartz
 6: Microcline feldspar (or, orthoclase)
 5: Apatite
 4: Fluorite
 3: Calcite
 2: Gypsum
 1: Talc

ADAMITE (Hydrous Zinc Arsenate)

It seems a joke to begin a list of Mother Earth's minerals with a material named after Adam, as if the mythical Judeo-Christian creation were being cited. Goddess forbid! We would prefer to begin with eveite, which is the manganese version of adamite. But this is only a joke; adamite has nothing to do with the biblical Adam. It was named after the French mineralogist Gilbert-Joseph Adam (1795–1881).[1]

Adamite crystals are found in many colors, but commonly range between yellow and green. The crystals make bright, sharp wedges. This is an interesting mineral that will reward close examination with a magnifier.

Books on crystal mysticism usually discuss the most readily available precious or semiprecious gemstones such as quartz, amethyst, fluorite, agate, beryl, turquoise, and so on. But adamite is not a gemstone. It is insufficiently hard, and it is considered a fairly rare mineral. Therefore, anyone who can recognize and identify a specimen of adamite is more mineralogist than mystic. Perhaps adamite may stand as a symbol of genuine knowledge of earth sciences and serve as a good beginning after all.

---

1. Sinkankas, *M. A.*, 415.

AGATE (Silicon Dioxide)

Agate is a form of chalcedony, or cryptocrystalline quartz, having many varieties, which are described by a long list of different names and nicknames. Among these are the following, all preceding the word *agate:* Aleppo, banded, blood, blue, Botswana, bouquet, brecciated, butterfly, cer,

circle, cloud, coral, cyclops, dendritic, dot, dryhead, fairburn, fire, fisheye, flame, flower, fortification, fossil, frost, glass, grape, horsetail, Iceland, Indian, iris, Kalmuk, lace, landscape, macaroni, mammillary, Mexican, milk, mocha, Montana, mosaic, moss, nipomo, occidental, ochoco, onicolo, oolitic, orbicular, oriental, owl eye, ox eye, pagoda, petoskey, picture, pigeon blood, pipe, plume, polka dot, pom-pom, rainbow, riband, ribbon, ring, river, rose, ruin, sagenitic, sard, scenic, seam, seaweed, shell, spectrum, star, sweetwater, tempskya, Texas, thunderegg, topographic, tree, tube, turritella, turtleback, Uruguay, variegated, view, wart, water, wax, white, wood, yellowstone, zebra, zigzag.

The name mocha stone, meaning a moss agate, came from the Arabian seaport of Mocha, which was also famous for its coffee.[1] Orbicular or eye-spot agates were invariably touted as protection against the evil eye, on the usual principle of "like affects like." Pliny said Sicilian agates would cure the bites of scorpions.[2] Moss or tree agates fastened by the farmer to himself or to the horn of his plow ox used to guarantee abundant crops.[3] Agates taken to bed were generally supposed to cure insomnia and bring pleasant dreams.[4] Ancient Britons believed that agates would ward off skin diseases. Syrians thought that triangular-shaped agates would prevent intestinal troubles. Women drank water in which green agates had been washed, believing that such water was a fertility charm.[5]

Bishop Marbodus of Rennes said in the twelfth century, and Pierre de Boniface repeated in the fourteenth, that agates make their possessors eloquent, prudent, amiable, and agreeable. These miraculous stones also sharpen eyesight, increase physical strength, and alleviate thirst. Moslems claimed that powdered agate drunk in water would cure insanity.[6] *The Book of Saxon Leechdoms* said in 1864 that agate prevents harm from thunder, sorcery, demonic possession, poison, disease, drunkenness, and skin eruptions.[7]

Modern notions about the powers of agate have obvious correlations with ancient ones. One New Age mystic says that agate will prevent nightmares, help the eyesight, improve blood circulation, strengthen the heart, stomach, and hair, protect children from falls, and prevent poisoning.[8] Another declares that kidney stones and gallstones can be "disintegrated and flushed out" by no more troublesome therapy than daily meditations with an agate.[9]

The principal difference between the ancient notions and the modern ones is that the latter usually support their prescriptions by bizarre pseudoscientific explanations having no relation to physical realities. For example, picture agate is said to assist in the body's assimilation of silica, although silica is not assimilated by a mammalian body; Botswana agate can bring about total "reoxygenation" of the body, whatever that may mean.[10] Or again, it is said that agate "reverses the flow of energy within the body or center that is upset, much like reversing the poles in a magnet." One would like to see a verifiable demonstration of this! Moreover, agate "has the interesting ability of defining truth or helping to bring it out," something that might profitably accompany such a demonstration.[11]

According to Edgar Cayce, agate carries "an incense to the finer self that makes for an awakening, an opening of the inner self for the receptiveness. And attunement is made through such vibrations."[12] The inner selves of crystal mystics, however, seldom open for the receptiveness when they approach the mysteries of syntax.

Diversity is perhaps the most obvious quality of agate, as may be seen from its many nicknames. Its patterns and colors are infinitely variable. Some agates of the "landscape" or "ruin" type can so closely resemble pictures that one can hardly believe they were not painted by an artist. Agates can be opaque, waxy, translucent, or almost transparent in thin slices. Lapidaries love agate because it is fine-textured and tough, fracture-resistant, yet easy to cut and polish. It takes dyes well. It is an excellent cabochon stone. Many a keyring charm or pocket "lucky piece" is a piece of agate. With all its diversity, agate can constitute the entire collection of a specialist and still look like a collection of many different stones.

1. Wodiska, 177. 2. Thomson, 62, 195. 3. Anderson, 45. 4. Kunz, 52. 5. Cunningham, 67–68. 6. Wodiska, 235. 7. Fernie, 168. 8. Stein, 201. 9. Bravo, 111. 10. Gurudas, 73, 76. 11. Richardson et al., 38–39. 12. *Scientific Properties,* 11.

ALEXANDRITE (Beryllium Aluminum Oxide)

Alexandrite is a chrysoberyl gem first discovered in Russia in 1830, and named after Czar Alexander II. Russian alexandrite has a unique property of color change, being green in daylight and red or purplish-red in artificial light.

There is an imitation alexandrite available, consisting of synthetic corundum colored by vanadium. This material has an odd purplish mauve hue that is bluish by daylight and pinkish under artificial light. It is accepted by most consumers as the real thing because they do not know how the true alexandrite looks. In 1973, however, a true chrysoberyl alexandrite was synthesized by a California firm. Good crystals are also produced by a Japanese company and marketed under the name of Inamori Created Alexandrite.[1]

Because of its recent discovery, alexandrite has no tradition of magical usage. But because it is unique and expensive, modern mystics hasten to remedy the lack with "newly channeled information" from Higher Whoevers to explain that alexandrite can heal leukemia and other diseases, and help one "attune to the energies of the earth."[2] It is said that alexandrite has an "impact" on the nervous system, spleen, pancreas, and testicles.[3] Strange future functions are being invented for this gem: "After a large block of Earth time has lapsed, the Alexanderite [sic] will become quite powerful and function similar to the Diamond, except that it will remain regenerative in operation and not be a physical healer. . . . This gem will have the peculiar knack of pulling the sacred fires together and keeping them stabilized."[4] But we do not know what causes the sacred fires to be scattered or unstable in the first place.

On the other hand, miracles are unnecessary for appreciation of this stone's real knack: its marvelous color change. The best specimens can pass from a daytime bright green to a fiery red in light that is rich in red rays, such as candlelight or the ordinary yellowish electric light. These extraordinary specimens are among the world's most expensive gemstones. Almost as expensive are the more common alexandrites that go from dull green to a brownish red. East Africa has produced a few garnets that show a similar color change, and these may be difficult to distinguish from alexandrite.[5]

1. O'Donoghue, *G. M. G.*, 150–152.
2. Parkinson, 125–126. 3. Gurudas, 76.
4. Lorusso & Glick, 30. 5. *Simon & Schuster's Guide to Gems and Precious Stones*, 116.

AMAZONITE (Potassium Aluminum Silicate)

Amazonite is the pale blue-green variety of microcline feldspar. It was named for a mistaken belief that its primary, and perhaps only, source was the Amazon River. Actually, amazonite is common enough. Its surface appears dull, but in a bright light it flashes with a silky, silvery brilliance, reflecting beams from thousands of tiny crystal faces. Some surfaces glitter like mica.

Amazonite takes a good polish and is sometimes used in jewelry. The crystal mystics have paid little attention to it, however, because it is not well known, is not expensive, is not usually considered a gem, and is not mentioned in either ancient or modern myths. Collectors and children seem to enjoy amazonite for just what it is: a pretty green stone showing some interesting surface features when closely studied. Its tender, minty green suggests springtime, refreshment, renewal. It is an excellent stone to preside over May Day (Beltane) festivals and other occasions of new life or new hope.

The green color is provided by a trace of copper, which used to be the metal sacred to the birthgiving Goddess. Sometimes, whitish amazonite is dyed a blue-green and falsely sold as turquoise. It is also treated in various ways to imitate jade.

AMBER (Organic Material)

Amber is the fossilized resin of long-extinct pine trees that flourished from forty to sixty million years ago—through a modern crystal mystic with a vague time sense refers to the amber trees as "almost extinct."[1] An ancient name for amber, *lyncurius* or "lynx stone," arose from the belief that amber was made of solidified lynx urine. The Romas knew better. Their usual term for amber was *succinum,* "sap-stone." Pliny mentioned the lynx urine theory only to refute it. Possibly it was related to the old Chinese tradition that amber was made of the souls of tigers, entering the earth when the animals died.[2]

Another name for amber was *electrum,* from which we derive "electricity," because amber provided the earliest demonstrations of static electricity. Like modern plastics, amber will attract small bits of paper and other light objects when rubbed to develop a static charge. In Germany, amber was named *Bernstein* or "burning stone" because it will burn, giving off a sweet, piney scent like the scent of its long-dead trees. Amber was often burned as a purificatory incense.

In Norse tradition, it was claimed that the tears of the Goddess Freya became gold when they fell into the earth and lumps of amber when they fell into the sea. Alternatively, amber originated as the beads of Freya's

magic necklace Brisingamen. Hellenic Greeks declared that amber was formed from the tears of the Heliads (sun nymphs) as they wept for their dead brother Phaethon after his ill-conceived and ultimately fatal attempt to drive the sun chariot. Sophocles, however, said that the amber tears came from bird incarnations of the sisters of the hero Meleager, as they flew around the world lamenting their brother's death. Such myths were Christianized by a later claim that amber was created by the tears of grief shed by "certain birds" over Jesus' crucifixion. A modern mystic in the throes of chronological confusion asserts that this Christianized version began with Sophocles—who lived five centuries before the time of Jesus and was certainly not a Christian.[3]

Many myths associated amber with the sun, and with immortality by extrapolation from the sun's perpetual rebirths. Some said that amber came from the apples of immortality in the Gardens of the Hesperides, brought by the sun hero Heracles. A similar Celtic sun hero was named Ambres. The basic word *amber* was a cognate of the Greek gods' elixir of immortality, ambrosia (from *ambrotos,* immortal), which was given to them by the Great Goddess Hera, keeper of the magic apples on the Tree of Life in the paradise-garden.[4]

Romans considered amber nodules so protective that they hung them on nets that defended the podium against wild beasts in the amphitheater. Roman gladiators hung amber on their weapons and armor. Pliny said that a small figurine of amber was thought more valuable than a healthy slave.[5] He also affirmed that amber would cure fevers, blindness, deafness, and other disabilities.[6]

Once it had been associated with eternal life, amber was often considered a general prophylactic against innumerable diseases. It was prescribed for stomachache, fits, scrofula, and jaundice—yellow stones usually were viewed as healers of jaundice, the "yellow disease."[7] In 1502, Camillus Leonardus wrote that amber will cure diseases of the throat and belly and prevent poisoning. Salmon's *Family Dictionary* of 1696 said that sitting over the smoke of burning amber would cure "falling fundament" (hemorrhoids?). Even up to the twentieth century, it was believed that amber necklaces would prevent sore throat and resolve "glandular swellings" of the neck. Dr. Fernie attributed these effects to amber's "innate sulfur," but then, Dr. Fernie knew very little about the composition of amber and even referred to it as a "fossil earth."[8] Although the cause of goiter is now well known and has no conceivable connection with either sulfur or amber, many Europeans still believe that goiter can be prevented by wearing an amber necklace.[9]

Oddly enough, the promotion of amber as a cure-all was spurred on by the decline of the rosary business in the seventeenth century. Having conquered pagan Prussia for Christianity in the thirteenth century and slaughtered most of its non-Christian inhabitants, the Teutonic Knights seized control of the amber trade as part of their payment and claimed every piece of amber found in the area. Gibbets were erected on the beaches for summary hanging of any person who took so much as a single nugget. What made the trade so profitable at the time was the fact that amber was a preferred material for both Christian and Mohammedan rosary beads. When rosaries began to fall out of favor, four centuries later, the church encouraged physicians to popularize amber as a medicine.[10]

It was the belief in amber's medicinal properties that led to its use for mouthpieces of tobacco pipes. Servants customarily lighted the pipes for their masters, and the amber mouthpieces were supposed to prevent infections originating in lower-class mouths.[11] Current recommendations for the uses of amber among crystal mystics are often as silly as this, and equally traceable to old-fashioned sources. Amber is touted as a treatment for depression, toothache, poisoning, malaria, goiter, hay fever, asthma, and urinary infections, among other things, because "amber's electricity resonates with brain wave patterns and aids the endocrine system."[12] Another source claims that amber strengthens the thyroid, inner ear, and "neurological tissue": it also cures diseases of the brain.[13]

It is asserted that amber's "high vibratory rate" can purify and clean the entire human body, by emitting a powerful "magnetic flow" that is said to balance the endocrine and digestive systems. Moreover, this magnetic flow can stabilize the heart, the spleen, and the base of the spine.[14] The vibratory rate is not measured; the alleged magnetic flow is never detectable. Or again, it is said that all internal organs can be "revitalized" simply by placing a piece of amber on the skin above. Physical nearness to amber is recommended for people with suicidal tendencies, presumably to prevent them from killing themselves.[15]

Modern mystics seem to be unaware of other fossil resins that are amberlike or closely related to amber.

Among these are gedanite, beckerite, stantienite, glessite, krantzite, and schraufite, none of which are mentioned in New Age books. The physical properties of amber itself seem to be a mystery to the mystics. Some say it is crystalline. Others say it is not. The truth is that amber has no crystalline structure, although it may sometimes contain within its mass a few crystals of succinic acid.[16]

The real magic of amber lies in its beauty and in the thought of its enormous antiquity, which helps to put ephemeral creatures like ourselves in the proper perspective relative to nature's great cycles. It is intriguing to realize that the trees whose lifeblood became today's amber were living organisms more than fifty million years before the first human beings walked on this earth. What our limited vision calls "antiquity"—that is, earlier portions of our own history—seems quite modern by comparison with the antiquity of a piece of amber.

An amber craftsman in Poland once wrote feelingly of the aesthetic response that amber can arouse: "To me, amber seems closer to human nature than any precious stone. It is warm in color and to the touch, gay, luminous, and full of surprises. . . . It gives me pleasure to find remains of ancient life when polishing a piece of amber. . . . What can be more beautiful than a lump of sunshine given the minimum of polish not to spoil its natural charm?"[17]

1. Harold, 175. 2. Rice, 130, 191. 3. Rice, 112, 115–116; Parkinson, 222. 4. Rice, 119, 122. 5. Weinstein, 221. 6. Desautels, G. K., 24, 31. 7. Wodiska, 235. 8. Fernie, 19, 324, 355. 9. Thomson, 25. 10. Rice, 53, 56. 11. Parkinson, 227. 12. Stein, 206. 13. Gurudas, 78. 14. Chocron, 62. 15. Raphaell, C. E., 136. 16. Rice, 143, 215. 17. Ibid., 98.

AMETHYST (Silicon Dioxide)

Amethyst is crystalline quartz colored purple by a small trace of ferric iron. One cubic foot of quartz can be turned into amethyst by as much iron as is contained in the head of a pin.[1] Early nineteenth-century mineralogists thought that the purple color of amethyst was due to manganese, which often produces purple coloration. This proved to be an error. Nevertheless, modern crystal mystics (some of whom are far behind on scientific information) are still attributing various effects to the "manganese content" of amethyst.

In antiquity, the word *amethyst* was indiscriminately applied to almost any purple gemstone, including purple garnet and purple corundum (sapphire). The word means "not drunken," because the purple stones were credited with the ability to keep drinkers sober no matter how much wine they consumed. A late myth described Amethyst as a nymph who loved the wine god. When he scorned her, Amethyst withered and hardened into a stone that would always oppose the effects of wine. Even in the twentieth century, it was seriously claimed that amethyst "subdues inebriety, and makes temperate, whilst maintaining a condition of pious calm."[2] Modern mystics therefore recommend amethyst for the treatment of alcoholism, as well as diseases traditionally associated with any form of overindulgence, such as gout, diabetes, or urinary troubles.[3]

The idea of amethystine sobriety in ancient times had a simple basis in the serving of wine in cups of carved amethyst. The purple stone naturally enhanced the color of the wine, making it possible for servants to water it down or even to serve plain water to masters who were already too drunk to know the difference. Medieval bishops also commonly used amethyst cups for similar reasons: either to be more parsimonious in serving wine to guests, or else to remain sober while seeming to drink freely. Therefore, the name "bishop's stone" was often applied to amethyst. The stone was also popular among Christian crusaders, who attached it to their rosaries as a magical protection.[4]

Because it is relatively common, desirable, and attractive, amethyst is a favorite of the crystal mystics, who distinguish it with some of their most extravagant claims. It is said that amethyst can "change the molecular structure of matter" and can "bring health and well-being to the entire planet," despite the fact that, so far, it has done nothing of the kind.[5] One mystic attributes the wholly mysterious "use" of amethyst "in the molecular and cellular alteration of organic substances" to the "ultraviolet spectrum" contained in the stone.[6] It is claimed that amethyst has "the highest vibration of all the gems . . . throbbing at the rate of forty-two trillion beats per second."[7] We are not told how this absurd figure could have been measured.

One mystic seems ignorant even of the identity of amethyst with quartz. He says that after a quartz crystal has been worn all day, it must be placed overnight on a cluster of amethyst crystals, because "the high rate of vibration of this species will serve to purify the rock quartz of all impurities."[8] Another mystic apparently believes that amethyst is not quartz but a variety of beryl (beryllium aluminum silicate), which is an altogether different mineral.[9]

Another declares not only that amethyst changes the molecular structures of things, but also that it can absorb "negative forces" like a sponge and "send them back into the ethers or repel them." However, there is a self-contradiction in the very next sentence: "This is not to infer [*sic*] that negative forces are sent back into the ethers." As if this were not enough confusion, the puzzled reader is told that amethyst can "differentiate between the right and the wrong, the pure and the unclean," and can also "purify and amplify all healing rays."[10] However, healing rays—impure or otherwise—have not been identified.

Amethyst is a busy healer. It "treats" eye problems, hypoglycemia, dyslexia, and headaches.[11] It will put dermatologists out of business, because any skin disorder can be cured by placing an amethyst cluster over it, with the points downward.[12] Amethyst dissolves blood clots in the veins.[13] It is "a major stabilizer, grounder, and sedative" and also "promotes all healing."[14] Amethyst even comforts people by "subliminally" broadcasting the information that there is no death![15]

Such wonderful effects are attributed to various causes. One writer says they occur because amethyst has "a very high magnetism."[16] (Like all quartz, amethyst is nonmagnetic.) Another says that amethyst "transmits the violet ray from the planet Mercury," though no such ray has ever been seen or recorded.[17] One unfortunate mystic admits that amethyst gives him a headache, which is only relieved by holding "a feminine or milky quartz crystal" over his head.[18] Indeed we have not come far from the old days when evil spells were counteracted by wearing amethysts along with feathers and baboon's hair.[19]

Some writers give weird pseudoscientific explanations purportedly based on chemical composition. Uyldert says, "It is through its titanium content . . . that the amethyst is the stone of *absolute power*" (italics original), and through its "manganese content" that it is the stone of creative thinking, as well as a cure for "impurities of the skin." Since amethyst contains neither titanium nor manganese, such explanations make little sense. This author even seems to have difficulty counting from one to six. She declares that amethyst crystals "are topped by four-sided pyramids," whereas amethysts are just as hexagonal as any other quartz crystals and their natural terminations are six-sided.[20]

The abundance of such nonsense does not, however, alter the fact that amethyst is a beautiful gemstone whose rich color may remind us that the Latin word for *purple* once meant "very, very holy." Some people favor amethyst with so much enthusiasm that they will not wear any other stone. The island of Sark in the English Channel became so proprietary of its amethysts that the islanders sold them under the name "Sark stones." Now the local deposits are exhausted, but the islanders still sell "Sark stones" that have been imported from Brazil.[21]

1. Bonewitz, 109. 2. Fernie, 169, 354. 3. Stein, 262–263. 4. Dake et al., 17, 86. 5. Parkinson, 56. 6. Chocron, 80. 7. Thomson, 30. 8. Harold, 135. 9. *Gems, Stones, & Metals,* 5. 10. Richardson et al., 40–41. 11. Parkinson, 58. 12. Harold, 41. 13. Richardson et al., 42–44. 14. Stein, 262–263. 15. Raphaell, *C. E.,* 78–80. 16. Richardson et al., 42–44. 17. Bravo, 55. 18. Harold, 42. 19. Anderson, 55. 20. Uyldert, 17, 96. 21. Webster, 213.

APATITE (Calcium, Strontium, Lead, Sodium, and/or Potassium Fluorine-Chlorine-Hydroxyl Phosphate)

The chemically complex apatite is a major constituent of mammalian teeth and bones. Ivory, being the tooth substance of slain elephants, walruses, narwhals, and other animals, is about 65 percent apatite—the rest is largely collagen.[1] Apatite was named from a Greek word for deception, because its mineral appearances imitate many other mineral species.[2] Its crystals may be violet, pink, blue, brown, gray, colorless, or the yellowish green that earned it the nickname "asparagus stone." A blue-green variety from Norway is called moroxite.

Despite its well-known occurrences in teeth and bones, crystal healers rarely associate apatite with these body parts. Instead, it is associated with muscles! Eight drops of water into which apatite has been dipped, mixed with one quart of distilled water and poured into a bath, "notably activates the throat chakra and balances muscular tissue."[3] Why muscular tissue should need balancing, or why such a tiny trace of "apatite water" should activate anything at all, must remain unexplained. The body has its own ample supply of apatite and hardly needs to bathe in the mere thought of it.

Apatite is useful in the manufacture of phosphate fertilizers. Because this mineral represents the phosphates that are essential to all life, it may well symbolize the intricate interaction between the organic and the inorganic throughout our mother planet. Some forms of apatite can be cut and faceted as talismanic gemstones, but the mineral is too soft to be considered jewelry material. Transparent crystals, however, can be very pretty.

1. Nassau, *G. E.*, 137. 2. Sinkankas, *M. A.*, 416. 3. Gurudas, 79.

APOPHYLLITE (Hydrous Potassium Calcium Fluorsilicate)

Popular items at mineral shows are the glassy, cubelike crystals of apophyllite: clear, faint pink, or faint green, often perched on other silicate material such as stilbite, heulandite, and prehnite. Apophyllite crystals are often beautifully shaped prisms with striated side faces and pearly end faces, their corners naturally cut at forty-five degrees to form small triangular facets. The symmetry of apophyllite is just as satisfying as that of quartz, although quartz crystals are more common and tend to grow larger. Apophyllite crystals are little jewels rather than table centerpieces. Sometimes they scatter themselves attractively over the surface of other, differently colored minerals so as to resemble dewdrops on flower petals. But such dewdrops as these, and such flowers as these, will easily outlast a million growing seasons of the botanical world.

Apophyllite is sometimes faceted as a collector's gem, but it is too soft and too brittle for use in jewelry. It has perfect cleavage, which means that a stone can easily fall apart without warning. Therefore, apophyllite is best appreciated in its own natural crystal forms, as a cabinet specimen, without interference by the cutter.

AQUAMARINE (Beryllium Aluminum Silicate)

Aquamarine is a blue-green variety of beryl, its name meaning "sea water." Natural aquamarine is usually rather pale in color, a blue with hints of yellow, green, or brown. Green aquamarine used to be preferred, but today the blue tones are more popular. The deep blue of modern aquamarine gems is artificially obtained by heat-treating paler, greener crystals. Temperatures of about 800 degrees Fahrenheit can suppress their yellowish tinge and enhance the blue.[1]

Aquamarine was long considered protective of sailors and ships, because of its name. It was also recommended for disorders of the neck and head and is still touted as a remedy for headache, toothache, jaw troubles, and swollen neck glands. It is said to "clear the throat of impure thoughts that are congested there"—assuming that there are thoughts in the throat.[2] Aquamarine helps students study, enhances concentration, and fosters psychic powers.[3] It also cures insomnia, vascular diseases, stomach troubles, choking, and difficulties of the liver, abdomen, kidneys, and vertebrae, and does the usual nonspecific "balancing" and "calming."[4] One writer insists that aquamarine was used in Atlantis to shape portions of the immune system.[5] We are not told which portions.

"Purification" is obtained by drinking "a gentle cleansing tincture" that consists of water in which aquamarine has rested for three hours under moonlight.[6] Aquamarine also "transmits the blue-violet ray from the planet Venus" and "works on the pineal gland located in the forebrain," although the pineal gland is not located in the forebrain. It is said that "when the pineal is not operating correctly, there is a tendency toward naiveté, immature gullibility, and openness to constant disappointment."[7] Thus it would seem that aquamarine would benefit nearly all crystal mystics.

The owner of a good aquamarine is not likely to be disappointed, however. It is a handsome gem whether natural or treated, combining well with gold or silver settings. Even imitation aquamarine is quite acceptable, because the material used to imitate it is synthetic spinel colored blue by cobalt. Spinel has the same hardness as beryl and just as much brightness and clarity, so the imitation aquamarine is not appreciably inferior to the original. Beware, however, of imitations made of some other material, such as glass.

Natural aquamarine crystals can be impressive objects. One spectacular example on record was a crystal nineteen inches long, sixteen inches around, weighing 243 pounds, transparent from end to end, with a blue center and greenish exterior. It was purchased by a dealer from Idar-Oberstein for twenty-five thousand dollars.[8]

1. Desautels, *M. K.,* 88. 2. Chocron, 73. 3. Thomson, 38–40. 4. Stein, 236; Parkinson, 72. 5. Gurudas, 79. 6. Cunningham, 75. 7. Bravo, 197. 8. Webster, 120.

ARAGONITE (Calcium Carbonate)

Aragonite has the same chemical composition as calcite, but it is less common and forms differently shaped crystals. One variety of aragonite, known as *flos ferri,* "flowers of iron," makes intricately curved, curled, coral-like or wormlike white intertwined branches. Other varieties often form hexagonal prisms, actually pseudohexagons created by twinning (merging of two crystals). Aragonite is the major constituent of pearls and other shell and skeletal structures of marine creatures. It was named after its first discovery in Aragon, Spain.

As a meditation stone, the pseudohexagonal kind of aragonite serves to remind us of the importance of six-sided symmetry in nature as well as in mythic symbolism, from the hexagonal cells of the beehive and the sixfold symmetry of many plants to the ancients' six-petaled Flower of Aphrodite and the holy hexagram of Tantrism, adopted a few centuries ago as the emblem of Judaism and now misleadingly called the Star of David, or Solomon's Seal. Many other minerals form six-sided crystals—quartz is perhaps the best-known example—but aragonite has closer associations with actual life forms. It also occurs in interesting aggregates, in which the prisms radiate outward in all directions from a common center, suggesting to the mind all kinds of progressions from singular to universal.

ASBESTOS

Any of three different minerals can provide the long, flexible, fibrous crystals that are spun into fireproofing material and called asbestos. One of the three is chrysotile, a variety of the phyllosilicate serpentine. A second is actinolite, a member of the actinolite-tremolite series classified as amphibole inosilicates, a series that also includes the type of jade known as nephrite. A third is crocidolite, a variety of riebeckite. When quartz encloses fibers of this mineral, the result is the silky-looking chatoyant (cat's eye) material named tigereye when it is predominantly yellow, or hawkeye when it is predominantly blue.

Crystal mystics seem unaware that asbestos can be identified with some of their favorite stones, such as tigereye and jade. They dislike the term *asbestos,* because asbestos fibers are known to be hazardous to human health. The lung disease asbestosis, caused by inhaling mineral dust, killed many workers before better manufacturing methods were instituted. Despite the dangers of its production, there is no better protection against fire than asbestos. The whole point of asbestos products is that they will not burn.

Since this fact is surely common knowledge, it seems almost perverse of a crystal mystic to write that asbestos "can be continuously burned" because it was used to make wicks for the perpetual fires in ancient Greek temples.[1] Perhaps as a consequence of bad karma, this writer will be set to work in the afterlife trying throughout eternity to light a bare asbestos wick.

Sometimes, asbestos fibers are found in compacted sheets resembling felt. Such a form is called mountain leather.[2] The long fibers can be spun like wool or cotton, and woven into cloth, to make fireproof garments.

1. Cunningham, 75. 2. Sinkankas, *M. A.,* 479, 487.

ATACAMITE (Hydrous Copper Chloride)

Atacamite is a favorite mineral for micromounting. Its crystals tend to be very small, but their rich, deep green color shows up beautifully under magnification. Atacamite forms green crusts on rocks near copper deposits in arid conditions. It also occurs as a sublimation product of volcanic gases. That means that the mineral has volatilized in hot vapor and recrystallized without passing through the liquid stage.

Atacamite was named after the Atacama Desert of northern Chile, where it was originally discovered. The best crystals, however, are said to come from the deserts of southern Australia. Before blotters were used for drying ink, atacamite sand was popularly used for this purpose.[1]

Although it is not very hard, atacamite might serve as a collector's gem if its crystals grew larger. As a rule, its beauty of form is revealed only to those who look with a lens. Having also beauty of color, atacamite symbolizes the many glories that Mother Nature hides in plain sight, awaiting the discerning eye.

1. Pough, 155.

AVENTURINE (Silicon Dioxide)

The name *aventurine* has been confusingly bestowed on two different minerals. One is an oligoclase feldspar also known as sunstone. The other is an opaque quartz rock with inclusions of glittering mica flakes, which may be either a medium green in color if the flakes are mostly fuchsite, or a reddish color if the flakes are a hematite, goethite, or iron mica. Generally, aventurine is understood to be the green quartz variety. Sometimes it is misrepresented as jade; quartz aventurine can resemble jadeite, but it is much more brittle.

The name was originally derived from a kind of glass manufactured in

Italy, said to have been discovered by mistake (*a ventura*) when some copper filings fell into a vat of molten glass and gave it a spangled effect. Glass of this sort is still manufactured and sold under the rather misleading name goldstone (or, "aventurine glass"). Natural aventurine shows the same spangled effect as light reflects from its included mica flakes. This is known as aventurescence.

Crystal mystics are uncertain about both the composition and the spelling of aventurine, which is rendered *adventurine* as often as not. Nevertheless, they confidently prescribe it for a variety of illnesses, including depression, headache, high blood pressure, sore throat, vascular problems, and the debilitating effects of grief.[1] Aventurine is said to "aid the bile ducts which effect [*sic*] the gall bladder," and green aventurine is the one stone worthy to be called an all-around healer.[2] In the United States at least, green color suggests money, so aventurine is recommended as a gambler's talisman of "money-attracting magic."[3]

Aventurine polishes well and makes attractive jewelry and accessories, in addition to lucky charms. It is pleasant to the touch. Its green color suggests springtime regeneration, shady trees, forest pools with glinting sunbeams.

---

1. Stein, 234. 2. Raphaell, *C. E.*, 163; *C. H.*, 190. 3. Cunningham, 76.

AZURITE (Copper Hydroxyl Carbonate)

Azurite has the same chemical composition as malachite. The two minerals often occur together, bright blue with bright green. Azurite tends to alter to malachite in time. Some medieval painters made their blue pigments of crushed azurite that has now altered to malachite, so the originally blue skies in the paintings have turned green.[1]

Mystics seldom agree on the powers of azurite. One envisions ill-defined but sweeping functions such as "the ability to restructure molecules," and a curious capacity to "work with the Lords of Karma on the inner planes in building new human bodies while they are still in their embryonic state. This will help the incoming races utilize the tools of the sixth and seventh senses in a more expanded fashion."[2] As usual, definitions of the tools, the incoming races, and the Lords of Karma are left to the reader's imagination.

Another claims that azurite stimulates the spleen, thyroid, and skin; treats arthritis (which this writer mistakes for a bone disease); and, in combination with malachite, will control any form of malignant cell growth.[3] But woe betide the unfortunate cancer patient who relies on such irresponsible statements, and seeks no further treatment. Taken at face value, this kind of prescription can too easily be life threatening.

A third source denies azurite's alleged stimulation of the spleen, saying on the contrary that azurite "comforts" the spleen but "does not have a strong vibration to be able to penetrate it." There is an earnest warning in capital letters: "DO NOT use carnelian or any orange stones with azurite" when dealing with children.[4] Why should a combination of blue and orange be harmful to children? No reason is given. Have toy manufacturers been advised, one wonders, to abandon their favorite marketing strategy of combining bright primary colors?

In reality, azurite is one of the few true blue minerals, ranging from azure to navy blue; in large crystals, the blue can be so dark as to look nearly black. In aggregates of small crystals, azurite can resemble a bunch of blue flowers, perhaps pointed up by leaflike touches of green malachite. Some specimens are cut and polished as gemstones, but they are fragile and easily scratched.

An alternative name for azurite is chessylite, after the vicinity of Chessy in France, which served as a leading source of the mineral. There are special names for azurite mixtures, such as azurmalachite or burnite, which is a combination of azurite and cuprite (copper oxide). Some of these mixtures create wonderful pattern effects and when polished resemble abstract art.

1. Medenbach & Wilk, 126. 2. Lorusso & Glick, 32. 3. Gurudas, 82. 4. Richardson et al., 47–48.

BARITE (Barium Sulfate)

The name barite means "heavy." Barite is the heaviest of the nonmetallic minerals. Because of its weight, finely powdered barite has long been used by dishonest dealers as an additive to foods sold by weight, such as flour and sugar.[1] Barite is tasteless, odorless, and harmless to the human digestive system, being chemically inert. Because it is opaque to X rays, barite "milk-shakes" or enemas are used for radiological study of the digestive tract. The ability to absorb radiation also makes barite useful in radiation shields.[2]

Barite has many different crystal forms and colors. Some are opaque, some translucent, some transparent.

They are interesting, and a few are cut as gemstones despite their softness (3 on the Mohs scale); but crystal mystics usually ignore barite because it is common and cheap, therefore not worth publicizing. They are, however, fond of celestite, which lies at the other end of a continuous barite-to-celestite series, with strontium substituting for the barium.

The typically tabular (platelike) crystals of barite create one of the various types of "desert rose" when they are filled with sand inclusions and arranged in rosettes.

1. Court & Campbell, 70. 2. Medenbach & Wilk, 132.

BENITOITE (Barium Titanium Silicate)

Blue benitoite was originally mistaken for sapphire when it was discovered in 1907 in San Benito County, California. So far, this material has not been found anywhere else. It is considered a rare gemstone, although the occasional colorless specimens of benitoite are not useful as gems. A pink color has been reported also.[1]

Benitoite is found embedded in white natrolite, which provides a pretty contrast with the deep blue crystals when the combination is displayed as a cabinet specimen. For many years, miners destroyed the rare benitoite crystals by trying to blast or chisel them out of the matrix. Eventually it was discovered that the natrolite could be dissolved by acid, leaving the benitoite unharmed.

Because benitoite is unique and valuable, crystal mystics have expressed considerable interest in it. Benitoite is said to emit "a powerful Lemurian vibration."[2] It is often shown that

Lemurian vibrations are keenly attuned to high twentieth-century price tags.

Gems cut from benitoite are small, because the natural crystals have many flaws and few clear, facetable areas. Although it is usually masked by the deep blue color, the dispersion of benitoite is equal to that of a diamond.[3] Jewels of benitoite are much prized, and priced accordingly.

---

1. Webster, 307. 2. Gurudas, 83. 3. Arem, 50.

BERYL (Beryllium Aluminum Silicate)

Color varieties of beryl include emerald (green), aquamarine (blue-green), morganite (pink), goshenite (colorless), and golden beryl (yellow). Even though "golden beryl" in Greek is *chrysoberyl*, golden beryl must not be confused with chrysoberyl, which is an entirely different mineral; an oxide, not a silicate.

Beryl was widely known in antiquity, when it was a favorite healing and divination stone thought to empower incantations.[1] Greek physicians practiced the gemstone elixir fraud by dosing patients with water into which beryl had been dipped as a cure for bladder and kidney stones. In the fourteenth century A.D., Konrad von Megenberg recommended the same treatment for asthma.[2]

Medieval doctors claimed that beryl could cure jaundice and liver disease, as well as laziness. It could also reconcile married couples, revive fading love, and bring victory in battle or litigation. *The Magic of Kiram* (published in 1685) named beryl the Panzoön, "All Life."[3] Ragiel's *Book of Wings* said that a beryl engraved with the figure of a frog would transform enemies into friends. Engraved with a hoopoe (a kind of bird), it would invoke the spirits of the dead and the spirits of waters.[4]

It used to be thought that the most suitable stone for crystal gazing was not quartz but beryl, especially during the waxing moon, when the stone was said to accumulate "lunar magnetism" (although beryl is nonmagnetic). Baron Reichenbach said in 1845 that when one gazes into beryl, "there streams from the human eyes an efflux of magnetism as projected from its reservoir in the lesser brain."[5] Theories as meaningless as this are still advanced, although the buzzwords now are either electromagnetism or etheric force.

Currently, beryl is recommended as a remedy for seasickness, upset stomach, ulcers, nausea, obesity, and *both* constipation and diarrhea.[6] It is said to cure eye troubles by a procedure that sounds like a surefire cause of eye troubles, namely, dropping grains of crushed beryl into each eye. After this treatment, the patient is told to lie still with closed eyes for a long time.[7] Perhaps this would enable the eyes to wash out the irritant grains with tears, but why bother to irritate the eyes in the first place? This is one more example of the truly dangerous kinds of "cures" that crystal mystics sometimes recommend, cures that make about as much sense as treating a headache with a hammer blow to the head.

At least one source categorically denies the findings of mineralogical science with regard to beryl by asserting that the entire family of beryl minerals did not take shape in the earth like other minerals but came from outer space, having been "seeded onto the planet Earth."[8] No evidence for this strange statement has ever been offered. Crystal mystics do not usually present evidence. Another source, not only confuses beryl with chrysoberyl but also unaccountably declares that golden beryl contains uranium![9]

The ancients' fondness for beryl as a gazing-stone for meditation is still valid today, however—even if it must be acknowledged that all beryls are products of the earth and not alien crystals from outer space. Beryl is beautiful, even when not transparent or of gem quality. The old name for golden beryl, *heliodor,* meant "gift of the sun," and indeed the stone seems to bring sunlight into its environment.

There are beryl rarities such as cat's eye and star stones (which may be confused with star sapphires) and the raspberry red beryl from Utah known as bixbite. The latter has not yet been found in crystals of any size. The largest gemstones of bixbite so far are less than two carats, and most specimens are badly flawed. There is also a green beryl colored by vanadium, as distinguished from emerald, which is a green beryl colored by chromium. Even though their greens are very similar and some specimens cannot be differentiated without chemical analysis, authorities insist that green beryl and emerald must be separately classified.[10] In addition to the many natural beryls, there are also successful synthetic beryls that have the same properties as nature's products.

1. Wodiska, 235. 2. Medenbach & Wilk, 192. 3. Fernie, 117, 131. 4. Kunz, 59, 133. 5. Fernie, 205. 6. Stein, 211. 7. Thomson, 55. 8. Lorusso & Glick, 37. 9. Uyldert, 107. 10. Webster, 107, 123.

BLOODSTONE, OR HELIOTROPE (Silicon Dioxide)

Although the name bloodstone has been given to nearly every red mineral, including garnet, ruby, hematite, and carnelian, it is now commonly applied to the jasper variety of chalcedony that is dark green with spots of red. Christian tradition held sometimes that the stone had been spotted by the blood of Jesus at his crucifixion, at other times that its spots were caused by the blood of Saint Stephen. It was often nicknamed "Saint Stephen's stone."[1]

The Leyden Papyrus declared that "the world has no greater thing" than bloodstone; it opens all doors for its owner, breaks down the walls of prisons, and averts many disasters. The Franciscan friar Bernardino de Sahagun claimed to have cured many Mexican Indians of the plague in 1576 by giving them a piece of bloodstone to hold; when they did this, their hemorrhages instantly stopped. A century later, Robert Boyle wrote of an acquaintance who was cured of chronic nosebleeds by holding a bloodstone.[2]

In 1622, the list of valuables of George, Earl Marischal of Scotland, included "one jasper stone for stemming of blood." The blood-stopping power of bloodstone was so frequently mentioned that Dr. Fernie tried to rationalize it with a few twentieth-century non sequiturs: "To wear a fragment of this stone externally on some part of the body will indisputably serve to stay any flux of blood from which the wearer may be suffering; doing so by reason of the diminutive specks of red iron oxide incorporated within its substance. This subtle effect is fully justified by the similar action which small doses of metallic iron given internally are found to exercise."[3]

The same specious argument is used by modern mystics who claim that "the iron oxide in the stone is an effective coagulator."[4] Many things, including air, encourage coagulation of blood, but never at a distance. One writer sidesteps the issue by saying that bloodstone is "useful where bleeding is involved," without describing any procedure, and claiming that bloodstone is "a major blood purifier," although blood is obviously never "purified" by anything outside the body. The same writer erroneously calls bloodstone "noncrystalline."[5] Another apparently believes that bloodstone placed in water will turn the water red.[6] The simplest kind of experiment, taking no more than ten seconds at most, would have demonstrated otherwise.

In addition to its various associations with blood, the bloodstone was traditionally credited with an ability to make its wearer invisible—another belief so easy to disprove experimentally that its persistence is quite amazing. *The Celestial Intelligencer* of 1801 rather unintelligently stated that bloodstone "so dazzles the eyes of men, that it causes the bearer to be invisible."[7] Some earlier works insisted that this effect depended upon taking some of the plant heliotrope along with the bloodstone.[8] Heliotrope, meaning "sun-turner," is an alternate name for bloodstone.

Confused by this, a crystal mystic speaks of the mineral "helitrope [*sic*]" as "a green chalcedony with red flecks of red jasper," apparently laboring under the belief that chalcedony and jasper are different minerals.[9] In fact, heliotrope or bloodstone is a green

jasper with red flecks of iron oxide. Mystics who have learned this much leap from the iron oxide to popular notions about iron-poor blood and proclaim that proximity to bloodstone will correct iron deficiency.[10] Proximity to a wrought-iron fence or a railroad track would carry a much higher dosage of iron, if it were possible for metallic iron to affect the iron content of hemoglobin from outside the body—of course, it isn't possible, in spite of one mystic's insistence that "the bloodstone has the ability to emit directly into the physical body."[11] This one does not mention iron, however, and fails to specify what it is that bloodstone is supposed to emit.

As in all magic, there are contingencies. Another source implies that the wondrous effects of bloodstone will not occur unless the stone is "amplified" through exposure to a pyramidal structure.[12] Therefore, if you do not keep your bloodstone under a pyramid, it will not cure anything. Thus the ancients, who did not have the benefit of a "pyramid power" fad, must have been deluded in their notions about this stone's curative qualities.

Appropriately enough, green jasper is known as *plasma* when it lacks the red spots that make it bloodstone.[13] Its green coloring is due to chlorite.[14] One of the crystal mystics confuses this with an altogether different kind of mineral and writes that plasma or bloodstone is opaque because its "green veins of asbestos prevent the passage of light."[15] When mystics refer to specific mineral inclusions, they may favor the first word that pops into their heads over the labor of looking it up.

Bloodstone is pretty, and a good meditation stone. It can suggest correlations between the red lifeblood of animals and the nurturing powers of the green plant world. It can be especially appreciated as an Earth symbol, because our Earth and her minerals constitute the basic support of both animals and plants.

1. Dake, Fleener & Wilson, 144–147.
2. Kunz, 61, 390–91. 3. Fernie, 268, 468.
4. Parkinson, 65. 5. Stein, 186.
6. Parkinson, 63. 7. Fernie, 182.
8. Anderson, 117. 9. Gurudas, 85.
10. Stein, 188–189. 11. Chocron, 60.
12. Gurudas, 85. 13. Schumann, 146.
14. Webster, 222. 15. Uyldert, 12.

BRAZILIANITE (Sodium Aluminum Hydroxyl Phosphate)

Brazilianite is a rare and unusual twentieth-century gem, discovered in 1945 in just one Brazilian locality. It was thought unique to that locality until some small deposits were found in New Hampshire.

The color of brazilianite ranges between yellow and green. Some specimens have been confused with chrysoberyl or topaz but brazilianite is softer than these. At 5.5 on the hardness scale, brazilianite is really too soft to be entirely successful as a gemstone. Nevertheless, its rarity makes it costly and desirable. It is a "prestige" or show-off kind of gem. As jewelry, it is best displayed in pendant or earring form because it will not stand up to the wear and tear endured by a ring or bracelet.

The fine, cool yellow-greens presented by this stone suggest spring sunlight or new white wine. Like most rare minerals, brazilianite fetches prices that are usually beyond the means of the average collector, but specimens are available for viewing in museums

and other displays. Complete crystals are rare indeed. Most of the brazilianite specimens in private collections are only pieces.[1] Therefore, museum specimens may be the best that the interested amateur will ever see.

1. Sinkankas, *M. A.,* 414.

CALCITE (Calcium Carbonate)

Calcite is a common mineral taking hundreds of different forms. Calcite can appear as limestone, marble, chalk, and the material that forms stalactites and stalagmites in caves, variously known as flowstone, cave onyx, or Mexican onyx, though it is not onyx at all. Calcite can be white, yellow, red, blue, gray, green, brown, black, or transparent. Calcite from Franklin, New Jersey, is famous for its brilliant red fluorescence. Water-clear calcite rhombohedra first found in Iceland, and therefore known as Iceland spar, are famous for their birefringence, which means that everything viewed through them appears double. Other varietal names for calcite include nailhead spar, honey calcite, amber calcite, blood calcite (with red hematite inclusions), and dogtooth spar (narrow, pointed, fanglike crystals).

Because calcite is common, specimens are usually not expensive. Every novice collector soon acquires a sample or two, but calcite has received little attention from crystal mystics. One recommends it as a "partner" to chiropractors and osteopaths, asserting that green calcite in particular will help heal bone and ligament trauma, sports injuries, arthritis, and tendinitis.[1] The imaginative connection perhaps extends from the calcium content of the mineral to that of bone. However, life in the presence of a marble tabletop or a marble-tiled floor would surely expose one to far more environmental calcium than a few calcite crystals. The body's real need for calcium is usually satisfied by any reasonably well-balanced diet, especially a diet that includes dairy products.

The more transparent varieties of calcite make wonderful meditation stones because they often show interesting internal features and planes of iridescence. It has been truly said that one may specialize in collecting only calcite specimens and never run out of new and different forms of this versatile mineral.

---

1. Raphaell, *C. H.,* 192.

CARNELIAN (Silicon Dioxide)

Carnelian is chalcedony with a reddish color imparted by iron oxides.[1] It is also called cornelian, cornaline, canary stone, Mecca stone, pigeon blood agate, demion, or sardoine. Named from Latin *carne,* "flesh," carnelian has been most frequently associated with blood, flesh, carnal passions, sexuality, earthiness, and the material world. In ancient Egypt, however, it symbolized the sacred heart-soul (*ab*) in the body of a mummy and the resurrection to be brought about through the stone, which was described as the blood, virtue, and magic power of the Great Goddess Isis.[2]

Moslems believed that carnelian could fulfill all desires. A carnelian or Mecca stone engraved with the names of the Twelve Imams placed in the mouth of a male corpse could bring him to paradise—a concept not far removed from the ancient Egyptian one, especially since the imams of

pre-Islamic Arabia were female. Mohammed himself wore a carnelian ring as a charm for a blessed afterlife.[3]

According to the *Lapidario* of King Alfonso X of Spain, the wearing of carnelian would strengthen a weak voice, enabling one to speak boldly and persuasively to achieve one's wishes.[4] Perhaps this is why a modern mystic claims that carnelian is beneficial to those who are "absent minded or confused and unfocused."[5]

As another kind of "bloodstone," carnelian was much recommended for blood disorders, menstrual troubles, wounds, nosebleeds, fever, infection, or "hot blood" (anger). It was a traditional remedy for tumors and a preserver of harmony between friends or relatives.[6] It is now called a "blood tonic," and also a stimulant for the bowels. It is erroneously described as "an important form of quartz though noncrystalline"; it is as crystalline as any other kind of chalcedony, even though its crystals may be microscopic in size.[7] It is also claimed that carnelian increases the heart rate, as well as "the thyroid and and adrenal output."[8] Alternatively, it is said that carnelian "feeds" those highly mysterious objects unknown to science, "energy molecules," directly through the skin into the body.[9] Or again, while resting with a carnelian in hand, one may pass the time by massaging it over the region of the liver, which will "cause the liver to throw off some of its own impurities."[10] The mechanisms of all these wonderful effects, as usual, are not described.

Some mystics seem unaware of the physical identity between carnelian and other members of the quartz-chalcedony family. One says that carnelian is not a "high-powered energy source" like the "higher vibration transparent stones" such as clear quartz—which is basically the same mineral. Yet, despite its shortcomings, carnelian "carries the stories and records of our planet," and can be used to "see into the past"[11] after a certain amount of advanced training. This does not mean advanced training in earth sciences, which is the customary way of learning how to read the records of Earth's past preserved in her rocks. On the contrary, it means training oneself to sit down quietly with a piece of carnelian in hand and let the mind drift, accepting any mental image that might appear as a revelation of a past reality. It is not the sort of training that is likely to strain one's mental faculties.

In addition to seeing into the past, at the same time one may stop bleeding and heal sores with carnelian, which "antidotes infection [*sic*] and blood-poisoning by its cleansing power."[12] Truly a remarkable stone.

Nonsense aside, to sit quietly with a carnelian in hand may be a comforting meditation exercise. One can contemplate its rich history of legend, or the cordial red glow of light projected through the stone, or the warmth that it develops after being held for a while. Rough carnelian often has a ripply, bumpy surface that is pleasant to touch. Polished carnelian is deliciously smooth and firm. It is also fairly tough, a dependable lifetime gem. As a talismanic mineral, carnelian has much to recommend it.

1. Sinkankas, *G. N. A.,* 379. 2. Kunz, 38, 226. 3. Stern, 42. 4. Kunz, 63–64. 5. Raphaell, *C. E.,* 140. 6. Wodiska, 236. 7. Stein, 197–198. 8. Bravo, 118. 9. Lorusso & Glick, 69. 10. Richardson et al., 53. 11. Raphaell, *C. E.,* 140. 12. Uyldert, 92.

CELESTITE (Strontium Sulfate)

Many specimens of celestite are colored a tender sky blue, which gave rise to its name, from Latin *coelestis,* "heavenly." The mineral can occur also in white and reddish shades. It forms a continuous series with barite, and so may contain barium as well as strontium. Because it is soft and fragile, it is not suitable for use as a gemstone, but display samples are found in many collectors' cabinets. Some mystics assert that it will relieve headaches and other symptoms of stress. It is also "worn or carried to create eloquence and to promote compassion for the Earth and our fellow creatures."[1] Certainly the earth and our fellow creatures are in need of all the compassion we can possibly spare, and if celestite can serve as a reminder of this, let us all acquire a piece of it.

1. Cunningham, 82.

CERUSSITE (Lead Carbonate)

Cerussite is one of nature's tricks. It has a wide variety of crystal forms, resembling glass houses, snowflakes, groups of tumbled jackstraws, stars, needles, networks, or earthy masses. Many of its forms look light and airy, as if they would float like feathers, yet they are extremely heavy. After all, cerussite is a compound of lead.

Cerussite is unsuitable for jewelry because it is fragile as well as heavy, but some forms are very pretty in their natural state. Transparent specimens may show iridescence. Those with fibrous inclusions show a silky cat's eye effect. The many guises of this chameleon mineral make it interesting to watch for. It always seems to show itself as something new.

Occasionally, cerussite is cut and faceted as a collector's gem to be displayed rather than worn. It can be lovelier than a diamond, because of its higher dispersion. Yet the mineral is so brittle and heat sensitive that cutting it demands extreme skill and patience. It is considered impossible to cut a large cerussite without breaking it.[1]

Cerussite is named from the Latin for "white lead."

1. Arem, 64.

CHABAZITE (Hydrous Calcium Aluminum Silicate)

Chabazite is named from Greek *chabazios,* one of the stones mentioned in the Orphic *Peri Lithon*.[1] The ancient original was probably not the mineral now named chabazite, which forms rhombohedral crystals in a broad range of flesh colors: subdued pink, faded peach, reddish tan, rusty brown, and occasionally white. Crystals have a glassy luster and a lively appearance. Though too fragile to be a gemstone, chabazite makes interesting specimens and is a good material for meditation on the theme of Mother Earth.

1. Sinkankas, *M. A.,* 470.

CHALCANTHITE (Hydrous Copper Sulfate)

Perhaps the most brilliant blue in the mineral world is shown by chalcanthite, which is found in the vicinity of copper deposits. Since this beautiful mineral is readily soluble in water, however, it cannot be a gemstone, nor is it likely to be a popular collector's item.

Commercial copper sulfate is an excellent material for the study of

crystal growth, though. Saturated solutions are easily made with hot water, and crystal deposition is relatively rapid. The attractive bright blue color interests children and encourages them to watch the crystals forming; therefore, home-grown chalcanthite may be one of the first specimens to appear in a young beginner's collection. The crystals are sharp, wedge-shaped, and usually good-sized for easy viewing. With a little experimentation, a beginner can learn to grow quite large individuals.

In this activity, some care is necessary. Children should always be supervised by an adult when dealing with copper sulfate solution, which is poisonous and somewhat corrosive and should not be put in metal vessels. Residues must be carefully disposed of where they can do no damage.

CHALCEDONY (Silicon Dioxide)

Chalcedony was named for the ancient Greek city of Chalcedon, across the Bosporus from Byzantium. Now it is a general term for many varieties of cryptocrystalline quartz, including agate, jasper, sard, onyx, carnelian, chrysoprase, bloodstone, chert, and flint. Common chalcedony, without a varietal name, is a bluish gray, slightly translucent stone often found in rock clefts, vugs (cavities), and geodes.

Chalcedony occurs everywhere and has been popular for millennia in all kinds of magical lore. It was thought to impart physical strength.[1] Worn with the hairs of an ass, it preserved its wearer from storms.[2] Bishop Marbodus wrote in the twelfth century that chalcedony would heal diseases of the gall bladder. Albertus Magnus said it would cure depression. Konrad von

Megenberg said it would confer fertility and attractive appearance. Adamus Lonicerus said it would cure snakebite.[3] Gonelli wrote in 1702 that chalcedony would drive away nightmares and phantoms because its "alkaline quality" dissipated the "evil humors of the eye" that saw such apparitions.[4]

New Age folk are not quite sure what to do with chalcedony. Some claim that ordinary gray chalcedony is not like other chalcedony varieties, because it "does not send out vibrations." One source murkily remarks that "if the energy pattern is continually raised, anything less than the highest vibration that it is at, will drop away."[5] Another says that a piece of chalcedony in one's bath will "increase oxygenation to the skin tissue."[6] Yet the porcelain of one's bathtub is largely silica, and therefore a near relative of the natural stone.

White chalcedony is associated with various ideas of whiteness in New Age prescriptions. It stimulates breast milk, purifies, "promotes chastity," and acts as an antiseptic.[7] Crystal mystics have not dealt effectively with the problem of dyed chalcedony, although they wish to assign different qualities to each of its different colors. Most chalcedony takes rather well to artificial dyes, so there can be some doubt about what color nature intended any given piece to be. One of the most common fakes is known as Swiss lapis—an imitation of lapis lazuli made by staining chalcedony or jasper a bright blue with ferric ferrocyanide.[8] Chalcedony can also be colored pink, red, yellow, green, brown, or black with man-made dyes. A great deal of inexpensive cabochon jewelry is made of chalcedony dyed to imitate jade, malachite, turquoise, and other stones.

These products can be advertised as "natural" stone, as opposed to plastic or ceramic imitations, which are wholly manufactured.

Polished chalcedony has a nice firm texture, a good "feel" about it, and an interesting repertoire of spotted or banded patterns. A chalcedony hand piece such as an egg or sphere is very pleasant to hold and contemplate.

1. Fernic, 354. 2. Wodiska, 236. 3. Medenbach & Wilk, 88. 4. Kunz, 65. 5. Richardson et al., 56. 6. Gurudas, 90. 7. Stein, 257. 8. Stern, 60.

CHAROITE (Complex Potassium/Sodium, Calcium/Barium/Strontium Hydrous Silicate)

Charoite is a comparative newcomer on the mineral scene, having been discovered in Russia in 1978 and exported as a material for gems and carved artifacts. It is pretty material, with a mixture of light and dark purple shades like the petals of an iris flower, and a mixture of hardnesses as well. The stone takes a high polish in some patches and remains relatively lusterless in others. No other mineral can provide quite the same intriguing purple-to-violet marbling or mottling.

Because it is still not widely known, charoite has attracted the attention of in-groups and of international dealers who hope to elevate its price as much as possible.

Charoite has a look that is all its own. Once seen, it can hardly be mistaken for any other mineral. Thus it may serve as a symbol of individuality. It is named for the Charo River, the location of its discovery.

CHIASTOLITE
(Aluminum Silicate)

Chiastolite is one of the "cross stones," named from Greek *chiastos,* "marked with an *X*," that is, with the letter *chi* (X). The *X* appears in the cross sections when prisms of chiastolite are cut. The dark core of the pattern is formed by a carbonaceous substance. Because of its mysterious internal patterning, polished slices of chiastolite were often worn or carried as amulets.

Chiastolite is a variety of the mineral andalusite, first found in Andalusia, Spain. Although its colors tend to be dull (grayish, brownish, greenish), its innumerable slight variations on the simple theme of the four-armed cross make chiastolite uniquely interesting.

CHRYSOBERYL (Beryllium Aluminum Oxide)

Although the name *chrysoberyl* means "golden beryl," chrysoberyl is not a golden or any other kind of beryl; it is a different mineral. Beryl is a silicate. Chrysoberyl is an oxide.

The chrysoberyl family includes some highly valued gems, such as alexandrite, cymophane, and chrysoberyl cat's eye (as opposed to quartz cat's eye). The latter, naturally, was usually recommended as a cure for eye troubles and a defense against the evil eye. Now it is said that water placed in the sun for three hours in a green glass jar containing a cat's eye stone becomes a "beauty tincture" and will beautify any face that is washed with it daily.[1]

It is also said that chrysoberyl "causes one to be more charitable toward their neighbor," and that chrysoberyl "has a 'yeast-like' quality in its energy pattern, in that it continues to expand. . . . The energy of chrysoberyl glances off the adrenal glands." A chrysoberyl stone should be worn in the navel.[2] This would seem to defeat the purpose of wearing an expensive gem, which is display; for if it were worn with a garment that shows the navel, such as a bathing suit, it might be too easily lost.

In recent years, a good imitation of chrysoberyl cat's eye stones has been provided by a glass product marketed as Cathaystone.[3]

1. Cunningham, 81. 2. Richardson et al., 58–59. 3. O'Donoghue, *G. M. G.,* 194.

CHRYSOCOLLA (Hydrous Copper Hydroxyl Silicate)

Chrysocolla is another of the vividly colored blue/green copper minerals, often found associated with chalcedony and quartz. Chrysocolla intergrown with malachite and turquoise is known as Eilat stone.[1]

A crystal mystic who describes chrysocolla as "gem silica," while misspelling it either chrysocalla or chrysocholla, says that it helps women who suffer from menstrual discomfort, and affects the balancing of menstrual hormones—although no one can say how. It also heals fevers and burns, neutralizes anger, and calms frazzled nerves—all, presumably, because of its cool color.[2] Another describes it as gentle, calming, soothing, loving, and feminine, adding that chrysocolla is "evolving to replace turquoise."[3] So far, though, turquoise does not seem to be on its way to extinction.

The innocent blue chrysocolla seems to inspire crystal mystics to some of their most untenable remarks. One calls it "a pinkish stone," whereas chrysocolla may be blue, bluish green, green, brown, or even black, but never pink.[4] Another claims that it "amplifies the medulla oblongata," in case anyone happens to need a larger medulla.[5] Another, still believing in the archaic four elements, writes that chrysocolla "carries the planetary influence of Uranus and is compatible to all of the elements except Earth . . . it filters up into the mental strata of the auric field via the solar plexus and helps alleviate personal fears and guilt."[6] A particularly confused "expert" declares (falsely) that chrysocolla "contains the compound borax," (which it does not) to account for its "therapeutic and beneficial effects."[7]

Chrysocolla can be confused with blue-dyed chalcedony, but it is softer. Although chrysocolla is sometimes cut and polished as a gemstone, especially en cabochon, it is too soft to withstand regular wear in jewelry. Its hardness varies between 2 and 4 on the Mohs scale. Its practical use is as a minor ore of copper.

Chrysocolla is sometimes found intermixed with various forms of silica. Chrysocolla mingled with jasper has received the nickname parrot-wing. Chrysocolla mingled with quartz is sold under the trade name of Stellarite.[8] Unfortunately, there is a different mineral called stellerite, a zeolite whose name is pronounced the same way; so this nomenclature has caused a certain amount of confusion. The mixtures tend to improve the mineral's wearing qualities, adding strength and hardness to overcome the fragility of pure chrysocolla, while retaining the latter's beautiful blue-green colors.[9]

As a symbolic meditation stone, chrysocolla evokes the beauty of calm summer seas and bright flowers, vividly suggesting an atmosphere of peace.

1. Schumann, 200. 2. Raphaell, *C. E.*, 101–104, 158, 164. 3. Stein, 238. 4. Cunningham, 83. 5. Gurudas, 90. 6. Lorusso & Glick, 33. 7. Hodges, 66. 8 Arem, 68. 9. Pough, 278.

CHRYSOPRASE (Silicon Dioxide)

Chrysoprase is a bright, apple green variety of chalcedony, long credited with wonderful powers. The ancients believed that, like emerald, chrysoprase would lose its green color in the presence of poison. Romanian folk tradition said that the owner of a chrysoprase would be able to understand the language of lizards. Medieval doctors prescribed it for relief of gout.[1] In the Middle Ages, it was believed that a piece of chrysoprase held in the mouth would make one invisible, so it was viewed as a stone that helped criminals escape punishment.[2]

One crystal mystic now states rather unnecessarily that the light emitted by chrysoprase is "taken into the body through the optic nerve into the glands of the brain."[3] Of course, the body has nothing that responds to visible light *except* the optic nerve, which transmits impulses to the brain's visual centers (not "glands"). Another mystic seems to think the heart responds to the "serene flow of light" emanating from a chrysoprase. "Its golden green light is also effective in feeding, recharging, and calming the heart."[4] This seems to imply that the heart eats light, recharges like a battery, and is automatically moderated in its action by the visual image of a stone, without the intervention of mind or emotion—hardly a series of implications that one can take seriously. The color of chrysoprase is, however, a serene green, reminiscent of sunlight shining through summer leaves, and many people may find just this shade of green soothing. Certainly it makes chrysoprase a pleasant gem, easy to wear and easy to like.

---

1. Wodiska, 138, 141, 236. 2. Dake et al., 141. 3. Bravo, 144–145. 4. Chocron, 72.

CINNABAR (Mercury Sulfide)

Because of its red color, cinnabar was named from the Persian word for "dragon's blood."[1] It is the principal ore of mercury, which can be seen in some specimens of cinnabar as tiny silvery droplets of the liquid metal.

A modern mystical book says of cinnabar in large capital letters: "WHEN PAINTED ON A SURFACE, IT HAS THE ABILITY TO REPEL ATOMIC RADIATION OR BOMBARDMENT."[2] The reader is told that safety from nuclear accident or holocaust can be assured inside any structure painted with cinnabar. Of course, to depend on this assurance is to risk a very nasty surprise.

Perhaps such a strange belief is somehow related to the magic "pills of immortality" that were made of cinnabar in China as much as 3600 years ago. In our own age of nuclear anxiety, any hint of immunity to sudden death seems welcome enough.

---

1. Boegel, 89. 2. Richardson et al., 139.

CITRINE (Silicon Dioxide)

Citrine is yellow quartz, sometimes misrepresented as the more expensive yellow topaz under such names as Madeira topaz or Bahia topaz. Natural citrine is relatively rare. Much commercial citrine is artificially created by heating low-grade amethyst to about 900 degrees Fahrenheit, whereupon it turns a golden color. Such "burned amethyst" tends to show red, orange, or warm bronze shades, whereas natural citrine is a cooler, paler, sometimes almost greenish yellow. Amethyst that "burns" green instead of yellow is called praseolite.

At least one crystal mystic expresses a preference for the heat-treated material (misspelled "madiera" citrine) as "superior for treatment of certain physical illnesses"—which are not, however, specified.[1]

Because color associations are so significant in crystal healing ideas, citrine is inevitably recommended for urinary troubles, jaundice, and liver and kidney ailments. It "aids" the gall bladder, even when it has not been ascertained that any aid is required. It "purifies the entire digestive and urinary tracts," even when these tracts have not been found impure. Citrine also "broadens reality."[2] These are far-reaching powers, indeed.

One mystic insists that citrine will cure gangrene and appendicitis, but it will be very dangerous to put any faith in this if you really need an appendectomy. Citrine also brings about regeneration of the red and white corpuscles, exerts an undefined influence on the lymphatic system, and has some equally undefined effect on the cells of the "flesh brain."[3] Another mystic prescribes citrine for depression, diabetes, and constipation.[4]

Others dismiss citrine with lofty contempt, saying that it "will not be of great benefit" and must not be confused with the more desirable topaz.[5] The same writers praise quartz to the skies, however, apparently unaware that citrine and quartz are the same material.

The transparency, pleasing color, and acceptable hardness of citrine make it suitable for cutting and faceting as a jewel. Also, because it is not expensive, it can be offered in large pieces. Buyers who are not knowledgeable about gemstones, however, should beware of citrines masquerading as more valuable materials or being sold at grossly inflated prices.

In recent years, the bicolored gem "ametrine" has been artificially produced by utilizing the tendency of heated amethyst to change its color haphazardly, in bands or blotches. If the process is halted before all the material has turned yellow, it can furnish gems that show both colors in the same cut stone.

---

1. Rea, 330. 2. Stein, 207–208. 3. Gurudas, 145–146. 4. Chocron, 63. 5. Richardson et al., 129.

COAL (Organic Material)

As everyone knows, coal is a decomposition product of plants that lived on earth during the Carboniferous period, more than three hundred million years ago. The cellulose of those plants and trees, buried and compacted, turned into lignite (brown coal), then bituminous coal, then anthracite coal; the end of the series is graphite, the soft form of pure elemental carbon. The hard form is diamond. This does not mean, however, that diamonds are found in coal beds. Different forces, much deeper underground, produce the carbon crystals that are now mined as diamond.

Coal was the major mineral resource that made the Industrial Revolution possible; so in a sense, the modern technological era was founded on coal. This fact has given coal aesthetic or metaphorical significance to some people in the industrial age. As the basis of manufacturing wealth and profit, especially in the British Isles, coal was sometimes viewed as a money-attracting amulet. To this day, some of the speculators in the London stock exchange carry a piece of coal in their pockets for luck and good fortune.[1]

The same good-luck wish may have been the origin of an obscure Christmas custom, that of placing a piece of coal in each child's Christmas stocking. More recently, the good-luck connotation was forgotten, and children were told that if they misbehaved, they might receive only coal in their stockings instead of toys and treats.

Some people misleadingly refer to coal as fossilized wood. Strictly speaking, coal is not a fossil. Fossils retain the exact cell structure of the organic material as it was in life, although the organic matter has been replaced by silica. Coal shows no such structure. The original matter has been destroyed by decay, compacted under pressure, and turned into a new substance altogether.

---

1 Cunningham, 84.

COPPER (Element)

Copper in the ancient world was sacred to the Great Goddess under her classical name Venus, or Aphrodite. One of her major temples stood at Paphos on the isle of Cyprus, whose name means "copper" because it had rich copper mines and colonies of coppersmiths who dedicated their art to the Goddess. Copper made the magic mirrors of divination used on the Goddess's day, Friday (named after her northern counterpart, Freya). The alchemical symbol of copper was said to represent one of these mirrors. It is still the astronomical symbol of the planet Venus and the biological/botanical symbol of femaleness.

Copper was essential to the economy of the Bronze Age, which was also the age of the Goddess. Bronze cannot be made without copper, which forms bronze when alloyed with tin. (Brass is made of copper alloyed with zinc.) The only two colored elemental metals are gold and copper.

Because copper was the Venus metal, it was often used as a love charm. Copper jewelry was supposed to enhance sexuality. In A.D. 1669, a Dr. Rowland was still writing that copper "sympathizeth with Venus in the Macrocosm, and with the generative parts in the Microcosm." It was said again in 1712 that copper will "strengthen the generative functions in men, and women."[1]

Edgar Cayce liked to recommend the wearing of copper for sundry purposes, but he seems to have been confused about its nature. He described his favorite mineral, lapis lazuli, as an essence or fusion of copper, an erosion of copper, or the exuding of copper—all nonsense, because lapis lazuli is a silicate rock containing no copper at all.[2] Evidently Cayce naively assumed that all blue minerals owe their blue coloring to the presence of copper.

The recent fad for wearing copper bracelets as a charm against arthritis has equally nonsensical rationales among New Age mystics. One claims that wearing a copper bracelet "antidotes the affects [*sic*] of

microwave radiation."[3] Another says that copper eliminates "metallic wastes" from the body, by "oxidizing through the pores."[4] Still another declares that copper can heal "because of copper's ability to balance the body's polarity."[5]

Such assertions return us to the ignorant Middle Ages, when medical diagnosticians were concerned only that their words should sound erudite, without having the least notion of physical and biological realities. Significantly, the miraculous effects are attributed to copper jewelry, whereas a purer copper might be found in any old piece of electric wiring or water pipe, not to mention the copper pots and pans that might occupy one's kitchen. Somehow, these are never medicinal. One might also expect invincible good health among the residents of Michigan's Keweenaw Peninsula, where some of the world's richest copper deposits were found. They were found, actually, by the Indians, who used Michigan copper for tools and ornaments. European settlers did not discover this source of Indian copper until 1840.

---

1. Fernie, 421–422. 2. *Scientific Properties*, 16, 23, 25. 3. Gurudas, 94. 4. Richardson et al., 140. 5. Cunningham, 155.

COPROLITE (Silicon Dioxide)

Coprolite means literally "excrement stone." It is fossilized fecal material, nicknamed "dinosaur dung." In order to have been deposited by a dinosaur, a given specimen of coprolite would have to be in the neighborhood of two hundred million years old. However, silicification of an organic substance like feces can proceed fairly fast under the right conditions; therefore, some coprolite may be no more than two or three million years old, and not the relic of a dinosaur but of some other, much more recent animal.

Coprolite specimens can bear a strong resemblance to the fake dog deposits perpetrated by novelty manufacturers for the amusement of practical jokers. Nevertheless, coprolite is stone, not plastic. It was not manufactured but actually excreted. Even if one can only guess about the animal that was its source, its outward appearance leaves little doubt of its original nature.

Crystal mystics tend to ignore coprolite, perhaps considering it an indelicate form of silica, not to be mentioned in the same breath with the "higher" spiritual forms. One might think, however, that coprolite would be a more appropriate prescription for intestinal troubles than some of the silicates that are generally prescribed. After all, one of the fundamental principles of all magic is "like affects like." If Nature can petrify wood, bone, coral, teeth, shells, footprints, insects, fish, crinoids, plants, or the excrement of land animals all impartially, why should we mere humans selectively ignore any of her works? As a symbol, coprolite may be more directly representative of earthiness than any of the daintier stones.

Some specimens of coprolite are cut and polished like agates. Thus treated, they often show inner patterns and colors of extraordinary beauty. Surely there is a lesson to be drawn from this.

CORAL (Organic Material)

Along with pearl and amber, coral is considered one of the organic gems,

although its mineral composition is mostly calcium carbonate (calcite). It is made of the calcified skeletons of the tiny coral polyps that, in their millions, build enormous submarine reefs and sometimes whole islands. Corals can occur in both salt and fresh water. The famous Petoskey stones of Lake Michigan are actually fossilized coral.[1]

Coral can be white, pink, blue, or black; but the most valued color has always been the red, known as "noble" coral. The ancient Greeks claimed that red coral was colored by the divine blood of Medusa.[2] Carved in the likeness of Medusa or Hecate, coral amulets brought victory in war. Bound to a ship's mast, coral was believed to ward off lightning and tempest.[3] Coral was used as a charm against fire, sorcery, and natural disasters.[4] Coral was the oceanic Tree of Life. Its red color was associated with the life-giving uterine blood supposedly bestowed by the Goddess upon all women. To this day the archaic connections between coral and the blood bonds of the maternal clan and feminine fertility still lead some Italian peasant women to believe that their coral jewelry will change color in rhythmic harmony with their menstrual cycles.[5]

According to Pliny, powdered coral drunk in water would cure fever and "griping pains in the bowels, affections of the bladder and urinary calculi."[6] Powdered coral was also used in ointments for skin infections. Coral amulets were supposed to help teething infants and to prevent convulsions in children.[7] Fading of the color of a coral amulet was taken as an omen of death but people believed that obtaining another coral amulet of a deeper color would preserve life.[8] Perhaps this helps to explain the general preference for corals of the more vivid colors. Coral amulets also drove away ghosts, hobgoblins, winds, storms, lightning, dreams, and illusions—though not, of course, the illusory ideas of coral's magical efficacy.[9]

Dr. John Schroder wrote in 1660 that coral strengthens the heart, stomach, and liver; purifies the blood; stops fluxes of the belly and womb; prevents epilepsy; and cures runny eyes and ulcers. Boyle's *Collection of Remedies* added that coral "sweetens" the blood and cures acidity. Early in the twentieth century, Dr. Fernie recommended coral as an antidote for children's diseases, such as whooping cough and croup.[10] Since coral amulets had always been considered protective of children, thanks to the archetypal associations with the blood mother and with mother-blood, these ideas were not without precedent.

Modern mystical uses for coral are not unlike these old ideas. Coral is said to cure colic, gallstones, hemorrhoids, hepatitis, jaundice, and warts.[11] It removes "impurities" from the blood and aura.[12] It is "heating, vitalizing and stimulating" to the bloodstream.[13] It cures diseases of the sexual organs.[14] It alleviates the pain of arthritis, and activates the thyroid gland, thus increasing metabolic rates and releasing muscle toxins. As a result, "emotional balance may develop."[15] But common sense, apparently, will not.

Coral is touted also as a cure for insanity and a charm for wisdom, provided its branches are never broken or cut with a metal tool.[16] This seems to be a safe bet, because coral branches that are neither broken off nor cut off are, of necessity, still part of their reef. Perhaps the insane can be sent down with scuba gear to partake

of the healing magic of living coral.

Common names for the favored red coral range from oxblood (deep red) to angel skin (light pink). "African star coral" is a commercial product stabilized, bleached, and dyed by various artificial processes before it is sold. Numerous coral imitations are made of plastic, porcelain, stained bone, powdered pressed marble, vegetable ivory, and opaque glass.

---

1. Wodiska, 107. 2. Stern, 69. 3. Anderson, 45. 4. Thomson, 22. 5. Kunz, 69. 6. Smith, 492. 7. Fernie, 355. 8. Thomson, 23. 9. Spencer, 232. 10. Fernie, 290–293. 11. Parkinson, 230. 12. Stein, 200. 13. Chocron, 59. 14. Bravo, 121. 15. Gurudas, 95–96. 16. Rutland, 161.

CROCOITE (Lead Chromate)

Wherever you see long, slender prismatic crystals of an intense flame color, between orange and cherry red, you will be in the presence of crocoite, a rare mineral highly esteemed by collectors. The colors of crocoite are among the most brilliant in the mineral world, but the material is seldom worked because it is extremely fragile. It must be handled with the greatest care.

Despite the difficulties, a few gems have been cut from crocoite—not for jewelry, because crocoite cannot be worn, but only as a challenge to the skill of the cutter. The material is expensive, and few cutters want to risk the well-known possibility of breakage. Most crocoite specimens are kept in the cabinet and never touched, though their flashing colors can provide delight to the eye that views them.

Crocoite is named from Greek *krokos*, "saffron." Nature produces only a few chromates, and crocoite is the only chromate generally found in mineral collections. Because of its rarity, its fragility, and its fine vivid colors, crocoite may be considered a glamorous eccentric—a hothouse flower of the mineral world.

CUBIC ZIRCONIA (Stabilized Cubic Zirconium Oxide)

In 1937, mineralogists first observed within a natural zircon the cubic form of zirconium oxide, otherwise known as baddeleyite after a nineteenth-century English mineralogist, Joseph Baddeley. At first thought too unstable to be useful in the gem trade, this "cubic zirconia" has become the most important man-made gemstone. It is the best diamond imitation so far, having a hardness of 8.5 on the Mohs scale and even more fire than a genuine diamond. Viewing a faceted cubic zirconia and diamond side by side, the average person cannot tell the difference. Cubic zirconia is almost twice as heavy as diamond, but this distinction is negligible in the case of small cut stones.

It used to be thought that zirconium oxide crystals could never be grown in the laboratory because of the mineral's extremely high melting point, close to 5000 degrees Fahrenheit (2750 degrees Celsius). The crucible could not be made of any known substance, because at such temperatures the container would melt before the contents. Finally a Russian scientist, V. V. Osiko, devised the "skull melt" technique whereby the molten zirconium oxide is contained within dry or unmelted walls of its own substance, the center portion being heated by radio waves while the external shell is cooled by water passing through copper pipes.

Cubic zirconia has been marketed under a great many trade names, some designed to suggest that it is a kind of diamond: Cerene, Diamon-Z, Diamonair, Diamonesque, Diamondite, Diconia, Djevalite, Fianite, Phyanite, Shelby, Singh kohinoor. Now that the gem is winning acceptance in its own right, such misleading names are being dropped, and "CZ" is respectable. It is available in a variety of colors. It is as durable as any natural stone of comparable hardness and is therefore a permanent addition to the minerals of this planet, even though it is a child of human ingenuity and not of nature. Indeed, these imitation diamonds may outlast the whole human species by millions of years. This thought is a provocative starting point for meditation on this new and most human jewel.

DANBURITE
(Calcium Borosilicate)

Danburite is named after its first find in Danbury, Connecticut. It is as hard as quartz and sometimes serves as a gemstone, although large crystals of suitable transparency are rare. Danburite gems lack fire because of their low dispersion, but they can be very bright when correctly cut. Danburite is a good material for the collector: attractive, unusual, not to be found (like quartz) in everyone's collection, yet reasonably available. Its crystals often bear a superficial resemblance to those of topaz.

DATOLITE (Calcium Hydroxyl Borosilicate)

Datolite is a transparent-to-translucent white, greenish white, or pale green mineral classified as a minor gemstone, because choice crystals are sometimes cut and faceted. Its hardness, however, is only 5.5 on the Mohs scale. Rough datolite crystals are interesting in their complexity. Crystal faces do not seem to be oriented in any particular way. Instead, individual crystals are scattered in a random manner throughout any aggregate, as if they were simply dropped there by the handful and stirred about. This makes datolite a puzzle for the crystallographer. Still, it is a pretty mineral. Some specimens may be tinted pink or red by copper inclusions, but the cool greenish white typical of datolite is attractive and restful.

In addition to the crystalline form, datolite also occurs in massive white nodules resembling porcelain, often handsomely mottled with specks of copper or other associated minerals. When it occurs in coarse granular masses, datolite easily crumbles: hence its name, from a Greek word meaning "to divide."[1]

---

1. Sinkankas, *M. A.,* 546.

DESERT ROSE

A desert rose is not a specific mineral, but rather a mineral formation. It appears when lamellar (flattened) plates of barite or gypsum become impregnated with sand during their crystallization and, in this condition, are arranged around a common center to form a rosette. Some desert roses are indeed remarkably flowerlike, except that the texture of the "petals" is rough and grainy instead of smooth.

On the ancient magical principle of like affects like, desert roses would be the logical sort of charm to place in a flower garden or in front of a potted plant. Some ingenious mineral fanciers have been known to use them as table centerpieces. Small ones also can be unusual party favors or gifts. As Nature seems playful in creating them, the little sand-flowers likewise lend themselves to playful uses.

DIAMOND (Elemental Carbon)

Diamond has been called the world's most beautiful stone, although 80 percent of all the diamonds mined are dull-colored and unattractive, useful only for industrial cutting and grinding machinery. Diamond is, however, the world's hardest stone: the hardest natural substance on earth. It is 140 times harder than the second hardest mineral, corundum, and 1000 times harder than quartz.[1] The only other substances that approach diamond in hardness are the metal tantalum and two artificial products: carborundum (silicon carbide) and borazon (cubic boron nitride).[2]

Yet the same mineral as diamond, pure elemental carbon, also takes the form of one of the world's softest substances, graphite: the "lead" in a common lead pencil, named from the Greek word for writing. Of the two, diamond is the more unstable form. Over the course of millions of years, diamond gradually turns into graphite.[3] Despite the popular advertising phrase, diamonds are not quite "forever."

Graphite and charcoal—both forms of carbon—are good conductors of electricity, but diamonds are nonconductors.

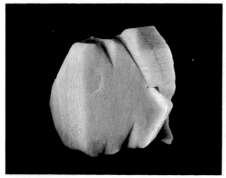

Amazonite

Apatite

Apophyllite crystals on stilbite

Adamite

Aragonite

Beryl

Asbestos (chrysotile) Courtesy of Joseph Cilen

Barite

Cerussite

Calcite

Celestite   Courtesy of Lisa Miller

Chabazite   Courtesy of Joseph Cilen

Chiastolite
Courtesy of Joseph Cilen

Coprolite

Chrysoberyl

Courtesy of the Morris Museum
of Arts and Sciences

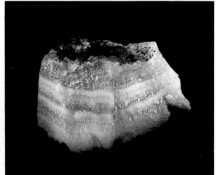

Chalcedony

Diopside (star cabochon)

Cubic zirconia

Danburite

Datolite

Enstatite

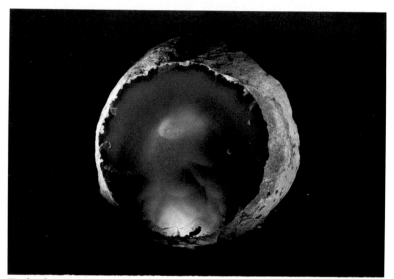

Enhydros

Galena

Epidote

Hexagonite

Herkimer diamond

Hemimorphite

Heulandite

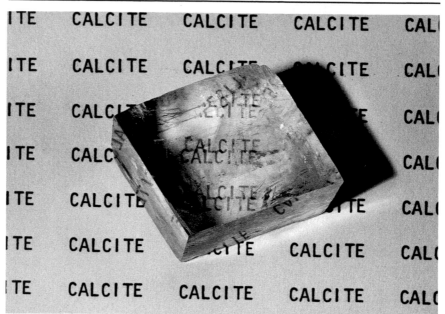

Iceland spar

Kutnohorite

Kunzite

Jet

Courtesy of Schiffer Lapidary

Meteorite

Marble

Lodestone

Courtesy of Nick Rochester

Mica (biotite)

Onyx

Moonstone (adularia)

Moldavite

Obsidian ("snowflake" variety)

Pumice

Pearl

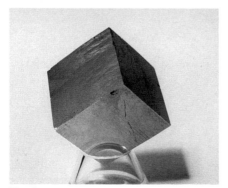

Pyrite

Petrified wood

Sapphire (natural crystal)

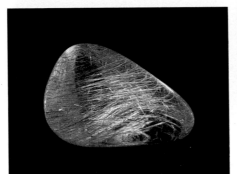

Rutile needles in quartz

Scapolite

Quartz

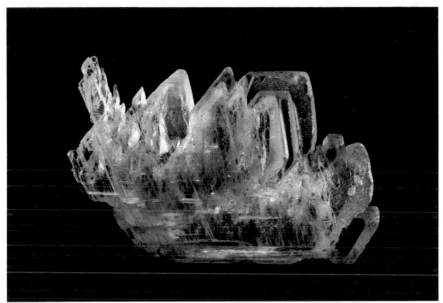

Selenite

Siderite

Smoky quartz

Sphalerite

Staurolite. Left: imitation. Right: natural.

Stilbite

Stibnite

Spinel crystals on calcite

Vanadinite

Topaz

Tektite

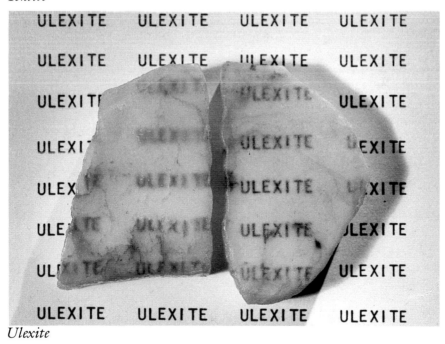
Ulexite

Witherite

Knitted crystal pouch

Zircon

Wavellite   Courtesy of Allan W. Eckert

Having been confused by the term *carbon*, at least one modern crystal mystic believes that diamonds are transformations of coal.[4] Actually, diamonds and coal are formed under quite different conditions. Diamonds are found in kimberlite rock, having been crystallized as deep in the earth as a hundred miles below the surface, under well-nigh inconceivable pressures—up to a million and a half pounds per square inch—and heat of perhaps 2500 degrees Celsius.[5] The difficulty of achieving such conditions technologically has been the major impediment to synthesis of diamonds.

A New Age "expert" claims that from ancient times, diamonds, rubies, and sapphires have been "reduced to ashes" to serve as medicine.[6] This claim is absurd. Rubies and sapphires are unburnable. Being carbon, diamond will burn, but only in air at a temperature of 900 degrees Celsius.[7] When thus burned, diamonds are reduced to carbon dioxide gas and leave no solid ash. Theophrastus in 300 B.C. knew better than our modern "expert." His *Peri Lithon* called diamond the unburnable stone.[8] Pliny noted that diamonds placed in a fire will not even become warm.

During the Middle Ages, people knew no way to test a diamond for genuineness except to scratch glass with it. This is a poor test, because glass can be scratched also by corundum, beryl, topaz, zircon, spinel, quartz, and other stones. Consequently, stones were often described as diamonds when they were actually something else.

A second-century Orphic poem recommended as a sure defense against the evil eye certain stones that were then called diamond, but they may have been quartz or white sapphire. Any stone called diamond was regarded as magical. Rabbi Jehudah described in the Talmud an occasion when diamonds were placed on the plucked, cooked, and salted carcasses of fowl that then came back to life and flew away. The fourteenth-century mystic Rabbi Benoni said that a diamond brings on spiritual ecstasy and makes its wearer "invincible," but his contemporary, the alchemist Pierre de Boniface, said "invisible." Bishop Marbodus said that diamonds cure insanity. Rabbi Simeon ben Johanan declared that Abraham had a magic diamond that would cure any person who looked at it. After Abraham died (in spite of looking at his diamond, presumably), God sealed the curative gem "in the planet of the sun."[9]

According to the *Speculum Lapidum* of Camillus Leonardus (Venice, 1502), diamond "disperses vain Fears; enables to quell all Quarrels and Contentions; is a Help to Lunaticks, and such as are possess'd with the Devil; being bound to the left arm, it gives Victory over Enemies; it tames wild Beasts; it helps those who are troubled with Phantasms, and the Night mare; and it makes him who wears it bold and daring in his Transactions." It also counteracts all sorcery and all poisons.[10] Mary, Queen of Scots, owned a talismanic diamond that was supposed to preserve her from poison and all other dangers.[11] Perhaps her diamond was not programmed to prevent beheading.

Doctors attempted to cure Pope Clement VII of his final illness in 1534 by dosing him with powdered gems, including a large diamond. Despite immense expenditure, the treatment failed.[12] Perhaps the pope died more bravely, for it was often said that diamonds taken internally would increase courage.[13] On the other hand, some thought that ingested diamonds were highly poisonous. Benvenuto Cellini claimed that his enemies tried to kill him by mixing diamond powder in his food. Fortunately, the assassin could not afford real diamond powder and substituted beryl instead, so "the powder had no effect."[14]

This superstition is still extant. One author declares that diamond powder was used as a poison because it tears apart the lining of the stomach and intestines.[15] Diamond powder may be indigestible, but it is hardly fatal.

Many stories about diamonds purported to explain how to feed them and make them grow, or how to get more of them. Even in the twentieth century, some have believed that the diamonds found in sands and gravels had a meteoric source and "have dropped from the skies . . . being literally a gift from heaven."[16] Though very small diamonds are sometimes found in meteoric material, this is not the source of gem gravels. Some people believed that two diamonds placed together in the right circumstances could mate and produce offspring. In the sixteenth century, Francisco Ruei's *De gemmis* gave the following crystal-mystical explanation: "The celestial energy in the parent stones, qualified by some as '*vis adamantifica*,' first changes the surrounding air into water, or some similar substance, and then condenses and hardens this into the diamond gem." Sir John Mandeville said that two mated diamonds would bring forth children, and when watered with May dew they would grow bigger.[17]

On the other hand, it was also believed that diamonds could sicken and die, losing their luster in the process. Jean de la Taille de Bonderay wrote in 1754 that diamonds "even take offense if an injury be done them and become rough and pale."[18] Most probably, they became just plain dirty.

Miraculous effects are still attributed to diamonds. Despite the numerous diamond wearers who are divorced or otherwise disappointed in love, diamonds are said to bring "constancy in lovers, and serenity in your life." A diamond also counteracts poison, nightmares, madness, strife, pestilence, epilepsy, dyslexia, tuberculosis, and autism. It "alters and corrects the muscle structure in the jaw and the shoulder blades. It arrests the progress of most diseases" and brings victory. "Because of its master number vibration," whatever that may be, diamond "has the capability of saving or breaking countries; of helping to win or lose wars."[19] Theoretically then, South Africa should be the leading world power.

Another mystic says that diamond can not only destroy most diseases, but also adjust the "plates" of the cranium, thus easing inflammation in the head.[20] Another, who says diamond is not a mineral, defines it as the strongest "energy absorber and transmitter" of the gem world because it "magnifies and transmits healing energy."[21] Another claims that diamond "magnifies" all other stones (making them larger?) and can "amplify and penetrate," though we are not told what it amplifies or penetrates.[22] It will, of course, penetrate solid rock when affixed to the business end of a drill.

Diamond is probably the world's most imitated gem. Colorless quartz, beryl, glass, spinel, zircon, corundum, and almost any other mineral that could even remotely pass for a diamond has done so. Recent synthetic products such as rutile, spinel, and sapphire have substituted for diamonds, also the artificial mineral lithium niobate ("Linobate"), cubic zirconia, YAG, GGG, and yttrium oxide ("Yttralox").[23] One of the popular imitations for a time was synthetic strontium titanate, marketed under such names as Bal de feu, Brilliante, Continental jewel, Diagem, Diamontina, Dynagem, Fabulite, Jewelite, Lustigem, Marvelite, Pauline Trigere, Rossini jewel, Sorella, Starilan, Wellington, and Zenithite.[24] This material has exceptional dispersion and luster, making a gorgeous jewel when it is freshly cut, but facet edges soon become worn down because the material is insufficiently hard to hold a high polish.

The desire to synthesize real diamond has motivated considerable research. One whose name is connected with the effort is the nineteenth-century Scottish chemist J. B. Hannay, who claimed the invention of synthetic diamond. He offered tiny quarter-millimeter crystals to the British Museum for testing, and the mineralogists accepted them as true diamonds. About seventy years later, Hannay's crystals were tested again with modern techniques, and found to be true diamonds indeed: natural ones. The first verifiable synthetic diamond crystals were grown by Howard T. Hall. Synthetic gem-quality diamonds are now available, but they cost more than natural stones.[25] It is said, however, that methods are improving, and the future will bring inexpensive synthetic diamonds to the jewelry trade.

This may well be a good thing. Overvaluation of precious stones in general, and of diamonds in particular, has caused much pain as well as gain. The history of the world diamond trade is replete with thievery, murder, exploitation, slavery, brutality, fraud, bribery, and every other manifestation of the greed and ruthlessness of acquisitive people. Moreover, diamond mining is extremely wasteful. It takes an average of five tons of rock to produce a single carat of diamond. Only 20 percent of diamonds are gem quality, and half of this is lost in cutting. Therefore, each carat of diamond jewelry is the result of digging up and crushing about fifty tons of rock. Multiplied by the number of carats annually produced, this is a staggering volume of the earth's substance.

Perhaps the prices that people have paid for diamonds are too high in more ways than one.

1. Spencer, 118. 2. Smith, 262. 3. Axon, 34. 4. Chocron, 41–42. 5. Rutland, 73. 6. Parkinson, 14. 7. Fisher, 53. 8. Medenbach & Wilk, 24. 9. Kunz, 72–74, 377. 10. Spencer, 111–112. 11. Stern, 23. 12. Kunz, 379. 13. Fernie, 2. 14. Desautels, *M. K.,* 12. 15. Gurudas, 33. 16. Fernie, 82. 17. Kunz, 41, 71–72. 18. Stern, 23. 19. Parkinson, 77, 81–84. 20. Gurudas, 4, 98. 21. Stein, 267. 22. Richardson et al., 66. 23. O'Donoghue, *G. M. G.,* 102–111. 24. Nassau, *G. M. M.,* 204, 216. 25. *Ibid.,* 164–178.

DIOPSIDE (Calcium Magnesium Silicate)

Diopside is one member of a series of pyroxene silicates that includes also hedenbergite and augite. There are many other varietal names. Colors are usually pale to dark greens, but specimens are also white, brown, or black, ranging from transparent to opaque. Diopside is especially interesting to crystal mystics because, like tigereye and cat's eye, it may contain fine inclusions that produce chatoyancy, the cat's eye effect. Some specimens even display asterism—that is, they are star stones, with two or more moving rays of light crossing each other. This effect is enhanced by polishing. Diopside stars are usually four-pointed, with two light lines making a cross. Since the earliest civilizations, all star stones have been viewed with reverence as the dwelling places of living spirits and as earthborn "eyes" that can see into the lives, motives, and doings of humans.

A deep violet or bluish variety of diopside, known as violane, is used for beads, inlay work, and other ornamental purposes. A green variety from the Ala valley in Italy is called alalite.[1]

---

1. Webster, 316.

DIOPTASE (Hydrous Copper Silicate)

Dioptase is a brilliant emerald green gemstone that may be cut for jewelry when found in crystals of sufficient size. Its color rivals that of the darkest emeralds, but its hardness is much less—only 5 on the Mohs scale. Small crystals of dioptase can form crusts and veinlets in matrix rock. These make pretty cabinet specimens. Some tiny crystals may be seen through the microscope to form starlike shapes, radiating from a common center. The major attraction of this mineral is its rich, luminous color, which is so intense in some specimens that it does almost seem to glow. One of the more misleading names for dioptase is "copper emerald."

DOLOMITE (Calcium Magnesium Carbonate)

Dolomite the mineral is often confused with dolomite the rock, which gave its name to an Alpine range in northeastern Italy, the Dolomites. Climbers like these mountains, because dolomite rock is notoriously firm, strong, dependable, and sandpaper-rough to provide friction; it includes calcite, clay, quartz, and pyrite.

Dolomite was named after the French mineralogist Déodat de Dolomieu (1750–1801). It appears in white, yellowish, tan, gray, or flesh-colored rhombohedral crystals. Sometimes it is transparent, and may be faceted as a gemstone, although it is not very hard. Its pearly luster has given it the nickname "pearl spar."[1] Crystals tend to form offset curved aggregates, resulting in saddle shapes. Dolomite is one end member of a series. The other end member, ankerite, includes some proportion of iron.

The pinkish, peach, or flesh-colored specimens of dolomite have placed it in the category of heart stones, according to crystal mystics. It is therefore "warming, soothing, cheering and comforting for depression and grief," also medicinal for skin and hearing problems, palsies, and heart disease.[2]

Dolomite clusters reward close inspection with a lens. Intricate connections can be seen between the shiny curved crystals, with interesting angles, spaces, walls, and tunnels. Dolomite is a labyrinth for the eye; and the tender shades of the flesh-colored variety do give an impression of warmth. Some specimens are attractively sprinkled with small, brassy crystals of chalcopyrite.

---

1. Schumann, 206. 2. Stein, 221.

EMERALD (Beryllium Aluminum Silicate)

Emerald is the grass green variety of beryl. Compared with other kinds of beryl, it is rare, because the chromium that provides its green color seldom occurs in the acid igneous rocks that produce beryl. Conversely, rocks that are rich in chromium seldom contain beryl crystals.[1] The same cause accounts for the rarity of the green variety of spodumene, hiddenite; more common is the violet variety, kunzite. Both hiddenite and emerald lose their green color when heated and regain it after cooling.[2]

Emeralds are characteristically much flawed. "A flawless emerald" is a lapidary's metaphor for the impossible. Jewelers refer to the internal fissures, inclusions, vacancies, and other flaws inside an emerald as the jardin (garden), because they sometimes resemble floral forms. The word *emerald* was first used in English in the sixteenth century, derived from French *esmeraude,* which was in turn derived from Latin *smaragdus,* "emerald".[3]

Emeralds have been greatly prized since antiquity. They were sacred to the Great Goddess, symbolizing her green-clad earth in spring festivals. Emerald remained the stone of Venus, or Aphrodite, to be worn on her holy day, Friday.[4] Her Greek consort Hermes, who became the god of magic because he was privy to her secrets, was said to have composed the famous Emerald Tablet, with the ultimate Words of Creation written on emerald. The Egyptians, who called him Thoth, said that his tablet was made of *uat,*

"matrix emerald." In the Middle Ages, Hermes became the mythical father of alchemy, Hermes Trismegistus. His magical tablet became the mythical prototype of the Koran, in Arabian tradition the Preserved Tablet, or Mother of the Book.

The emerald's established sacredness led a biblical writer to describe the throne of God as surrounded by a rainbow that looked like an emerald (Revelation 4:3). Rabbinic legend said that emerald was one of the four precious stones that God gave to Solomon.[5] Medieval tradition insisted that the Holy Grail was carved from a single huge emerald, which had fallen from Satan's crown during his descent from heaven to the underworld.

This same Holy Grail was identified by the Italian church with an "emerald" vessel revered in Genoa as the Sacro Catino (Tazza di Smeraldo). Subsequent investigations proved that the holy vessel was made of green glass.[6] Similarly, the famous emerald of Reichenau Abbey, allegedly a gift to the church from the emperor Charlemagne, was finally studied only two hundred years ago and found to be a lump of green glass.[7]

At the time of the Spanish conquest of Peru in 1531, the Peruvian city of Manta was dominated by an Emerald Goddess, Umiña. Her image was an enormous emerald crystal. Her priests had collected a great store of her "daughters," smaller emeralds offered by the faithful. All this booty was seized by the conquistadores.[8] Their missionary priest, Fray Reginaldo de Pedraza, encouraged the soldiers to "test" the stones by smashing them with hammers, for he claimed that real emeralds would not shatter and those that broke were only imitations, inhabited by devils and fit only for destruction. "But it was observed that the good father did not subject his own jewels to this test." Later, the missionary sold his large personal collection of emeralds in Panama for huge prices.[9]

As a result of the church's hostility to the Emerald Goddess, Peruvian Indians later became convinced that their emerald mines and the gems that came from them were inhabited by evil spirits.[10]

The only medicinal use of a gemstone mentioned by Theophrastus in the third century B.C. was the prescription of emeralds to rest the eyes. According to this tradition, the emperor Nero had a famous emerald through which he watched gladiatorial games. On the other hand, emeralds were said to be bad for the eyes of snakes, even to cause them to go blind. A thirteenth-century Arabian gem merchant, Ahmed Teifashi, claimed that emeralds "dissolved" the eyes of snakes. By this time it was being written that emeralds would cure such things as dysentery, ophthalmia, hemorrhage, and intestinal troubles. They would even act as laxatives.[11]

During the seventeenth century, the list of illnesses curable by emerald grew very long. The gems not only protected the eyes; they also stopped "all Fluxes whatsoever," promoted liver function, stopped bleeding, strengthened the memory, removed "acrid humors," and cured the bites of venomous animals. An emerald hung at the neck was "good against the Falling Sickness."[12] Emeralds also cured malaria, blood poisoning, and demonic possession.[13]

Modern crystal mystics repeat many of the old-time prescriptions, with further embellishments. Emerald cures biliousness, colic, heartburn, colitis, eye problems, diseases of the heart, skin, liver, kidneys, pancreas, spleen, gall bladder, adrenals, also diabetes and "demonic possession." Emeralds soothe pain and are antiseptic.[14] It is recommended that everyone should drink water in which an emerald has lain. This is an effective healing potion because "Emerald is a living energy field that represents universal intelligence."[15]

Even more than that, emerald is declared extraterrestrial, having been brought to the earth by mysterious beings from the planet Venus.[16] Or, according to another source, emerald "transmits a green ray from Saturn."[17] This ray "transmutes" illness, because it is like a laser beam that amplifies, focuses, directs, and even magnetizes—although what these functions might have to do with illness, no one can say.[18] As far back as 1937 it was claimed that emerald was "one of the sacred stones of the Atlanteans," and that women develop occult powers by wearing emeralds after the age of menopause.[19]

Methods of using emeralds for their wonderful curative effects are simple in the extreme. Mere contact will do it. Emerald rubbed on the right hand, which is then rubbed on the back, "creates a force which can be used in the healing of the back."[20] Emerald "enhances" parts of the vertebrae (we are not told which parts), and also assists the chlorophyll in the blood,[21] despite the fact that there is no chlorophyll in the blood. The mystic who makes this claim seems unable even to distinguish clearly between human beings and plants.

Except for the most expensive gem quality stones, most emerald specimens are disappointing to the average person, who expects them to be clean, transparent crystals. Emeralds are more often opaque, or semi-translucent, and rather dull. Before being cut and polished, most emeralds look undistinguished. Some crystal mystics insist that a miracle-working emerald need not be anything like gem quality. Even if it looks like nothing more than a lump of green rock, it will "work" the same as any gem from a set of royal crown jewels. Of course, all emeralds *are* alike in basic crystalline lattice form and chemical composition; otherwise, they would not be emeralds. But very often, as innumerable charlatans and counterfeiters have discovered over the centuries, green glass is prettier than real emeralds, and more believable. Still on the market today, and even quite popular, are the so-called Soudé emeralds whose name has deceived many. A Soudé emerald consists of a thin layer of dark green glass sandwiched between an upper crown and lower pavilion made of colorless beryl or quartz.[22] It can be an attractive gem, despite the fact that it has no component of real emerald at all.

Real emeralds have always been somewhat puzzling to the nonexpert. Green stones in ancient Egyptian jewelry are often erroneously identified as emerald, when they are in fact green jasper, malachite, chrysocolla, fluorite, or even glass. If the word *emerald* has become a synonym for green, the contrary is also true: green (stone) is often thought synonymous with emerald. Another semantic confusion is the so-called Indian emerald, actually cracked quartz ("craquelees") penetrated by green dye. When a red dye is used instead, the product may be called Ancona ruby, Chinese ruby, or fire stone.[23] In the gem trade, you can't always believe what you hear, or

even what you see. To disguise their surface flaws, emeralds offered for sale are frequently oiled. When they dry out, the buyer finds that they are not as attractive as they first appeared.

Green stones in general have been particularly invested with mystic connotations, possibly because of their widely recognized association with the Mother Goddess in antiquity, and modern mystics are quick to supply their own outré interpretations. "When the Sun, Earth and Moon were still one, [green] stones received a *potential existence* through the Sun-force which also works in the diamond and in gold. This is the power of *light,* and we can consider these stones together with magnesium and gold as gifts from the Sun sent to us earth creatures to remind us of our royal lineage." This remark is dropped without further explanation of the "lineage," but it is also asserted that the stones' green color "attracts helium out of the atmosphere." What use this might be to "us earth creatures" remains undisclosed. The same author still believes the ancient superstition about emeralds and eyesight, declaring that lapidaries use emerald "to refresh their tired eyes."[24] No lapidary has ever mentioned this. The more imaginative sort of crystal mystic apparently is not deterred from making statements, however, by so trivial a detail as their baselessness.

In truth, emeralds will not improve the eyesight, attract helium, or convert ordinary folk into descendants of royalty; but they are handsome stones, justly admired throughout human history. Fine gem-quality emeralds may be beyond the means of the average collector, but the more common and less transparent emerald specimens can be surprisingly inexpensive. An emerald need not be an item of jewelry. It is always admirable for its fresh green color, or its crystal shape, and/or its historic and symbolic significances.

1. Shaub, 182. 2. Sinkankas, *G. N. A.*, 157. 3. Rutland, 62. 4. Fernie, 136. 5. Kunz, 78. 6. Rutland, 159. 7. Weinstein, 296. 8. Kunz, 247. 9. Weinstein, 66. 10. Fernie, 130. 11. Kunz, 158, 380–81. 12. Fernie, 2, 127, 137, 354. 13. Anderson, 112. 14. Stein, 231. 15. Parkinson, 97–98. 16. Lorusso & Glick, 37. 17. Bravo, 56. 18. Chocron, 68. 19. Thomson, 34. 20. Richardson et al., 71. 21. Gurudas, 101. 22. O'Donoghue, *G. M. G.*, 196. 23. Nassau, *G. M. M.*, 284. 24. Uyldert, 58, 110, 127.

ENHYDROS (Silicon Dioxide)

Enhydros is a singular noun, though some people think it is plural and call a single one "enhydro." From the Greek meaning "water inside," an enhydros is a chalcedony or agate nodule that contains liquid water, often with a bubble of air as well. These objects are carefully sliced down to a point where the water can be seen through a remaining thin layer of translucent chalcedony, but the central cavity is not opened. Thus, the observer can have a view of nature's pure "million-year-old water," as it is often called.

Naturally, the enhydros seems a very magical object. Perhaps it could serve as a focal point for rituals symbolizing the refreshment of earth's now polluted waters. The image of free-flowing water trapped and enclosed forever in its stone prison is piquant. From what rains, or from what streams, how long ago, might that water have come?

Owners of an enhydros are cautioned never to leave it outdoors in winter. Some collectors have told sad tales of specimens that had insufficient inner space to allow for freezing of their "million-year-old water," and when it expanded in the cold, the whole nodule cracked open.

Most water-containing nodules will dry out eventually. The rock is porous enough to allow very slow evaporation. Some collectors keep their specimens immersed in water to retard internal drying.

ENSTATITE (Magnesium Silicate)

Enstatite is a dark green-gray, brown, blackish, or yellowish member of the pyroxene group of silicates, which also includes diopside and spodumene. Enstatite rarely forms large crystals. An iron-bearing variety (ferroan enstatite, also known as bronzite) has numerous tiny inclusions that impart a bronzy luster to the stone. Some specimens are cut and polished for a cat's eye effect. Some furnish star stones, usually with a four-pointed star. Enstatite is not widely known as a gemstone, but certain types can make striking gems, especially if strongly chatoyant. This quality places enstatite in the category of "moving light" stones.

EPIDOTE (Calcium Aluminum Iron Hydroxyl Silicate)

Having a good hardness almost equal to quartz, epidote is sometimes faceted as a gemstone, but its color is usually so dark that even transparent crystals tend to look opaque. Another name for epidote is pistacite, from its typical pistachio green.[1] The green is often tinged with brown or gray. Deep-colored crystals can appear black, and may be mistaken for schorl (black tourmaline) because they form long slender prisms like the crystals of tourmaline. Lighter-colored yellowish crystals are found occasionally. A rare emerald green variety from Burma is known as tawmawite.[2]

Epidote is really a mineral series or group, including piemontite (or piedmontite), a manganese-bearing member; mukhinite and hancockite, rarities; allanite, a dark material containing radioactive elements; clinozoisite, an iron-poor member; and zoisite, which in turn has two submembers, pink thulite and blue tanzanite. Beside these, there is unakite, a granite rock consisting of green epidote and pink feldspar; it is a popular material for polished cabochons.

Ruby crystals in a matrix of green zoisite are found in Africa and may be polished, matrix and all, for attractive red-green contrast. Pink, massive, manganese-bearing thulite and violet-blue tanzanite are also gem zoisites. The latter was named by the New York firm of Tiffany and Company, who first imported it from Tanzania and promoted it as a new gemstone. Scientists prefer the simpler and clearer designation "blue zoisite."[3]

It is clear that epidote is a large and interesting family.

---

1. Schumann, 184. 2. Arem, 90.
3. Schumann, 160.

FIRE AGATE (Silicon Dioxide)

Fire agate is a variety of chalcedony in which crystals of goethite (iron hydroxide) are interspersed between thin layers of silica in such a way as to present an iridescent play of colors when light passes through the layers. This material does not show its iridescence until it has been polished. The background color is a rather rusty brown, in which opalescent gleams of green, yellow and red can be seen through a polished surface.

Fire agate is a popular material for jewelry. It makes handsome cabochon pendants and rings. Inspired by its warm, earthy colors as well as by its name, crystal healers like to call it a "heating" stone, to be prescribed for chills, colds, frostbite, or an excessively inhibited temperament. Or again, like any agate, it can be used to cool fevered skin. Well-known sources for fire agate are Mexico and the southwestern United States. It is typically a mineral of arid regions.

FIRE OPAL (Hydrous Silicon Dioxide)

The term *fire opal* is somewhat controversial. Some authorities insist that it is synonymous with precious opal, the kind that has a lot of "fire" or flash of various colors. Others apply the term to the flame-colored opals found mostly in Central America, which have little or no multicolored flash of opalescence but are monochromatic bright orange. These can also occur in paler shades of apricot, peach, or even lemon yellow. Some specimens are transparent, but most show some turbidity.

Crystal mystics give fire opal a wide variety of meanings. One says that it will draw money.[1] Another says that it represents passion.[2] Another says that it can "make the solar plexus nervous" and should be worn only with caution.[3] Another most cryptically calls the fire opal a gem of specific times: six o'clock in the evening, in summer. The reader is left to guess whether the fire opal should be worn only at six o'clock in summer, or whether its magic works only at such times, or whether there is any relation at all between the time and the gem, and if so, what its nature can be.[4]

The flame-colored fire opal is an attractive gem, considerably less expensive than precious opal. Like all opals it is somewhat fragile, but with reasonable care it will readily provide a lifetime of aesthetic pleasure.

---

1. Cunningham, 122. 2. Bravo, 125. 3. Richardson et al., 102. 4. Parkinson, 173.

FLUORITE (Calcium Fluoride)

Fluorite is a common mineral with many diverse forms and colors, some much prized by the ancients. Romans admired the blue-purple fluorite mined in Britain, now known as Derbyshire Blue John. Pliny's "most precious" *murrhine* was fluorite, as in the valuable vase taken from Alexandria by Augustus. Pompey took six such vases from Mithridates' treasure and presented them to the temple of Jupiter. Artifacts of carved fluorite were found in the ruins of Pompeii.[1]

The cleavage planes in fluorite form natural octahedrons, which resemble two four-sided pyramids joined base to base, each exposed face being an equilateral triangle. This geometric precision apparently inspired the modern mystical concept of fluorite as an "intellectual" stone. One source says it "aids in the integration of knowledge," but this does not seem to include knowledge of spelling, because this source and others frequently misspell the mineral's name as *flourite*. Another claims that fluorite straightens out one's thoughts, and "strengthens

its user's analytical abilities."[2] It brings "clarity and peacefulness of mind."[3]

It is sometimes said that fluorite is calming "because of the calcium content." But if holding calcium in one's hand is all that is needed to become calm, then a piece of chalk, marble, bone, plaster, or any of dozens of other common materials would do just as well.

It is also claimed that clusters of fluorite crystals are like computers, for the reason that fluorite is not a product of this earth; it was mysteriously conveyed into the rocks of our planet by unnamed powers from "higher dimensions."[4] Geologists will be surprised by this information, because they have been fairly certain all along that fluorite is formed by natural earth processes, like any other mineral.

Fluorite is too soft and too easily scratched to make wearable jewelry, but it may be cut and polished into beautiful ornaments and collectors' gems. It comes in a broad range of colors, and many pieces are attractively streaked with contrasting areas of purple, green, yellow, or blue. Fluorite shaped into spheres, pyramids, obelisks, and wands can be found in many crystal shops. It is a versatile mineral: diverse, interesting, and affordable. Pink fluorite from the Alps is much prized by collectors, and is expensive, but charming little octahedrons are readily available by the millions for mere pennies apiece, to grace the embryonic collections of children and other beginners. Carved artifacts of Blue John and other fluorite varieties are still popular. Such creations are sometimes impregnated with plastic epoxy resin to make them stronger and more scratch-resistant than the untreated mineral.[5]

1. Weinstein, 162–163. 2. Cunningham, 96.
3. Stein, 254. 4. Raphaell, *C. E.,* 107–108.
5. Nassau, *G. E.,* 135.

GALENA (Lead Sulfide)

Galena is a primary ore of lead. The name *galena* was bestowed on it by Pliny. To Aristotle, it was *itmid stone.*[1] Galena forms cubic, opaque, silvery gray crystals that feel very heavy in the hand (specific gravity about 7.5). It resembles lead, but it is not lead, despite the crystal-mystic book that calls it a metal.[2]

The old-fashioned "crystal radio" crystals were galena. For this reason, the mystics regard this stone as somehow connected with communication. One says, "The radio is metaphysical because it uses unseen waves. The radio was a direct result of the planet Uranus."[3] By this reasoning, is everything that cannot be seen metaphysical? Another says that galena can act as a radio to "receive the thoughts of others," and even to "trace back through time," as well as to see into the future.[4] The humble lead ore is given extraordinary powers.

Despite its lack of transparency, or brilliance, or lively color, however, galena is an interesting mineral to contemplate. A sizable piece shows fascinating patterns on the cleavage surfaces, patterns that change perspective with every change in the angle of light, and often resemble architectural structures.

1. Boegel, 88. 2. Richardson et al., 141.
3. Bravo, 33. 4. Richardson et al., 141–142.

GARNET (Calcium, Aluminum, Magnesium, Manganese, Chromium, and/or Iron Silicate)

Garnet is not one mineral but a group. The commonest member, almandine, has many colors. Pyrope is usually red; spessartine, orange-red or brownish. These two may be combined in a mix known as malaya. Rhodolite is purplish red, or pink. The rare uvarovite is dark green. Grossular, also known as hessonite or cinnamon stone, includes submembers hydrogrossular, xalostocite, landerite, rosolite (pink), tsavorite (green), and green massive material called Transvaal jade. Andradite garnet includes demantoid (rich green), schorlomite, melanite (black), and topazolite (yellow-green). There are also garnet rarities called goldmanite, henritermierite, kimzeyite, knorringite, majorite, yamatoite, aplome, and colophonite. Every color is represented except blue. A modern mystic seemingly unaware of all this, distinguishes only two kinds of garnet: masculine (dark red) and feminine (light red).[1]

Red garnets are inevitably associated with blood. Albertus Magnus said that garnet improves blood circulation and strengthens the heart. Everyone believed this except a few skeptics like Johann Gmelin, who wrote in 1778 that the garnet's powers are "fully fictitious."[2] Garnets stopped heart palpitations and spitting of blood in the seventeenth century and could also dissolve "tartar in the body."[3] Garnets averted the plague and dangerous thunderstorms.[4] A lion's figure carved on garnet would preserve health, honor, and safety.[5] It was believed that garnets could not be stolen, because they would bring the thief catastrophically bad luck until they were given back to their rightful owner.[6]

Indian soldiers fighting the British in Kashmir used garnet bullets, hoping to cause very bloody, nonhealing wounds. At the same time, European folklore claimed that garnets would help heal any bleeding injuries.[7] Garnet blood magic was left over from ancient ideas of the lifegiving powers of uterine blood. Garnet was named from *granatum,* the pomegranate, a red-jeweled womb symbol ever since the matriarchal age. Because of these ancient connections with feminine life force, it was sometimes thought that garnets should be worn only by women.

New Age folk have taken over many of the old ideas about garnets, with embellishments. It is still said that garnets avert accidents and thunderstorms, control hemorrhages, and "detoxify the system."[8] They improve blood circulation and relieve menstrual troubles. They provide "warmth" for soothing the pain of arthritis. They "aid the imagination"—although most New Age folk probably do well enough even without their garnets.[9]

One New Age "expert" learnedly declares that garnet is "formed of silicate and oxygen" (*silicate* actually means silicon plus oxygen) and goes on to say that garnet "transmits the rays of Pluto into our bodies through the 'Mind Power Center of Life,' the thinking area of the actual mind system located in the generative organs. . . . The ray-wave of Pluto, entering the brain through the hypothalamus and descending to the generative organs, can be used constructively to heal sexually related negative mind-set psychosomatic diseases."[10] Others say that the "vibration" of garnet can "free the membranes which bind the

thought-forms . . . so that the thought-forms can be freed into the ethers." In addition, garnet has mysterious effects on the spleen, "an organ which has difficulty in being stimulated properly. There is constantly a residue in the average person that needs to be stirred and cleansed." No one seems to know what this supposed residue in the spleen consists of, but the reader is assured that garnet, held over the spleen, "cleanses, purifies, enhances and magnifies."[11] All those who need a larger and cleaner spleen, take note.

Some people are confused about the synthetic products called Yttrium Aluminum Garnet (YAG) and Gadolinium Gallium Garnet (GGG). Actually, these are not garnets, because they contain no silica. They have a garnetlike internal structure but lack any real counterpart in nature. YAG was a popular diamond substitute in the 1960s, sold under such names as Alexite, Amatite, Circolite, Dia-bud, Diamite, Diamogem, Diamonique, Diamonite, Geminair, Kimberly, Linde simulated diamond, Nier-gem, Regalair, Replique, Somerset, and Triamond.[12] GGG replaced YAG in the 1970s, having a more diamondlike appearance even though it is somewhat softer.

1. Harold, 178. 2. Medenbach & Wilk, 176. 3. Fernie, 158. 4. Wodiska, 236. 5. Anderson, 147. 6. Thomson, 76. 7. Desautels, *G. K.,* 100. 8. Parkinson, 48–49. 9. Stein, 188; Chocron, 59. 10. Bravo, 128–129. 11. Richardson et al., 75–76. 12. Nassau, *G. M. M.,* 224.

GEODE (Silicon Dioxide, *et al.*)

A geode is a rounded cavity in sedimentary rock lined with one or more layers of a cryptocrystalline material such as chalcedony and containing crystals growing inward from the walls. When the hollow space in the center of a geode has been completely filled in, it is usually called a nodule. Thunderegg is the name given to agate nodules with starlike interior patterns, found especially in Oregon.

Geodes come in all sizes from tiny to enormous, as rough balls or egg-shaped nodes in surrounding rock. They are cut open and polished across the slice, to reveal their interior beauty. Clear quartz and amethyst crystals are found in geodes; also, colorful fillings of agate, jasper, sardonyx, and crystals of other minerals, such as calcite. Some collectors specialize in geodes only. The aesthetic variety to be found in this kind of formation is literally endless.

A geode symbolizes inner space, a private world, or a hidden beauty known only to its possessor. It may also represent the disguises of Mother Nature, who does not necessarily flaunt her best works in the open but sometimes conceals them in dark places, not caring whether or not they will be admired. In consideration of this, a geode can remind us that in relation to the great cycles of the natural world, human ambition and praise-craving are pointless indeed. A geode may also serve as a symbolic model earth. Its name, meaning "earthlike," refers to its rounded shape. One of its nicknames, "potato stone," suggests its dull-colored, undistinguished-looking exterior hiding an inner substance of high-quality nourishment—spiritual and aesthetic nourishment, that is, in the case of the geode, rather than the physical nourishment of the potato.[1]

---

1. Webster, 13.

GOLD (Element)

From the earliest civilizations, gold was revered for its untarnishable brightness and for its malleability, which made it suitable material for many artifacts. Gold became a standard of value because of the spiritual implications that were drawn from its manifest resistance to the effects of time. Immune to rust, corrosion, dirt, water, acids (except aqua regia), or any other agents of deterioration, gold always represented immortality—the ultimate desire. In some cultures, it was believed that only gold could bring about the resurrection of the dead, who therefore required it in burials.

The Golden Calf of Egyptian religion, adopted by the Old Testament Hebrews under Aaron, was a resurrected form of the savior god Osiris, when he was reborn as Horus from the Goddess Isis: the Golden Cow. The Bible claims that Moses took the holy calf and "burnt it in the fire, and ground it to powder, and strawed it upon the water, and made the children of Israel drink of it" (Exodus 32:20). This passage actually speaks of a pagan ritual custom. Drinking gold powder in water was considered a sovereign remedy, and/or a resurrection charm. It was still so used by medieval alchemists, who sought the "true potable gold" as a heal-all. Some said that every infection was curable with lemon juice in which gold had rested for twenty-four hours, mingled with white wine and angelica root (an early version of a wine cooler?). Paracelsus declared that eating pulverized gold would cure epilepsy, fainting, melancholia, and leprosy.[1]

Physicians of the late nineteenth century continued to believe that certain diseases could be cured only by gold. A treatise written in 1879 claimed that gold would heal dropsy, syphilis, scrofula, and heart trouble. The widespread custom of rubbing a sty with gold dates all the way back to Pliny (A.D. 79). It was sometimes stipulated that the gold must be wet with saliva from a fasting person. Dr. Fernie suggested that the gold is "probably superficially dissolved by the saliva," though he should have known better.[2] Gold is not dissolved by anything, except aqua regia, a formidable mixture of nitric and hydrochloric acids.

Gold is the heaviest of naturally occurring minerals, up to more than nineteen times as heavy as water, as compared to lead, which is only eleven times as heavy as water. This makes it possible for prospectors to pan gold from stream beds. After the matrix rock has weathered away and released a gold nugget into the water, it may sink to the bottom and remain undisturbed for thousands or millions of years. The famous Golden Fleece of Greek myth probably originated with the ancients' practice of hanging a sheep's fleece in goldbearing streams to trap gold particles.[3]

Gold may be found naturally alloyed with silver, a combination known as electrum, from a Greek word for sunshine. The same word used to refer to amber. It was claimed that a cup made of metallic electrum would emit warning rainbow flashes if filled with something poisonous.[4] The name of the alloy might have inspired the New Age myths about the "electricity" of gold. Like most metals, gold is a good conductor of electrical current, but hardly a generator of the same. Yet gold is said to be "more electrical than warm, reaching a higher octave of aura levels."[5]

Gold is much recommended in New Age healing lore, which often alludes to the fact that physicians sometimes treat arthritis with injections of gold salts, such as gold thioglucose, gold sodium thiomalate, gold sodium thiosulfate, or gold thioglycanide. In reality, gold salts cannot be considered identical with gold, any more than common salt (sodium chloride) can be considered identical with either of its component elements, sodium or chlorine. For one thing, gold salts are soluble and therefore assimilatable in the body. Metallic gold is insoluble in aqueous solutions and cannot be assimilated in any way. That is why the gold fillings in your teeth do not melt away.

Wearing gold jewelry or holding gold in the hand is hardly likely to affect the interior of the body. Nevertheless, Edgar Cayce declared that these external acts will "rebuild the nervous system [nerve tissue does not regenerate] and is good for multiple sclerosis." According to one mystic, ether influenced by gold is converted into the life force. Gold also causes regeneration of "neuron structures within the cranial capacity," or, to put it more directly, brain cells—which ordinarily do not regenerate.[6] In an equally funny physiological jabberwocky, the inimitable Lama Sing says that gold "would be thought of in terms of affecting significantly the first and second endocrinal positions, though can sometimes imbalance the third. . . . If it is added with a stone can be improved somewhat to balance between the upper three endocrinal and the lower three."[7] Uyldert even believes that the jeweled gold crowns of royalty were worn not for ostentation but for magic, for gold conducts the mystic powers of the gems and "turns the monarch into a powerful battery of force."[8]

The real magic of gold perhaps lies in the romantic and turbulent human stories that have been connected with it. Gold has represented the fulfillment of dreams: striking the mother lode, discovering El Dorado, returning to the Golden Age, acquiring the Midas touch, finding the secrets of the Golden Flower or the Philosopher's Stone, which could make unlimited quantities of gold out of almost anything. Thousands of hopeful European peasants migrated to the New World in the belief that gold could be found there for the taking. Even in the twentieth century, Dr. Fernie believed that gold could be picked up from the streets in Brazil after a rain.[9] True stories originating in the Californian and Alaskan gold rushes often exceed the most garish colors of fiction.

Gold is the symbol of eternity, the universal metaphor of excellence, the perennial lure. The alchemical sign of gold is the same as the sign of the sun. Ancient Hindus called gold the Mineral Light, believing that it was formed by sunlight that was swallowed up by the earth. It would seem that gold is poetry.

---

1. Medenbach & Wilk, 14. 2. Fernie, 366–369, 381. 3. Rutland, 140. 4. Cunningham, 156. 5. Stein, 203. 6. Gurudas, 106–108. 7. *Gems, Stones & Metals,* 11. 8. Uyldert, 76–77. 9. Fernie, 68.

GOLDSTONE (Glass)

Goldstone is a misleading name. The substance is not gold, and it is not stone. It is a man-made glass containing tiny particles of copper or some other bright metal to create a sparkly effect. Sometimes it is called "aventurine glass." The mineral aventurine (quartz with mica inclusions) apparently received its name because of its resemblance to this kind of glass. Germans call the substance *Goldfluss.*

Goldstone is usually a reddish tan with golden glitters, but it also comes in other colors, such as a midnight blue that is confusingly named blue goldstone. Goldstone is cut and polished for use in jewelry as an inexpensive substitute for sunstone. It makes handsome cabochons or pendants, but like any glass it is subject to chipping and cracking.

Rough pieces of goldstone are often sold by mineral dealers to unsuspecting customers who assume that they are buying a pretty rock. When asked, a dealer can say truthfully that the material is goldstone, without bothering to add that it is a man-made glass. Naive buyers have been known to jump to the conclusion that the shiny metallic flakes are actually gold. Crystal mystics have been known to use goldstone as a healing charm in the belief that it is a product of nature.

HALITE (Sodium Chloride)

Halite comes from *hals,* the Greek word for salt.[1] Halite is salt, the same substance that we sprinkle on our food or on our icy roads. Natural halite crystals can show beautiful colors—rich pinks, purples, and blues—which may fool the unwary into thinking them rare gemstones. Like table salt, however, they will deliquesce in damp weather and dissolve away completely if placed in water. Unscrupulous dealers have been known to sell necklaces with beads made of halite. Naturally, these will become sticky against perspiring skin, and when an attempt is made to wash them, they will disappear forever.

Halite crystallizes in cubes, as anyone knows who has ever looked closely at the miniature cubes that come out of the salt shaker. In esoteric lore, the cube is a symbol of the Earth Goddess, and so is salt, with its taste like the taste of blood and its preservative qualities. The "salt of the earth" originally represented the Goddess. Cabalistic tradition said that the sacred name of Queen Mother Earth was Malkuth, from Hebrew MHL, "salt," which may explain the archaic paganism underlying the biblical myth of Lot's wife—the Goddess image as a pillar of salt.

The Christian practice of "blessing" altars, bells, icons, chalices, and most other ecclesiastical knickknacks with salt was very deeply rooted in ancient paganism. The Egyptians also blessed their altars by sprinkling them with salt, and Rome's Vestal Virgins sprinkled every sacrificial animal with consecrated salt and flour. In Hawaii, it was an ancient custom to mix halite with iron-rich red clay as an imitation of sacred blood for purifying rituals.[2]

The age-old association of salt with purification has filtered down to New Age healers, who recommend "clearing and cleansing" the magic crystals with sea salt. However, some sources warn that salt might "strip" a healing stone of its stored energies.[3] Others insist that nothing will do an adequate job except salt. Some specify sea salt and nothing else; others accept ordinary rock salt. Some say the salt must be thrown away after each use. Others say it can be used over and over, indefinitely.

Of course, these distinctions are absurd. Salt and quartz do not affect each other in any way, no matter how long they remain in contact; both are chemically inert. Moreover, all salt is sea salt. The underground deposits from which salt is mined today were once ancient sea bottoms, accumulating saline sediments through millions of years as the seas dried up. The Dead Sea, surrounded by its Old Testament pillars of salt, is one of the last remaining puddles of a larger sea that has been drying up throughout human history. So is Utah's Great Salt Lake, surrounded by the famous Bonneville salt flats, which once lay at the bottom of the vast inland sea that geologists have named Lake Bonneville and that covered nineteen thousand square miles when our early ancestors were chipping their first flint axheads.

In a sense then, any halite crystal serves as a symbol of the origins of life in the amniotic soup of the primitive seas, whose salty legacy we and all other vertebrates still carry in our very blood. Salt is the mineral that we eat in its inorganic form, just as it comes out of the rocks. It is the only inorganic substance that most mammals genuinely crave in their diet. We could eat and assimilate other water-soluble minerals, but they seem to taste bad. Only salt has a likable flavor.

Salt came to represent immortality in early civilizations because it was one of the few preservative substances known. The ancients reasoned that if salt could preserve meat from spoiling, it would also preserve the bodies of the dead; this was the beginning of the art of mummification. Egyptian mummies have lasted for thousands of years because they were carefully pickled in brine. Today we follow a similar custom, but we no longer use salt. We pickle our dead in formaldehyde.

1. Medenbach & Wilk, 58. 2. Cunningham, 130. 3. Stein, 150.

HEMATITE (Iron Oxide)

The literal translation of *hematite* is "bloodstone." The ancients believed that the stone could bleed, because of the red fluid it produced when mixed with water for the purpose of cutting or grinding.[1] Massive hematite can be silvery, reddish brown, or black, but its streak is always blood-colored. The earthy form of hematite, red ocher, was often used to line Stone Age graves and colored everything in them to imitate the blood-filled womb of rebirth. Red ocher is still used by primitive peoples as a sacred blood imitation. Egyptian mummies were usually provided with headrests made of hematite. A gem treatise by Azchalias of Babylon in 63 B.C. said that amulets of hematite obtained the favor of kings and judges.[2]

In addition to its time-honored association with sacred blood, with rebirth, with Rome's red god Mars, and with the protection of warriors, hematite is a primary ore of iron and was considered almost as valuable as gold during the early Iron Age. Much later, high-ranking Nazis during the Hitler era in Germany used hematite as their symbol of "blood and iron."[3] Crystal mystics now prescribe amulets of hematite for high blood pressure, bloodshot eyes, muscle cramps, ulcers, inflammation, and bladder and kidney troubles.[4] It is also recommended for menstrual difficulties, anemia, and other blood conditions even though

iron oxide and blood really have nothing in common except color.

Hematite is imitated by an artificial substance, hematine, made of stainless steel with chromium and nickel sulfides. Hematine is magnetic; natural hematite is not.[5] When cut as a gem, hematite is called "black diamond."

One confused crystal mystic insists that hematite, rhodonite, and magnetite (lodestone) are garnets.[6] This makes about as much sense as saying that tulips, gardenias, and chrysanthemums are all roses.

1. Medenbach & Wilk, 74. 2. Kunz, 38, 80. 3. Rutland, 161. 4. Stein, 185. 5. Arem, 110. 6. Uyldert, 121.

HEMIMORPHITE (Hydrous Zinc Hydroxyl Silicate)

Hemimorphite is one of the chameleon minerals that can appear in several different forms: as pale or transparent crystals, fan-shaped coxcomb aggregates, mammillary (breastlike) or granular masses, or in layers with a dark matrix. Together with its usual companion, smithsonite, hemimorphite used to be called calamine—an ingredient of the oldtime zinc oxide ointment known as calamine lotion.

Hemimorphite has precisely the same strong pyroelectric and piezoelectric properties that crystal mystics so enthusiastically praise in tourmaline. It can develop a static charge when subjected to either warmth or mechanical stress, just as tourmaline can. Crystal mystics have not paid much attention to hemimorphite, however, because it is not a popular gemstone like tourmaline.

The massive form of hemimorphite can be found in a delicate blue color that makes attractive cabochons, but it is not well known. Hemimorphite crystals can be extremely pretty. The mineral's name comes from Greek, meaning "half-form," because the crystals are differently formed at opposite ends of the same long axis.

HERKIMER DIAMOND
(Silicon Dioxide)

Herkimer diamonds are unusual kinds of quartz crystals named after a particularly famous deposit in Herkimer County, New York. They are typically double-terminated (pointed on both ends) and exceptionally clear, at least in smaller specimens. In the larger sizes, Herkimer diamonds tend to be much broken and full of inclusions, because the crystals crack almost at once when removed from the rock matrix, and they contain sheets and spots of black oil and other extraneous materials.

Quartz crystals of this sort are found in other places as well as in Herkimer County, and have received many other names, depending on their place of origin. Among the alternative names for these "diamonds" are: Alaska, Alençon, Arabian, Arkansas, Baffa, Bergkrystall, Bohemian, Bornholm, Brazilian, Briancon, Brighton, Bristol, Buxton, Cape May, Cornish, Crystallus, Cubaite, Dauphiné, Dragomite, Dragonite, Euban, German, Hawaiian, Horatio, Hot Springs, Irish, Kiesel, Lake George, Mari, Marmarosch, Marmora, Mexican, Mountain, Mutzchen, Occidental, Paphros, Pecos, Quebec, Rhine, Royite, Schaumberg, Stolberg, Tasmanian, Vallum, and Zabeltitzten.

Nevertheless, the Herkimer County stones are reputed to be the finest and clearest. They are much sought after by crystal mystics, who regard naturally double-terminated stones as more powerful magical tools than single-terminated ones. Double-terminated crystals do not form by growing outward from a rock wall or from the side of a cavity, as most quartz does. They are formed while floating free in the semiliquid or plastic mass of molten silica, so the crystal lattice is able to establish its natural outlines in all directions.

At least one crystal mystic, however, does not seem to know even the basic fact that Herkimer diamonds are quartz. He claims that Herkimer diamonds would be better for use in computers than "silica chips," defining the Herkimer diamond as "a colorless stone that is often crystalline in structure." (Herkimer diamonds are always crystalline, and always silica.) He believes that quartz crystals and Herkimer diamonds have "similar properties," but apparently does not know that they are the same substance.[1] He is unaware of the fact that natural quartz in any form is not suitable for use in electronic equipment, because of its frequent internal twinning (merging of crystals). Such equipment requires the uniformity of structure that is found in laboratory-grown quartz.

Herkimer diamonds are excellent meditation stones, however. The very cracks and inclusions that disfigure their crystalline symmetry can provide interesting internal shapes, rainbow iridescence, and random structural deformations for visual study. Their water-clear substance can glitter and sparkle, in certain lights, like an actual diamond. Contemplation of a good specimen makes one easily understand how the Herkimer diamond came to be so universally admired.

---

1. Gurudas, 114.

HEULANDITE (Hydrous Sodium Calcium Aluminum Silicate)

Named after the English mineralogist who identified it, heulandite forms coffin-shaped crystals of white, pink, or brick red, sometimes with brownish tones. It is one of the zeolite group of silicates, along with several other popular collectibles, such as stilbite and chabazite. Crystals are lustrous and form glittery clusters. This attractive material is a welcome addition to almost any collection, another example of the rich diversity to be found in the crust of the earth.

HEXAGONITE (Calcium Magnesium Iron Silicate)

Hexagonite is a relative of asbestos and of nephrite jade; it is a form of tremolite with manganese substituting for iron [1] It is therefore not green, gray-green, or white, like most of the tremolite–actinolite series, but pinkish violet. Its pretty color makes it suitable for cutting and polishing as a gemstone, when crystals of sufficient size can be found. As a general rule, crystals are small and imperfect, however. A layperson might describe the average hexagonite specimen as an ordinary rock of a decidedly odd color. Magnification, however, reveals a fascinating world of shapes and crystalline reflections.

---

1. Sinkankas, *M. A.*, 488.

HIDDENITE (Lithium Aluminum Silicate)

Sometimes known as "lithia emerald," hiddenite is the green gem variety of spodumene, sister to the lilac gem variety kunzite. Indeed, hiddenite and kunzite are the same mineral with different colors produced by slightly different conditions in the environment. When exposed to gamma rays, kunzite will turn green, thus becoming hiddenite. This induced color does not last, however. Upon subsequent exposure to light, the stone fades back to its original color. [1]

Hiddenite is rarer than kunzite, owing to the usual scarcity in its native rocks of the chromium that furnishes its greenness. A paler, yellow-green or yellowish spodumene is sometimes marketed as hiddenite, but this is not the true emerald green stone. Yellow transparent spodumene was given the name of triphane.

Hiddenite is considered a rare gemstone, not only because it is not naturally abundant, but also because it is difficult to cut and facet. Like kunzite, hiddenite has perfect cleavage and a strong tendency to fall apart in the lapidary's hands. Therefore, to produce a jewel of hiddenite requires great skill and experience on the part of the cutter. It may seem preferable to leave a hiddenite crystal in its natural condition as a cabinet specimen.

The name hiddenite sounds like a romantic reference to its obscurity and mystery; however, that is not so. Prosaically enough, the mineral was named in 1881 after William E. Hidden, a mining director in North Carolina, where the first specimens were identified. Now there is a town named Hiddenite at the location of the original find.

---

1. O'Donoghue, *G. M. G.*, 64.

ICE (Hydrogen Oxide)

Yes, ice is a mineral. Like other minerals, it retains its crystalline form as long as the ambient temperature remains lower than its melting point. People who live near polar regions or in permanently glaciated mountainous areas can readily comprehend the mineral nature of ice. Most people know how delicately beautiful ice crystals can be when they form in midair, as snowflakes, or on twigs and grassblades, as hoarfrost. Icicles grow in the same way as stalactites in caves. The specific gravity of ice is a bit less than that of water; therefore, ice floats on water and can grow into drifting mountains, the icebergs.

Compact crystalline ice is a lovely mineral having as many interesting internal features as any other transparent crystal. Observe the play of winter sunlight through transparent ice on a pond or puddle, or the fascinating splash patterns around a waterfall in January. One some winter days, our own windowpanes can show mystic silvery landscapes painted by ice. Sometimes, when the sun shines after an ice storm, this amazingly versatile material can coat our whole world with a blaze of crystalline brilliance. Even in summer, one can observe high stratospheric cirrus clouds made of tiny ice crystals. Ice is Mother Earth's diamond tiara, crowning her waters, without which no life could exist anywhere on her surface.

Think about this, perhaps, the next time you take one of your tame ice cubes out of its little tray to plop into your drink. That mineral is the world's most valuable resource—far more essential than gold or diamonds or oil. Look at your ice cube and meditate. Will Mother Earth's vast deposits of the drinkable mineral remain drinkable? This is a thirsty world. Human beings must not be allowed to turn its lifeblood into poison.

ICELAND SPAR (Calcium Carbonate)

Iceland spar is a variety of calcite, first discovered in Iceland and formerly used in the manufacture of polarizing prisms. It occurs in glassy clear, sharp-cornered rhombohedra, which possess the interesting property of birefringence—that is, they double the image of anything that is viewed through the crystal. It is a standard trick of mineral dealers to put a crystal of Iceland spar on a piece of paper with some printed words, so that novices may marvel at the striking effect.

The phenomenon of birefringence is sometimes applied to magic rituals. It is said that when a piece of Iceland spar is worn by the celebrant, or placed on the altar, it "doubles the power" of the ritual.[1]

Iceland spar is not only birefringent, it is also highly attractive to the meditative gaze. Some specimens show splendid iridescent dispersion. The character of each crystal seems to change with alterations in the ambient light. Since Iceland spar is easily available, most beginners' collections include at least one sample.

---

1. Cunningham, 79.

IRON (Element)

Edgar Cayce maintained that iron (or steel) should be carried "in the groin pocket—it will prevent, it will ionize the body—from its very vibrations—to resist cold."[1] These mysterious vibrations prevent colds and flu. Consequently, some modern "authorities" insist that iron or steel can help those with colds or virus infections and that iron supports "tired bodies." Since iron has always been the prime metaphor for strength, this is hardly surprising. One mystic states that the wearing of iron draws out illnesses and gives more strength to athletes. A steel knife can drive away "negativity"; kept under the bed, it prevents nightmares.[2]

Because of its propensity to oxidize (rust), free iron is very rare in the rocks of the earth's crust, although it does occur—usually combined with nickel—in meteorites. The discovery of techniques for smelting iron out of its ores was a technological turning point in ancient civilizations, marking the division between the Bronze Age and the Age of Iron. At first, iron was considered more valuable than gold. Throughout most of its history, it has been used as a metaphor and a charm for strength.

1. *Scientific Properties*, 5. 2. Cunningham, 160, 171.

IVORY (Organic Material)

No true lover of Mother Earth and her life forms would tolerate an artifact of animal ivory, no matter how beautiful it may be. Endangered creatures are brutally slain to obtain ivory, which is simply their teeth, or sometimes their bones. Elephants, narwhals, walruses, hippopotami, and cachalot whales are the usual sources of dental ivory. Although exquisite artworks have been carved from ivory, aesthetics can hardly justify the decimation of living species only to rob the animals of their teeth. Yet, for all their vaunted ecological

sensitivity, some New Age writers seem oblivious to the fate of these species, noting that ivory may be used in "gemstone healing."[1]

A perfectly serviceable substitute for animal ivory is vegetable ivory, obtained from the hard white "Corozo" nuts of the South American ivory palm (*Phytelephas macrocarpa*) or from the kernels of the African Doum palm (*Hyphaene thebaica*).[2]

Those who wish to boycott the needless destruction of animals should avoid not only ivory but also other animal products, such as tortoise shell, "hornbill ivory" (from the beak of the hornbill bird), deer and rhinoceros horn, whalebone, pearl, fur, snakeskin, alligator leather, and so on through a long list of so-called luxury items produced by the taking of life.

1. Stein, 173. 2. Webster, 595–598.

JACINTH

The term *jacinth* currently refers to a red zircon, an orange hessonite garnet, or sometimes a topaz. *Hyacinth* is an alternate reading. We no longer know what stone it was that the ancients called jacinth or hyacinth. Some authorities suggest the sapphire.

In any event, medieval folk believed that the jacinth (whatever it was) would protect travelers, cure madness, relieve pain in the heart, and avert lightning.[1] When ground to a powder and taken internally, it was supposed to be a heart stimulant and an antidote to poisons. Barrett wrote in *Natural Magic*, 1801: "Jacinth possesses virtues from the Sun against poisons, pestilences, and pestiferous vapours . . . [it] conduces also to gain money."[2]

Modern mystics claim that jacinth

cures polio, tuberculosis, insomnia, and anxiety; it protects travelers, averts lightning, and "aids astral projection."[3] If you can decide which stone you should consider a jacinth, that is. One would not wish to be astrally projected by the wrong stone, and then discover one's mistake too late. Who knows what awfulnesses might result?

Perpetuation of the word *jacinth* is considered necessary, chiefly because it is mentioned in the Bible. Nevertheless, holy writ notwithstanding, mineralogical texts generally ignore the word. It has been dropped from the experts' vocabulary.

---

1. Kunz, 82. 2. Fernie, 3, 161. 3. Stein, 201.

JADE (Nephrite: Calcium Magnesium Iron Silicate, or Jadeite: Sodium Aluminum Silicate)

Jade is two minerals: nephrite, of the amphibole group, and jadeite, of the pyroxene group. Chinese jade artifacts manufactured before the eighteenth century were nephrite. Today, jadeite from southeastern Asia is preferred as "imperial jade." Both minerals are very tough. Jade is not exceptionally hard (5 to 7 on the Mohs scale), but it is so unbreakable that it was used for anvils and axheads.

There are many jade imitations, which lack the toughness of the real thing. Plastic, crushed stone, aventurine, and natural or dyed chalcedony are presented as jade. Victoria stone, Kinga stone, or Meta-jade are imitations made of partly crystallized glass. "Pink jade" may be dyed quartz. "Siberian jade" is dark green glass. "Mexican jade" may be calcite. "Styrian jade" is pseudophite

(hydrous aluminum magnesium silicate), a serpentine relative with a hardness of only 2.5. "Transvaal jade" is green garnet. Korean jade, Indian jade, soft jade, or new jade are names given to different kinds of fakes.[1] Amazonite and prehnite are also used.

Jade is the sacred stone of China, where it is known as *yu.* Chinese bridegrooms used to present carved jade butterflies to their brides as a symbol of love. Newlyweds often drank together from a jade cup in confirmation of their vows.[2] The Chinese dosed themselves with powdered jade in water, believing that it would cure many diseases. They claimed that taken just before death, such a decoction would preserve the dead body from corruption.[3]

Jade was also revered by Mexican Indians, who thought it could cure fever, gout, and skull fracture and could even resuscitate the dying.[4] Jadeite, known as *chalchihuitl,* made the "green heart amulet" inserted into a corpse to ensure resurrection. Maoris of New Zealand likewise loved jade, which they called *punamu,* "green stone," or *hei-tiki,* "carved neck amulet." Mohammedan Pekdash sectaries carried jade talismans to ward off every kind of injury.[5]

Nephrite, meaning "kidney stone," owes its name to the European belief that it could cure kidney diseases.[6] Nineteenth-century physicians believed that jade tied to the arm or hip would expel kidney stones.[7] The word *jade* echoes the same belief. It comes from Spanish *piedra de ijada,* "stone for the loins." The belief in jade's magical effect on the kidneys is still extant, and has even expanded. Jade treats not only the kidneys, but also the heart, liver, and spleen; it "cleanses" the blood, and brings on astral projection.[8] It influences "the production of bile by the liver" and cures hemorrhoids.[9] Yellow jade placed on the back "is an aid to the pancreas." Any jade "affects the glands in such a way that it causes them to give up their impurities," despite the fact that glands do not become impure.[10] In a highly contemporary application, nephrite jade is said to "detoxify" persons exposed to radiation poisoning.[11]

With the usual pseudoscientific confusion, one mystic calls jade a noncrystalline gemstone, although it is certainly crystalline.[12] Another claims that jade is not a product of this earth but a "mutation" from a planet not in our solar system—therefore, presumably, located in another solar system encircling some other star.[13] Anyone who can credit this kind of nonsense has no room to scoff at the ancient Chinese belief that jade was the semen of the celestial dragon, deposited in the rocks during his matings with the Goddess Earth.

In the United States, where money happens to be green, the green varieties of jade are said to attract money. Pieces of green jade should be held and fondled by anyone contemplating financial deals or engaged in gambling.[14] One might assume that this magic would not work in other countries, where money is printed with inks of different colors. In any event, one can never be sure about the natural color of any given piece of jade. Both nephrite and jadeite are often dyed to achieve the favored (and more expensive) green or lavender colors. Jadeite is the more porous of the two and takes dye somewhat better. Some of the dyes used are not light-stable, however;

their color will fade in the course of time.[15]

1. Weinstein, 151. 2. Kunz, 85. 3. Smith, 431; Kunz, 385. 4. Sinkankas, *G. N. A.,* 256. 5. Kunz, 86, 88, 246. 6. Wodiska, 236. 7. Fernie, 285. 8. Parkinson, 232. 9. Bravo, 155. 10. Richardson et al., 80, 82. 11. Gurudas, 133. 12. Stein, 232. 13. Lorusso & Glick, 44–45. 14. Cunningham, 103. 15. Nassau, *G. E.,* 140.

JASPER (Silicon Dioxide)

Jasper is another name for certain kinds of chalcedony. Jasper colors range through the browns and reddish browns, also including the dark green, red-spotted bloodstone or heliotrope. Medicinal jasper of the Middle Ages was described as grass green, so it may have been chrysoprase.[1]

Galen wrote that a green jasper hung about the neck would "strengthen the stomach." Much later, in the eighteenth century A.D., doctors claimed that a green jasper or bloodstone would stop bleeding and prevent bladder stones, especially when engraved with the figure of a scorpion at the time when the sun entered Scorpio. It also cured epilepsy, stomach pains, fluxes of blood, and "scour of the guts."[2]

Healing jasper has been popular since antiquity. Both Galen and Dioscorides recommended jasper tied to a woman's thigh for easy childbirth.[3] A wearer of jasper was said to be safe from drowning, lung disease, and the attacks of scorpions.[4] And jasper was considered a magic stone in both hemispheres; an American Indian name for the stone meant "rain bringer."[5]

Superstitious medieval Europeans attached all sorts of bizarre notions to their jasper amulets. In the fifteenth century, Bartolomeus Anglicus said that jasper stones are to be found in the heads of adders. Fourteenth-century writers declared that a jasper engraved with a dog, stag, or huntsman would confer on its owner the power to cure demonic possession—an assertion disliked by churchmen as an encroachment on their territory. A thirteenth-century manuscript treated the jasper as holy, stating that a jasper engraved with either the god Mars or a maiden with a laurel branch (Daphne the Laurel Goddess) should be "consecrated with perpetual consecration."[6]

If modern mystics are to be believed, jasper still serves as a multipurpose remedy. It soothes the stomach and nerves. It "works on" kidneys, liver, and gall bladder. It improves the sense of smell. It changes "vibrations rising from the lower centers" when it is dipped in "magnetized water" that is later drunk.[7] Although there is no such thing as magnetized water, the recipe for this nonsubstance is simple enough. "Put a piece of jasper in water, and allow it to sit for two-three days, and then drink the water. . . . This can be considered as a general body tonic."[8]

Jasper is also recommended as a protection against the ever-dangerous vibrations of "negativity." So assiduously does it absorb these vibrations that it sometimes becomes dull from overwork. Red jasper seems particularly prone to such exhaustion.[9] Then, of course, one's faithful jasper stone requires some magical refreshment and the usual "cleansing." The simple translation of this is that if a stone becomes dirty, you wash it. But that is much too simple for crystal mystics. Every cleaning process is a ritual to be savored—even when, like the recommended immersion in dry sea salt, it doesn't really clean.

Like its close relative the agate, jasper has many varietal names. Jaspagate and jasponyx are stones that cannot be classified either way. Jasper containing hematite is sometimes called jaspillite. Jasper dyed blue is German lapis or Swiss lapis. Jasper dyed green is Swiss jade, or molochites. Brown jasper with yellow specks is vabanite. Brecciated jasper (containing angular fragments) is sometimes called creolin. Jasper stained various colors is Italian lapis. Orbicular (eye-spot) jasper may be labeled kinradite. Other varieties are darlingite, herbeckite, torrelite, and xyloid. Because there is no clear distinction between jasper, agate, chalcedony, onyx, or carnelian, these terms sometimes can be used interchangeably. "Picture jasper" creates scenes that closely resemble desert landscapes or hills, plains, and rivers, the same as "landscape agate." These attractive specialty stones are made by color variations in different layers of the mineral. Yellow-brown jasper nodules are "Egyptian pebbles." Light green jasper may be called plasma; dark green, prase. Basanite, a fine-grained black jasper, is used as a touchstone for determining the purity of metals.[10] When the metal is rubbed on the stone, assessment can be made from the color of the streak.

1. Kunz, 90. 2. Fernie, 173–175. 3. Anderson, 46. 4. Wodiska, 236. 5. Cunningham, 104. 6. Kunz, 91, 135, 140. 7. Stein, 191. 8. Richardson et al., 85–86. 9. Chocron, 59–60. 10. Webster, 227.

JET (Organic Material)

Jet was named from *gagates,* because Pliny said the material was first found in the river Gages. In German, it is *Gaget*.[1] During the sixteenth century A.D., jet was called black amber and was widely used for rosary beads.[2] During the Victorian era, jet jewelry became popular as a result of Queen Victoria's fondness for wearing it in her widowhood as part of her perpetual mourning costume. Consequently, jet came to be considered the only proper adornment for those attending funerals, or for women in mourning.

Because jet is a form of coal, it will burn and produce obvious smoke. Such smoke was formerly used to drive away demons, repel snakes, bring on menstruation, and serve other magical purposes. Powdered jet in water was also given as a drink to girls whose virginity was in doubt. If the black material was retained, virginity was verified.[3] The recipe neglected to say, however, just how long after drinking it was supposed to be retained. British fishermen's wives used to burn jet as a charm to preserve their husbands' boats at sea.[4]

Modern mystics still cling to the old belief that the coal smoke from burning jet will repel fevers, infections, hysteria, hallucinations, epilepsy, and stomach troubles.[5] Powdered jet drunk in water or wine is also "good for" colds, gout, cramps, toothache, palsy, tumors, and premenstrual syndrome.[6]

If you possess some old and treasured jet jewelry, however, do not be induced to burn or crush it. It is much better left alone as a family heirloom, because no mistreatment of it will cure your ills anyway.

Like all popular gem materials, jet has been imitated. False substitutes include anthracite, Scotch cannel coal, vulcanite (hard rubber), obsidian, black-dyed chalcedony, plastic, and the black glass known as "Paris jet."[7]

1. Weinstein, 237. 2. Kunz, 264. 3. Anderson, 117. 4. Cunningham, 106. 5. Stein, 185. 6. Parkinson, 234. 7. Webster, 583.

KAEMMERERITE (Magnesium Iron Aluminum Hydroxyl Silicate)

Kaemmererite is a varietal name for one of the chlorite group of minerals, clinochlore, when colored a vivid magenta or violet by traces of chromium. The common color of chlorite minerals is dark green. Kaemmererite may be found in crusts of tiny crystals coating the surface of other minerals. Large crystals are rare. Collectors like this variety because its assertive color creates an aesthetic accent among other specimens. Kaemmererite is occasionally cut as a gemstone, though it is much too soft to serve well in this capacity. The natural material, however, presents another example of the brilliant coloring that sometimes hides in ordinary rocks to astonish the eye of the digger.

Kaemmererite was named for A. Kämmerer, once Director of Mines at St. Petersburg.

KUNZITE (Lithium Aluminum Silicate)

Kunzite is the pale lilac–colored variety of the mineral spodumene, which was first identified early in the twentieth century and named after the prominent gemologist George Frederick Kunz (d. 1932). The same mineral, spodumene, is called triphane when it is yellowish or colorless, and hiddenite when it is emerald green.

Because of kunzite's recent appearance on the mineralogical scene, crystal mystics evidently have had to invent some "traditions" for it. We are told that "traditionally" kunzite provides treatment for diseases of the eyes, kidneys, and lumbar region.[1] This is a tradition of very short standing. It is being claimed that, although nothing was known about kunzite before Kunz's time, more ancient "valuable information" about it has been "channeled psychically" in the past few years.[2]

Among the assertions of this "valuable information" is that kunzite worn over the heart chakra can send penetrating energy through emotional "blockages" and cause the wearer to "experience the purity" of his or her inner heart, which sounds rather like loosening a rusted bolt with penetrating oil.[3] A piece of kunzite passed over "tension-ridden parts of the body unknits the muscles."[4] (Possibly this means "unknots.") When held over the shoulders, "two-three inches away from the body, it has the effect of bombardment of the nerves in the shoulders, which eases and relaxes them."[5] One is not told what the "bombardment" consists of, but the statement is not as unsettling as it seems. Kunzite is not radioactive. It is quite inert. One mystic claims that "electrical impulses run the length of the crystal," but in truth, kunzite is a nonconductor.[6]

Some specimens of kunzite will fluoresce a pale orange under ultraviolet light. One New Age authority garbles this phenomenon by calling kunzite "phosphorescent under the influence of radium."[7] There is no radium in an ultraviolet lamp, nor is there any in kunzite. Moreover, fluorescence and phosphorescence are not the same.

Kunzite is strongly dichroic; that means that its color is many shades deeper when viewed along the length of the crystal than crosswise. Therefore, cut gems are usually oriented with the table at right angles to the crystal's long axis, to make the most of kunzite's delicate tints. Even with this precaution, some kunzites will fade after prolonged exposure to sunlight.[8]

1. Gurudas, 121. 2. Parkinson, 225. 3. Raphaell, *C. E.,* 115. 4. Cunningham, 107. 5. Richardson et al., 88. 6. Chocron, 65. 7. Richardson et al., 88. 8. Webster, 167.

KUTNOHORITE (Calcium Manganese Carbonate)

Kutnohorite (also spelled kutnahorite) is one of the dolomite–ankerite series, rarer than its relatives but equally attractive. Showing shiny rhomb-shaped crystals, like dolomite, it is colored a delicate pearly pink similar to the tint of rose quartz. Unlike rose quartz, however, kutnohorite is opaque. It breaks in sharp, brittle, acute-angled fragments that lend an interesting piquancy to the softness of its color.

Though not common, kutnohorite is not one of the expensive rarities. Therefore it offers to the collector of modest means a mineral that is different, will not be seen in everyone else's collection, but provides eye-catching specimens nevertheless.

LABRADORITE (Sodium Calcium Aluminum Silicate)

Labradorite is a plagioclase feldspar, a member of the albite–anorthite series. Named for the place of its original discovery, labradorite gave another standard term to mineralogy: *labradorescence,* the luminous blue-green, gold, or red sheen that appears on polished surfaces when they are turned at a crucial angle to the light. Gem quality labradorite showing a brilliant play of colors has been found also in Finland and has been given the trade name Spectrolite.

Labradorite is an astonishing stone. It seems to be a modest, ordinary, dull, dark gray rock without any remarkable qualities; then in handling a piece, one tilts it just the right way, and suddenly it is aflame with the shimmering blue iridescence of a tropical butterfly wing or the sparkle of gold dust. All at once, dowdy Cinderella is dressed for the ball. Surely such a mineral must symbolize the hidden beauty that can be found in improbable-looking places, or the spiritual richness that can be concealed in apparently uninteresting aspects of everyday life. It is fun to play with, to watch it go from dark to brilliant and back to dark again with miniscule changes in position. Few of the New Age mystics have yet discovered labradorite, but when it is better known among them, undoubtedly it will be found to be quite miraculous. One such writer, whose knowledge of rock-forming conditions seems virtually nonexistent, opines that the radiance of labradorite is like ancient sunlight, because it "has been preserved from the time when the Earth was still united with the Sun."[1]

A colorless variety of labradorite, darkened by needlelike inclusions, is sometimes called black moonstone.[2] Possibly the mystic would like to date the formation of this stone from a dream time when the Earth was still united with the Moon.

---

1. Uyldert, 142. 2. Webster, 197.

LAPIS LAZULI, OR LAZURITE
(Sodium Calcium Aluminum Sulfate Silicate)

Lapis lazuli is not a distinct mineral but a rock, consisting mostly of the bright blue mineral lazurite in combination with hauynite, sodalite, diopside, white streaks of calcite, and golden specks of pyrite. It was the "sapphire" of the ancients, as we know from Pliny's description of sapphire as containing "spots like gold"—the characteristic pyrite.[1] Powdered lapis lazuli was the original coloring matter in ultramarine blue pigment.

The bright color and handsome appearance of lapis lazuli aroused admiration from the oldest times. The stone was often considered holy. The Bible claims that God's throne was made of it. Early Christians declared it sacred to the virgin Mary—probably copying the idea from Egypt's Goddess Isis, known as the "throne of the god," that is, of Horus, the Holy Child, who sat on her lap as the resurrected savior.[2] Lapis lazuli was sacred to Isis long before either the Bible or Christianity existed. It symbolized her in the guise of Truth (Maat the Mother), and was worn by Egypt's chief justice as the sign of her All-Seeing Eye.[3] One of the oldest Sumerian mythologies stated that the palace of the Great Goddess in her underworld aspect lay beneath a mountain of lapis lazuli.[4]

Today's crystal mystics frequently confuse lapis lazuli with other blue minerals, such as azurite (copper carbonate) and lazulite (magnesium iron aluminum phosphate). Though their names are derived from the same Arabic word for "blue," there is no excuse for such false statements as "lazulite is similar to lapis lazuli,"[5] or "noncrystalline . . . lapis is also called lazulite."[6] Lapis lazuli *is* crystalline, and it is *not* lazulite.

Edgar Cayce produced particularly muddled descriptions of lapis lazuli, which seems to have been one of his favorite prescription minerals although he falsely called it "the essence or fusion of copper," or "an erosion of copper," or "the exuding of copper" (lapis lazuli has no copper), or sometimes "lapis linguis," which is an old name for amber.[7]

Other mystics confuse the two names of lapis (lazuli and lazurite), claiming that they are different minerals. One says that, though lapis lazuli is a natural stone, lazurite is not natural but was artificially created with mental energy in Lemuria.[8] The blue color of lapis lazuli is "a celestial sulphur which still floated in the atmosphere in Lemurian times and subsequently solidified into this stone." The blue color "attracts oxygen" out of the atmosphere.[9] Thus in a few simple sentences, all the world's painfully acquired knowledge of history, archaeology, geology, chemistry, and physics is blown into a meaningless rubble.

Because of its many sacred connotations lapis lazuli has been a popular healing stone from remote antiquity. It was used as an antidote to snakebite.[10] It was said to purge melancholy, strengthen the heart, and heal boils and other sores.[11] Lapis amulets were used to cure apoplexy and blood disorders and to give confidence to timid children. In the eighteenth century, mystical beliefs about lapis were rife, and the stone was so much desired that a gem price list set its value at fifteen times that of emeralds.[12]

Modern crystal mystics give lapis the usual assortment of occult functions, such as general improvement of the wearer's mental, physical, spiritual, emotional, and psychic condition. It is said to alleviate fevers, heal blood diseases, and improve eyesight.[13] It prevents ulcers and "forms of intestinal cancer."[14] It soothes burns, infections, earaches, swellings, and wounds. It opens the third eye, and should be worn on a headband over the brow.[15] It cures depression and painful nerves, and water into which it has been dipped should be used as eyewash[16]—an appropriate term.

Lapis lazuli is often imitated. Various forms of chalcedony, dyed blue, are sold as "Swiss lapis" or "German lapis." Some people think tiny golden flakes of pyrite will identify genuine lapis, but the better imitations will add those too. Gilson-created lapis is a synthetic ultramarine with pyrite specks that can fool even an expert.

1. Smith, 436. 2. Thomson, 68. 3. Kunz, 119. 4. Anderson, 126. 5. Richardson et al., 130. 6. Stein, 248. 7. *Scientific Properties*, 16, 23, 35. 8. Gurudas, 123. 9. Uyldert, 58, 136. 10. Anderson, 46. 11. Fernie, 2, 355. 12. Thomson, 68–69. 13. Cunningham, 108. 14. Bravo, 177. 15. Stein, 249. 16. Uyldert, 137.

LEAD (Element)

The symbol for lead is Pb, from Latin *plumbum,* which also gave us "plumber," one who deals with lead pipes; "plumb," to drop straight down like a lump of lead; and "plumb line," a cord attached to a lead weight for ascertaining verticality.

Ancient Romans used lead for their water pipes and for many table vessels, such as cups. It is now well known that upper-class Romans often died of cumulative lead poisoning, because they drank wine and other acid juices from goblets of lead, the metal dissolving slightly in the liquid and entering their bodies. Metallic lead is not excreted, so a marginal annual accumulation can prove fatal in the long run.

Appropriately enough, lead was sacred to Saturn, the Lord of Death. Because Saturn was revered as the underworld god who knew the ultimate secrets of the future, his metal was often used in divinatory procedures, and it still is. "Pendulum scrying" began with the use of lead weights. By immemorial tradition, during the Christmas season (the ancient Saturnalia), Europeans throw a spoonful of molten lead into cold water, to take omens from the shapes assumed by the metal as it solidifies.

By a similarly ancient tradition, coffins were made of lead to curry favor with the Dark Lord. The custom was followed by Christians until they began to inter corpses in crypts beneath a church, rather than underground. It became unpleasantly evident that the soft metal could not contain the gases generated by the body's decomposition. Lead coffins were "liable to bulge out because of the lethal gases generated within, and then to burst, thus throwing out into the church above these deadly gases."[1]

Despite the poisonous nature of metallic lead, doctors continued to use it as a medicine for many centuries. It was administered for ulcers, inflammation, blindness, and to "open the spleen." A seventeenth-century authority called lead "a great anodyne, and easer of pain."[2] But then, of course, so is death.

Elemental lead does not occur in nature. Its major ore is galena (lead sulfide), of which enormous quantities are mined, because our civilization could hardly get along without the many industrial uses of lead. It was undoubtedly one of the first metals to be smelted, if not *the* first, because its low melting point makes smelting relatively easy. It has been with us from the beginnings of prehistory, and it is with us still. And still it represents death in common parlance, for "lead" is a synonym for a bullet.

---

1. Fernie, 444. 2. *Ibid.,* 451.

LEPIDOLITE (Potassium Lithium Aluminum Hydroxyl Fluorsilicate)

Lepidolite has no occult traditions from the past. It has been only recently discovered by the mystics. It is an attractive variety of mica. Lepidolite can be yellowish or grayish, but its usual colors range from pink through lilac and violet. Sometimes it occurs in rich purple layered "books," easily cleavable into thin sheets, like others of the mica family. It is common to find sparkling, sugary masses of lilac lepidolite enclosing crystals of pink tourmaline (rubellite), a particularly pretty combination.

Lepidolite is one of the minerals that crystal mystics frequently insist on misspelling; some seem convinced that it is "lapidolite." One declares firmly that "lapidolite" is a natural mood balancer.[1] Another claims that it is a calming influence; a whole house can be quieted by the magical process of placing pieces of lepidolite in a circle around a pink candle.[2]

New Age artisans shape lepidolite into spheres, wands, and rounded "stroking tools" for soothing the nerves. Tourmaline-containing lepidolite can be polished to provide interesting artifacts and cabochon jewelry. Because lepidolite is a mica, with the perfect cleavage characteristic of micas, it is almost impossible to facet. Nevertheless, it is a handsomely ornamental stone even without lapidary improvements.

---

1. Bravo, 5. 2. Cunningham, 111.

LODESTONE, OR MAGNETITE
(Iron Oxide)

The natural magnetism of lodestone (magnetite) was noticed early in the history of civilization. The obvious attraction between lodestone and iron encouraged expressions of the wish for some other attraction, frequently sexual. Prostitutes used to wear lodestone to attract customers. East Indian kings were crowned on lodestone seats, to attract gifts and affection. A temple of Venus and Mars described by Claudian (fifth century A.D.) had a lodestone image of the Goddess and an iron image of her consort, to celebrate the sacred marriage by allowing the two statues to rush together. Chinese called lodestone *t'su shi*, "loving stone." In Sanskrit, its name was *chumbaka*, "the kisser."[1]

Pliny said that magnetite was named after the shepherd Magnes, who discovered it clinging to the iron nails in his shoes. More probably, the word came from the district of Magnesia in ancient Thessaly, where lodestone could be found.[2] The name *lodestone* was originally "lead stone," because of the mineral's use as a direction finder.[3]

A fourteenth-century alchemist, Rabbi Benoni, thought that lodestone would cause sleepwalking, and when combined with diamond and sapphire in an amulet, it would "attract such powerful planetary spirits as to render the bearer almost invisible." (It is interesting to imagine how an almost invisible person might look.) Leonardus

believed that lodestone would not only cure gout and cramps, by "drawing out" the pain, but also reconcile estranged lovers and spouses.[4]

Lodestone's Venus-and-Mars magic persisted through the centuries in its use as a cure for sexual dysfunctions—male ones, at least. For better sexual performance, men were told to rub their genitals with oil into which lodestone had been dipped. Sometimes it worked, probably owing to the oil rather than the stone. Some men in Mexico still believe that wearing a lodestone in the belt buckle will guarantee not only sexual success but also success in other areas, such as gambling and business deals. Women believe that lodestone worn on a coral necklace will bring about easy childbirth and draw back philandering husbands. Healers "draw out" diseases with lodestone. It is widely thought that lodestone set in silver will improve the eyesight; set in gold, it strengthens the heart.[5]

Like the ancients, modern mystics insist that lodestone will draw illness out of the body, and also that the stone's magnetism will draw other people. Some seem to believe, however, that lodestone and magnetite are different minerals instead of two words for the same one. They are listed separately, and magnetite is said to be "more organically bound" than lodestone. It is also claimed that a child's bedwetting problem can be cured by a pre-bedtime drink of water into which lodestone, black pearl, dark opal, and petunia have been dipped.[6] If the child is convinced that it will work, it might; but drinking water before bedtime is not generally a useful therapy for bedwetters.

It is said also that lodestone causes "man's mind to be released to some extent from his body," an effect that would be interesting to see. Two pieces of lodestone applied to the chest of a tubercular patient will improve health by causing "the blood vessels or cells to begin to churn," another unprecedented occurrence that certainly would interest a medical observer. Unfortunately, however, "it doesn't show any visible effects."[7] No one but the mystics can know that it is happening. It is another one of those amazing mineral operations that seem fated to remain unrecognized.

Lodestone is still much used in love charms. An ordinary magnet would do just as well, since it is only the quality of magnetism that is wanted; but the natural stone is usually preferred over anything manufactured. Lodestone is not one of the pretty minerals, but it is interesting, and always surprising to the lay person who "knows" that a magnet cannot stick to a rock. Touch a magnet to a piece of lodestone and behold! the rule is refuted.

---

1. Kunz, 94–96. 2. Medenbach & Wilk, 72. 3. Desautels, M. K., 127. 4. Fernie, 319. 5. Cunningham, 164–166. 6. Gurudas, 125, 127, 185. 7. Richardson et al., 145–146.

MALACHITE (Copper Hydroxyl Carbonate)

Malachite is named after Greek *malache*, "mallow."[1] It occurs commonly around copper deposits, and it is familiar as the green tarnish on copper. Being so closely associated with the Venus metal, malachite was admired by ancient followers of the Goddess and thought to possess great powers. In Rome, it was sometimes called peacock stone, dedicated to the Great Goddess Juno, whose totem was a peacock. It was a protection against the evil eye when cut in a triangular shape, the triangle being another of the Goddess's classic emblems.

Malachite attached to a baby's cradle would keep away evil spirits, or warn of approaching danger by suddenly cracking.[2] Malachite amulets could keep children from all harm.[3] Malachite gave protection against lightning and other perils of nature; relieved vertigo; cured insect bites; healed stomach ailments when powdered and drunk in milk; stopped bleeding of wounds when mixed with honey; relieved rheumatism in the elderly and teething pains in infants; and, of course, due to its eyelike spots, guarded against the evil eye.[4] Pliny's *smaragdus medicus* (medicinal emerald) seems to have been not emerald but malachite.[5]

According to Russian legend, anyone who drinks from a malachite goblet will understand the language of animals.[6] During the Renaissance, physicians claimed that their patients' sores could be anesthetized with malachite.[7] In China, a twelfth-century medical text advised malachite for treatment of colds and diarrhea, calling it "acid, cooling, nonpoisonous."[8]

Some modern mystics disagree, regarding malachite as poisonous if taken internally.[9] One claims that malachite dust is highly toxic, but goes on to say that the stone "promotes complete tissue regeneration" and counteracts the effects of radiation absorbed from computer terminals.[10] Another says that malachite is toxic and should never enter the body, yet malachite "elixir" (water) should be drunk freely to relieve general infection, colic, cholera, malignant tumors, leukemia, rheumatism, ulcers, and vertigo.[11] Another says that although malachite is poisonous, it cures asthma, colic, epilepsy, spasms, joint pain, toothache, and wounds; it purifies the digestive system, bladder, liver, pancreas, and spleen; and it balances blood sugar and bile levels.[12] Another says that wearing malachite will heal all diseases of the teeth and gums.[13] Still another source disagrees with everything and commands: "*Never* attempt to use this stone in healing."[14]

The most notable feature of malachite is its vivid greenness. Some mystical impressions of it seem to recall the dedication of that color—as well as copper metal—to the Great Goddess of love. It is said that malachite attracts love, especially when engraved with a Venus sign and placed in a setting of copper. To draw a loved one to you, burn a green candle behind the stone for fifteen minutes each day, visualizing "yourself in a loving relationship." Green malachite also attracts green (United States) money. It is called the salesperson's stone. Business people are advised to carry a piece of malachite to meetings, or to keep it in the cash register.[15]

Perhaps the silliest remark based on the greenness of malachite is that it is experienced "as a liquid chlorophyll."[16] How in the world does one experience liquid chlorophyll?

Mysticism aside, malachite is one of the world's most decorative stones for cut and polished artifacts. It shows stripes, swirls, and spots of dark and light shades of green, no two patterns alike, but all striking. It is often shaped into small ornaments, spheres, eggs, obelisks, and cabochons. It takes a polish well, and its polished surface is always filled with interesting pictures. This, together with its attractively rich color, makes malachite an excellent meditation stone.

1. Boegel, 172. 2. Kunz, 97, 137. 3. Rutland, 161. 4. Thomson, 66. 5. Fernie, 167. 6. Medenbach & Wilk, 128. 7. Desautels, *G. K.*, 24. 8. Hay, 48. 9. Harold, 181. 10. Parkinson, 238. 11. Gurudas, 128–129. 12. Stein, 213. 13. Bravo, 159. 14. Richardson et al., 95. 15. Cunningham, 112. 16. Rea, 322.

MARBLE (Calcium Carbonate)

Marble is a rock made of recrystallized calcite, sometimes combined with other accessory minerals such as graphite, ilmenite, quartz, mica, plagioclase, tremolite, and talc. Marble is found all over the world. Some regions became noted for certain types and colors of marble, such as the famous white statuary marble found at Carrara in Italy, used by Michelangelo and other sculptors after him.

Marble is common in home decoration, accessories, and furniture, so one would not think of it as a magic stone ordinarily. Some crystal mystics do, however. Marble tables and fixtures are said to be "protective for the home."[1] Living with marble about also causes deeper penetration of the red corpuscles into the ductless glands, which leads to increased longevity—a rather astonishing result, to say the least. People who need marble are "too passive to the accord of apathy," but also mentally too aggressive.[2] This would seem to cover just about everyone.

In one sense, marble may be viewed as a sacred building stone. It is favored for ecclesiastical buildings, mausoleums, and tombstones. Perhaps some of the dead decently interred under marble got there by letting too many red corpuscles get into their ductless glands.

Like calcite, marble is a chameleon. Different types of marble display so many different colors and patterns that it is almost impossible even for a specialist to collect a sample of each. Marble may well serve as a symbol of Nature's inexhaustible variety.

---

1. Cunningham, 113. 2. Gurudas, 130.

MERCURY (Element)

Mercury is the unique metal that shares with water the unusual property of remaining liquid at ordinary temperatures. Mercury will not freeze (crystallize) until the temperature falls to 38 degrees Fahrenheit. Unlike water, however, mercury will pour but will not wet. It rolls itself into little balls on a dry surface. It is nearly fourteen times heavier than water. Iron will float in liquid mercury. The vapor of mercury is very poisonous. Mercury is a good conductor of both electricity and heat. It sometimes occurs as tiny liquid globules in its ore, cinnabar, but as a rule it is chemically bound in the form of the sulfide.

Alchemists were fascinated by mercury. They named it quicksilver, that is, "living silver." It was sacred to the mythical founder of alchemy, Hermes Trismegistus (Hermes the Thrice-Great), a medieval version of Hermes the Greek god of magic, whose Roman name was Mercury. There were some who called mercury the Philosopher's Stone, maintaining that when mercury could be colored yellow by sulfur and solidified (the marriage of Hermes and Athene, or of Mercury and Minerva), the result would be true gold. Alternatively, the esoteric goal of the alchemist was to discover in nature the Anima Mercury, or mercurial soul, another term for the spirit of creation. Once that secret was understood, the alchemists thought, they could then create any substance, organic or inorganic.

Because the Mercury of old was also a god of tricksters, thieves, and gamblers, mercury became a special mineral for risk-takers. Modern gamblers may still carry a good-luck charm consisting of a hollow nutmeg filled with mercury and sealed.[1] The tricky god's ancient connection with the Triple Goddess of Fate (Venus Fortuna)—and with her later counterpart, Lady Luck—led to the use of small pools of mercury as scrying mirrors, to seek a view of one's future fate. Later, mercury amalgam became the backing used on ordinary glass mirrors.

With so many strands of belief in the various magic powers of mercury, it is hardly surprising to find that doctors used to prescribe mercury as a medicine to be taken internally, and continued to do so for centuries, even though the results were nearly always distressing. Like other heavy metals, mercury will accumulate in animal tissues and is poisonous rather than medicinal. In sufficient quantity, it is a relentless killer. So, in a way, the bright, pretty, interesting, and magical "living silver" is a trickster indeed: a sly villain in a handsome guise. Even handling liquid mercury can be dangerous, for lengthy contact can pass its poison through the skin and cause inhalation of its toxic vapor. On the ecological front, mercury has proved to be a major environmental polluter even though modern industrial society regards its use as indispensable. Thus the old trickster god still plays macabre jokes on his admirers. Nevertheless, he is still our basic thermal informant. He tells us the temperature of our bodies and our environment. Meteorologists and medical professionals consult him every day.

---

1. Cunningham, 166.

METEORITE (Elements: Nickel-Iron)

Meteorites are classified as either stony or metallic. The metallic types consist largely of a nickel-iron combination. Both of these elemental metals are virtually unknown on earth in their free or pure form; they occur only in their ores, chemically combined with nonmetals such as oxygen, sulfur, or carbon. Out in space, a metallic meteor might travel for millions of years without encountering oxygen, so it would be unable to rust (oxidize). In earth's abundant water vapor and oxygen, however, meteoric metal rusts rapidly. It must be kept dry and preserved with care.

Inevitably, some crystal mystics tend to regard meteorite material as a medium of communication with alien beings on UFOs, as well as with distant planets in "various constellations."[1] One writer seems to believe that a constellation is a single locality instead of a chance juxtaposition of stars as they are seen from earth: stars that may be millions of light-years apart in our line of sight. Of course, the alleged communications are chimerical.

Nevertheless, meteorite material is exciting simply because of our awareness of its origin. It invokes for us the vast cosmos, the dark depths of empty space, the immense distances it

might have traveled before falling on our planet's surface. Pieces of meteorites are the only commonly available objects that are unquestionably extraterrestrial. They are not especially pretty, but they are wonderful just because of what we know about them. A meditation on a small chunk of meteorite can be a whole science-fiction adventure in the limitless reaches of the imagination.

---

1. Gurudas, 131.

MICA (Complex Potassium Sodium Magnesium Iron Aluminum Hydroxyl Silicates)

Most people are familiar with the thin, shiny little flakes of "mica" seen as components of many rocks. But mica is not a single mineral. There are many micas, some of them hard to tell apart, forming a distinctive mineral group. Micas are valuable industrial minerals. Some are used for electrical and heat insulation, in the manufacture of paints, porcelain, and paper, as dry lubricants, fillers, and other useful substances. Transparent sheets of muscovite mica were long used in Russia as insulating windows in stoves, vehicles, or houses, and were popularly known as Muscovy glass or isinglass.

Muscovite has a number of varieties. Sericite and pinite are fine-grained; fuchsite or mariposite is colored green with chromium; alurgite is colored red with manganese; roscoelite contains traces of vanadium; paragonite and illite are poor or lacking in potassium. Other micas similar to muscovite are phlogopite and biotite. The pinkish or lilac lithium mineral lepidolite is also a mica; so is glauconite, which tends to form tiny blue-green crystals.

"Brittle mica" is yet another variety, margarite.

The typical characteristic of mica is its perfect cleavage into flexible, easily separable laminae (sheets), which may be very thin. Platy crystals are sometimes called "books" because their "leaves" readily come apart. Perhaps this is why crystal mystics associate mica with learning. To read the mica book, however, requires no real study. One need only hold a piece of mica in moonlight, move it gently, and "let its shimmer drowse your conscious mind."[1] This is supposed to increase psychic awareness and confer the gift of prophecy. Mica is also recommended for "protection," which may be an imaginative transformation of its insulating qualities. Many forms of mica make attractive cabinet specimens, bringing their own unique qualities to the enhancement of a collection.

---

1. Cunningham, 113.

MOLDAVITE (Glass)

Moldavite is a noncrystalline, glassy material initially found along the Moldau river in Czechoslovakia—hence its name. It may be yellowish or brownish, but it is usually a muddy green. Some mineralogists say moldavite might be hardened drops from the outer surfaces of meteorites, fused and melted during their passage through the atmosphere and splashed about on impact. Others say it might be terrestrial rock melted by the heat of a meteorite's strike.

Either way, moldavite has some connection with outer space, and this hint is enough for the crystal mystics. Although it is not a crystal at all, it is described as the "green crystal from space" that was secretly promised by

an Alien Master. It is even proposed that moldavite—rather than emerald—was the substance of the Holy Grail, and that the legend of the jewel's fall from Satan's crown during his descent was a metaphoric description of the green jewel arriving from space: that is, from the "higher planes."[1] The typical rough, ripply striations on the outside surface of moldavite chunks are sometimes interpreted as a sort of runic code, carrying messages of extraterrestrial origin.

Moldavite has other names, depending on where it is found. Moldavite from Australia is australite. Moldavite from the state of Georgia is called georgiaite.[2] Moldavite is sometimes cut and faceted as a gemstone, but it is still basically nothing but cut glass, and therefore not as durable as other gemstones. Any faceted piece of a darkish green glass can be passed off as moldavite. After its characteristic ripply surface has been polished away, it can resemble any other glass. The buyer is usually unable to tell whether it came from the site of a meteorite strike or from the bottom of a bottle. In fact, one of the names of moldavite is Bouteillenstein (bottle stone).[3]

---

1. Parkinson, 12, 248. 2. Schumann, 212. 3. Webster, 278.

MOONSTONE (Adularia Orthoclase: Potassium Aluminum Silicate; or Albite Plagioclase: Sodium Aluminum Silicate)

The name moonstone is given to either of two feldspars with somewhat different composition. In appearance, both have a pale silky sheen. Moonstones can be white, blue-white, cream-yellow, brown, or pale yellow-pink shades like peach and apricot.

Greeks called the moonstone Aphroselene, a composite of Moon Goddess names, Aphrodite and Selene.[1] Some crystal mystics confuse moonstone with selenite, which is an entirely different mineral, even though its name means "moonstone." Selenite is a form of gypsum (hydrous calcium sulfate), soft and fragile, unsuited for gem use. Nevertheless, Parkinson insists that selenite is the same as adularia moonstone.[2]

On the basis of its name, everyone supposes that moonstone must be connected with the moon. One mystic even states that the mineral waxes and wanes along with the lunar phases.[3] Inevitably, it is also connected with women's menstrual cycles and the "balancing" of monthly hormone levels.

In India, moonstone was sacred to lovers, and was supposed to confer prophetic powers when kept in the mouth during a full moon. Indian gem merchants display moonstone on a cloth of yellow, the sacred lunar color.[4] The Basques believed that the moonstone would make its owner "serene and placid" and would cure epilepsy.[5] It was commonly thought in Europe that moonstone could foretell the future during the "crone time" of the waning moon.[6]

Even today, the mystics say that this stone can tell "all that has been and will be."[7] It also aids "travel to the astral plane," which is the modern version of the ancients' spirit journey to the sphere of the moon.[8] Even up to the nineteenth century, it was believed that moonstone could make the wearer invisible, after the manner of one who walks only in the spirit.[9]

It is still said that moonstone

protects travelers, especially over water. Swimmers may avoid accidents in the water by wearing moonstone rings.[10] Moonstone also "realigns" the spine, "enhances" pituitary secretions, and helps childbirth.[11] Moreover, it "treats" cancer, edema, ulcers, and emotional problems. Hung on fruit trees, it will increase their yield.[12]

Even if (as seems likely) moonstone does none of these things, it is still an attractive mineral because of its pearly sheen, known as *schiller*. It makes handsome jewelry that has always been especially prized by women.

---

1. Wodiska, 148. 2. Parkinson, 114. 3. Stein, 256. 4. Kunz, 98. 5. Thomson, 46. 6. Wodiska, 147. 7. Richardson et al., 98. 8. Raphaell, *C. E.*, 149. 9. Fernie, 333. 10. Cunningham, 114. 11. Gurudas, 132. 12. Parkinson, 116, 118.

OBSIDIAN (Glass)

Obsidian is a natural glass, a volcanic melt that was suddenly exposed to air and cooled too rapidly to form crystals. One crystal mystic erroneously defines obsidian as "a crystal formed too quickly to develop facets," and also erroneously states that clear quartz is a natural glass like obsidian.[1] Quartz is crystalline; obsidian is not. Another mystic, even farther off the mark, refers to obsidian as a fossil.[2]

The ancient Mexicans made divinatory mirrors of polished obsidian and also obsidian images of the god Tezcatlipoca, whose name means "shining mirror."[3] Obsidian itself was called *iztli* or *teotetl,* "divine stone."[4] Older civilizations had many reasons to revere obsidian. It was extremely useful. When carefully chipped and polished, obsidian makes razor-sharp knife blades, arrowheads, spear points, scrapers, and other tools. It is also ornamental and talismanic, serving for personal adornment and as a gift to divinities.

Popular talismans nowadays are small tumbled nodules of black obsidian known as Apache tears—although why Apaches should have wept black tears remains a mystery.

Obsidian is usually a hard, shiny black mass, translucent at the edges. There are color variations. Mahogany obsidian is reddish or marbled with streaks of brownish red. Snowflake obsidian (also called flower obsidian) shows gray-white star-spots of included spherulites (spherical grains). Golden sheen and silver sheen obsidian contain inclusions that display a silky luster under bright light. There is also rainbow sheen obsidian. Another form is "Pele's hair," named after the Polynesian Goddess of volcanoes, consisting of long thin filaments: nature's spun glass.

To the mystics, obsidian is "a magnet that draws the spirit forces into the body," and is somehow involved in "interbreeding a higher form of awareness" here on earth. This alleged interbreeding is brought about by drawing the qualities of souls into bodies, while "lesser vibrations" are cleared away, all by the ineffable magic of inert volcanic glass.[5] This seems to imply that "soul qualities" are not part of one's self, but must be brought from somewhere else. The only justification for this premise would be a belief like that of the ancient Polynesians, that the Goddess Pele kept all souls of the dead in her volcanoes, occasionally sending them back to Earth's surface along with her lava, to be reincarnated in new life forms.

The shiny surface of obsidian is frequently embellished with faint flow lines, in which images may be seen,

recalling the tradition of the divinatory mirror. Golden, silver, and rainbow sheen obsidian makes beautiful objects for contemplation in a bright light. Out of their inky black surface, luminous clouds unexpectedly appear, suggesting the numerous symbolic connotations of light emerging from darkness. Sheen obsidian serves as a metaphor of creation or birth. Its own history is compatible with the metaphor. Obsidian has emerged from Earth's (or Pele's) fiery womb, and is itself the very substance of that womb. In the same sense as the old belief that each child was formed of its mother's retained uterine blood, so obsidian is formed of Earth's inner fluid. Once born, it is congealed but not crystallized. Just as meteorites come suddenly from the heavens, so obsidian comes suddenly from the depths.

1. Stein, 181. 2. Gurudas, 78. 3. Kunz, 204. 4. Sinkankas, G. N. A., 506. 5. Raphaell, C. E., 93–100.

ONYX (Silicon Dioxide)

Onyx is a banded chalcedony, usually with white streaks alternating with black, or brown (sard-onyx), or red (carnelian-onyx). It is often used for cameos and other jewelry in which its contrasting colors are utilized, but onyx may be a solid color also when bandings are very thick.

The name *onyx* has been misapplied to streaked or banded calcite, such as "Mexican onyx," which is too soft for jewelry.[1] Brazilian onyx, Algerian onyx, Yava onyx, cave onyx, and onyx marble are similarly misleading names for stalagmitic calcite, which is neither onyx nor marble.[2]

Onyx can be dyed. Dull colors can be made glassy black with the burnt sugar treatment. This means impregnating the stone with a sugar solution, and then with concentrated sulfuric acid, which turns the sugar into a tenacious carbon black.[3]

Black onyx used to be prized for rosary beads. Christians also copied pagan ideas of the stone's medicinal properties, believing that it would help wounds to heal and would assist women in childbirth. The Abbey Church of St. Alban's preserved a miraculous healing onyx that was accepted as a Christian fetish even though it was engraved with the image of the pagan god of medicine, Aesculapius (Greek Asklepios).[4] *The Magick of Kiram, King of Persia,* published in 1686, stated that one could become invisible by wearing an onyx ring.[5]

To some, the darkness of onyx stones suggested a connection with the dark side of nature and with powers of the underworld. A medieval Arabic text claimed that Chinese miners so fear the onyx that "they dread to go into the mines where it occurs. None but slaves and menials, who have no other means of gaining a livelihood, take the stone from the mines. When it has been mined, it is carried out of the country and sold in other lands."[6] Ragiel's thirteenth-century *Book of Wings* said that an onyx engraved with the likeness of a camel or two goats would produce "terrible visions in sleep."[7] Other sources claimed that onyx incites quarrels, especially between married couples, because the stones themselves were of two different sexes.[8]

Some modern mystics transmute such dark hints from the past by saying that onyx is helpful to those who fear death, or who are dealing with death. The stone's quarrelsome reputation is reinterpreted as a control over sexual desires.[9] Onyx "is working on the black ray from the cosmos," which, it seems, has a direct effect on the immune system.[10] It also improves the skin, nails, hair, and heart; treats ulcers; alleviates hearing difficulties; and keeps records of the wearer's "physical herstory."[11] Furthermore, onyx is "a plug that will not allow the body to be drained of any of its forces," and it "stabilizes the pancreas."[12]

Anyone who is worried about having a wobbly pancreas had better wear onyx.

Aside from this questionable benefit, onyx is a fine ornamental and gem stone with good wearing qualities. Like other forms of chalcedony, it appears often as cabochon rings, pendants, decorative boxes, bookends, figurines, knife handles, and such objects. Onyx is a stone of many uses.

---

1. Wodiska, 180. 2. Webster, 93. 3. Stern, 63. 4. Thomson, 20. 5. Fernie, 313. 6. Rutland, 161. 7. Kunz, 133. 8. Fernie, 179. 9. Cunningham, 120. 10. Bravo, 259. 11. Stein, 183–184. 12. Richardson et al., 100–101.

OPAL (Hydrous Silicon Dioxide)

Opal is a noncrystalline gem, a gel of silica containing varying amounts of water, up to as much as 30 percent. Precious opals can dry out, and in losing too much of their water, lose their iridescence.[1] Varieties are: white, black, moss, wood, fire, water, liver, harlequin, peacock, boulder, ironstone, and common (potch) opal; also hyalite, cachalong, hydrophane, girasol, and more.

Opal was named from Sanskrit *upala,* "valuable stone."[2] The *opalus* stone mentioned by Pliny was probably not opal, because opals are not found in the localities Pliny cited, nor were Europe's main sources of opal known to the Romans. Pliny's wonderful stone with soft reddish fire, the brilliant purple of the amethyst, the sea green of the emerald, and the flame of burning sulfur, could have been clear quartz with iridescent cracks. Pliny said the Indians could make glass imitations of the *opalus* that he praised so highly.[3] Iridescent quartzlike glass is not hard to make, but true opal is almost impossible to imitate. The *opalus* may have had an archaic connection with the Opalia, Rome's annual festival of the Goddess Ops.

Whether or not the Romans' opal was the same stone that now bears this name, it is clear that the Romans prized it. They believed that such stones would confer foresight and the power of prophecy.[4] When Mark Antony tried to buy a famous opal from the senator Nonius in order to give it to Cleopatra, the senator fled from Rome and voluntarily accepted exile rather than part with his stone.[5]

Eastern traditions said that many-colored stones could protect the wearer from all diseases. Blond women valued opals in the belief that the stones would preserve the golden color of their hair.[6] In the Middle Ages, it was believed that opals would improve the eyesight of their wearers, yet also dim the eyes of a beholder so the wearer of the stone could become invisible. Thus it was called the stone of thieves, making possible the most secret thefts.[7]

The latter tradition may have been one source of the opal's evil reputation as a bad-luck stone, although the origin of this belief is often traced to the fictional bad-luck opal in Walter

Scott's *Anne of Gierstein*. Long before Scott, the opal aroused fear in some regions. Superstitious Russians would buy nothing if they should catch sight of an opal among goods offered for sale. They believed that any subsequent purchase would bring them bad luck.[8]

Modern mystical ideas concerning opal tend to be equally irrational. One source says that opals "treat" autism, dyslexia, epilepsy, depression, leukemia, and all disorders of the blood, eyes, and physical coordination; also, black opals were "used in Lemuria when the race, at first genderless, was divided into sexes."[9] Another unaccountably claims that "the physical makeup of an Opal corresponds to the physical properties of the brain."[10] Yet opal seems to be of little or no benefit to the brain, because it must not be worn by teenagers, whose tender age makes them too unstable to withstand the opal's changing vibrations.[11] On the other hand, opal is recommended for "spiritual awareness," for easing stress, and for encouraging achievement, all of which would seem helpful to teenagers.[12]

Another "authority" distinguishes between different types of opals for different mystical properties. Fire opals draw money. Black opals are power stones for magicians.[13] Another misleadingly refers to opal as "a distant member of the quartz family."[14] Because, apart from their water content, opals *are* quartz, "distant" is perhaps not the right word. Unlike other forms of quartz, however, opals are fragile and require special care. Owners of precious opals may be advised to keep them in water, oil, or glycerin to retard cracking. For reasons imperfectly understood, some opals craze and crack anyway, while others remain crack-free virtually forever.

Few stones are better suited to leisurely contemplation and meditation than the opal. Its changing lights and colors can be fascinating. A millimeter's difference in the angle of vision can reveal a world of different colors in a good opal. The magic of this stone's appearance is real enough; it is not necessary to load the innocent mineral with fictional magic.

Because of its great beauty and desirability, innumerable attempts have been made to synthesize or imitate precious opal. None has been completely successful. John S. Slocum invented a silicate glass imitation known as Slocum stone. Experts pronounced it attractive but not very much like opal. A better imitation was produced in the 1970s by Pierre Gilson. Various combinations of colored, translucent, or milky glass are sold as opal simulants. Their appearance is sufficiently unlike the real thing that few people would be deceived by them.[15]

Another kind of simulation, however, is harder to detect. Unsalable white opals are sometimes turned into black opals by the same sugar-and-acid treatment that turns ordinary chalcedony into black onyx. Black opals should be studied with care. They are not always what nature intended them to be. Another way to make worthless "potch" or common opal salable is to impregnate it with plastic. By this means it can often be induced to show a play of colors, resembling precious opal.[16]

Construction of opal doublets or triplets is common practice. This may create a better gemstone than one solid piece. The composite stone is less prone to craze or crack, because it is held together by the cement. Also, fragile opal is protected from bumps and scratches by its covering of transparent quartz or other material that is harder and more resistant. A special black glass made in Belgium and marketed under the name Opalite often serves as a backing for opal doublets.[17]

1. Schumann, 150. 2. Boegel, 89. 3. Kunz, 145. 4. Thomson, 61. 5. Stern, 53. 6. Kunz, 143, 148. 7. Webster, 65. 8. Fernie, 249. 9. Parkinson, 174. 10. Bravo, 252. 11. Richardson et al., 103. 12. Stein, 261. 13. Cunningham, 122. 14. Raphaell, C. H., 197. 15. O'Donoghue, G. M. G., 173. 16. Nassau, G. E., 147. 17. Webster, 233.

ORPIMENT (Arsenic Trisulfide)

Orpiment is named from Latin *auripigmentum,* "golden pigment." Under its old name of "king's yellow" it was widely used in paints and dyes. This name is now applied mostly to synthetic orpiment. The natural material occurs in masses or veins near hot springs and volcanic fumaroles. Orpiment is an ore of arsenic. The arsenic monosulfide, realgar, forms brilliant red crystals, but realgar is light-sensitive, altering to powdery yellow orpiment when exposed to daylight. Though it is more stable than realgar, orpiment itself tends to crumble if kept in a light and airy environment. This poisonous mineral likes the dark.

Both orpiment and realgar were known to the ancients. Aristotle referred to realgar as sandarach. Arsenical copper alloys were found useful in metallurgy. Alchemists knew that arsenic would dispose of noxious insects, rats, mice, weeds, and even inconvenient people. Over the centuries, a fair number of people have died with symptoms of murder by arsenic—symptoms that include nausea, diarrhea, headache, muscle pains, and eventually coma.

Nevertheless, inorganic arsenic compounds like orpiment are still eaten in some parts of central Europe as a tonic or as a cure for such diseases as leukemia, anemia, malaria, rheumatism, and syphilis. In other areas it has been recognized that organic arsenic compounds such as salvarsan (arsphenamine hydrochloride) can indeed treat syphilis and a few other diseases. The inorganic material, however, is dangerous.

As a mineral specimen, orpiment is often obtained inadvertently by collectors who originally admired it in the form of bright red realgar crystals, then failed to keep them in the dark. Thus they received yellow orpiment whether they wanted it or not.

PASTE (Glass)

Paste is the jeweler's term for cut glass faceted to imitate a jewel. Owners of valuable gems may have them copied in paste for ordinary wearing to avoid risk to the originals. Paste is extensively used in costume jewelry, providing precious-stone look-alikes at low cost. Needless to say, paste imitations have also figured in innumerable frauds, being sold to unwary buyers as real gems.

Another word for paste is strass, named after Joseph Strass, who invented a glass formula in 1758 to imitate diamonds. Some say that Strass's formula included chert, iron oxide, alumina, lime, and sodium. Others claim that the ingredients were silica, potash, borax, and lead oxide.[1] Today there are various formulas,

devised to strike a balance between desirable hardness and optical properties. Lead glass (the commercial "lead crystal") provides sparkle but is soft and easily scratched. At the other extreme, borosilicate glass has a good hardness, equal to quartz, but does not look very lively.

Glass gems have been given many trade names designed to suggest that they are something other than glass. A popular term for such imitations is Royalite. The hopeful title True Star has been applied to a poor imitation of star corundum, consisting of a glass cabochon with a marked foil cemented to its back. A more successful star-stone imitation is a molded, ridged opaque glass cabochon covered by a colored glaze.[2]

An experienced hand can tell glass from gemstone by its touch. Glass feels warmer than a natural crystal because it is amorphous and cannot conduct heat away from the skin as fast as a crystal can. Plastic imitations are even warmer to the touch.

Another way to distinguish paste from a gemstone is to study facet edges. Cut gems have sharp, clean edges. In glass imitations, facet edges look a little softer and rounder. If the glass is pressed (molded) rather than cut, the edges are even less sharp. Of course, this test cannot apply to cabochon stones in settings.

Well-made paste imitations can look very good, and are substituted for the real thing more often than the layperson might think. For one who knows little about gems, the sure way to avoid being thus cheated is to deal only with a reputable lapidary and to keep away from gemstone "bargains" that are offered informally nearly everywhere in the world.

One of the fanciful names applied

to a paste gem is Aurora Borealis Stone. This is not a stone, of course, but cut glass backed by a thin interference coating such as those used on camera lenses. A "gem" of this kind can show a lot of sparkle when it is new, before scratches appear. Sometimes, paste jewels are given a backing of mercury amalgam— essentially, a thin layer of mirror. Such a jewel is called a chaton.[3]

---

1. O'Donoghue, *G. M. G.*, 210. 2. Nassau, *G. M. M.*, 272. 3. Webster, 440.

PEARL (Organic Material)

Natural pearls are produced by pearl oysters, as coating of nacre (largely aragonite, i.e., calcium carbonate) applied to seal off small foreign bodies that get inside the oyster's shell and cause irritation. There is a popular myth, always retold with immense assurance, to the effect that some lucky diner found a very valuable pearl in one of the appetizers. In reality, pearl oysters are not edible, and edible oysters do not produce pearls—at least, not good ones. The pearls found in edible oysters resemble small chips of ordinary porcelain.[1]

Nowadays, nearly everyone knows what pearls are and how they originate—except for some of the crystal mystics. A writer admits that pearls are "producted [*sic*] by certain mollusks," but he will not allow the mollusks full credit. On the contrary, he says that pearls were originally created by mental energy in Lemuria.[2] Edgar Cayce believed that pearls are magnetized, and can be "demagnetized" by exposure to ultraviolet light for one-tenth of a second, thus programming the pearl "for better body vibration."[3] Cayce was almost unsurpassed at packing many scientific blunders into one short sentence.

In the ancient world, pearls were sacred to the Great Goddess as Aphrodite Marina, whose body sexually symbolized the Pearly Gate of paradise, and whose "pearls of wisdom" were dispensed by her priestesses. Her Syrian form was known as Lady of Pearls.[4] She was Christianized as the mythical Saint Margaret, whose name means "Pearl," as well as the Virgin Mary (Maria), who inherited the Goddess's sea blue robe and necklace of pearls. Nonetheless, her gem retained pagan connotations. Pearls were often associated with moon worship. It used to be thought that pearls were formed by a combination of seawater and moonlight. In the fifteenth century it was said that oysters generate their pearls by leaving the seabed and rising to the surface to take in "celestial dew," which was thought to emanate from the moon.[5]

Hindu brides traditionally wore pearls as a symbol of feminine sexual magic. With the advent of patriarchal gods in India, it was claimed that the tradition began with Krishna, who adorned his daughter with pearls for her wedding. Krishna was an incarnation of the god Vishnu, whose followers claimed that he had created pearls.[6] Perhaps because of such associations with heathenism, some Europeans insisted that pearls were unlucky gifts for brides or engaged girls, signifying tears later in life.[7]

In China it was thought that "pearl drops" falling from the sky, to be swallowed by the oysters, were either the blood or the semen of celestial cloud dragons.[8] To use this miraculous substance, the Chinese still grind up millions of small seed pearls to be sold as medicine.[9]

European doctors similarly prescribed powdered pearls for such complaints as weak eyes, unsteady nerves, consumption, plague, and "the decay of old age." Leonardus wrote in 1750 that "bruised" pearls, drunk with milk, will heal putrid ulcers; with sugar, they will cure pestilential fevers.[10] Pearls were said to cure skin diseases and stomach troubles.[11] Today, mystics are still saying that powdered pearl placed on the tongue will alleviate stomach ulcers—surely the world's most expensive antacid.[12]

Paracelsus evidently remembered and believed the impossible old story about Cleopatra dissolving a valuable pearl in either wine or vinegar and drinking it in Mark Antony's presence. A modern mystic actually approved Paracelsus's prescription of pearls dissolved in vinegar or lemon juice to "kill the acids of the stomach" and relieve ulcers.[13] The major flaw in this reasoning is that pearls do not dissolve in wine, vinegar, or lemon juice. If Cleopatra had drunk any liquid that would dissolve a pearl, it would have dissolved her digestive tract also.[14]

Some mystics still claim that powdered pearl is good for the stomach, and/or can cure ulcers and cancers of the digestive system.[15] Lama Sing obscurely remarks that pearl "does affect the abdominal, does affect somewhat the absorption of drosses in the body."[16] Others claim that "the pearl has no effect on the physical body," but subsequently assert that it has an important "soothing effect" on the pituitary gland, which does seem to be part of the physical body.[17]

Of course one of the major considerations about pearls of good quality is that they are worth a lot of money. Therefore, all kinds of charms, spells, and chicanery have been used either to increase or to imitate them. Some pearl fishers of southeastern Asia believed that one pearl, kept with rice in a bottle stoppered by a dead man's finger, would give birth to more pearls.[18] Since the seventeenth century, credible imitation pearls have been made by coating hollow glass beads on the inside with *essence d'orient,* a fish-scale preparation, and filling them with wax. Cheaper imitations simply coated beads on the outside. One of the disadvantages of real pearls as gemstones is that, in time, they "die" and turn black because their organic conchiolin decays after about a century and a half.[19]

Ninety percent of the pearls sold today are cultured artificially by inserting shell beads into living pearl oysters, so the beads can be coated with nacre in three or four years (provided the oysters survive and remain healthy). Pearl farming is hard on oysters, and many die. Consequently, certain ecology-minded women's groups are now boycotting pearls for the same reason that they refuse to buy fur coats: they do not want to have living creatures sacrificed for their adornment.

Not only are pearls artificially cultured; they are also artificially colored. Off-color pearls are treated in various ways to improve their appearance. Pearls can be dyed a rich black by a solution of silver nitrate in dilute ammonia. Pink pearls can be produced by a solution of eosin. Many pearls are found to be insufficiently white, so they are bleached before being sold.[20] In short, one who thinks of pearls as pure, unspoiled products of nature is probably wrong.

1. Wodiska, 237. 2. Gurudas, 137. 3. *Scientific Properties,* 34. 4. Cunningham, 123. 5. Spencer, 229. 6. Stern, 32. 7. Thomson, 44. 8. Cunningham, 123–124. 9. Weinstein, 81. 10. Fernie, 3, 300. 11. Wodiska, 237. 12. Gurudas, 138. 13. Bravo, 106. 14. Desautels, *G. K.,* 17. 15. Parkinson, 108; Gurudas, 138. 16. *Gems, Stones, and Minerals,* 17. 17. Richardson et al., 104. 18. Kunz, 41. 19. Smith, 475. 20. Nassau, *G. E.,* 150.

PERIDOT (Magnesium Iron Silicate)

Peridot is the gem variety of olivine. It is yellowish green, sometimes green enough to pass as an emerald in dim light—hence its nickname, "evening emerald."

The old name *chrysolite* was once applied indiscriminately to both peridot and topaz, which engendered enormous confusion, especially since peridot came from the Red Sea island of Zebirget, which was identified with the legendary topaz isle, Topazin. In some ancient writings, *topaz* means peridot.[1]

Some crystal mystics have not yet worked out the confusion of names. They think peridot and chrysolite are different minerals, although they are called first cousins to one another.[2] Some attribute one set of healing powers to "chrysolite" and a different set to "peridot."[3] One calls chrysolite "a very soft stone," which describes neither peridot nor topaz—nor, for that matter, any other stone, since chrysolite is an obsolete name.[4]

Whatever it was that the ancients called chrysolite, however, it was credited with wonderful powers. It could drive away evil spirits and spells when attached to the left arm with the hair of an ass. Engraved with the figure of an ass, it would give prophetic powers; engraved with a vulture, it would control demons.[5] Now it is said that "chrysolite" (as opposed to peridot) alleviates viral infections, toxemia, and appendicitis.[6]

Peridot is a modern wonder drug. It is recommended for lung congestions, fevers, ulcers, colitis, and constipation. It was a "major healing gemstone of fabled Atlantis."[7] It stimulates "tissue regeneration" in the entire body.[8] It "works with the adrenals and the liver."[9] It also develops human mental capacities, "because of its high content of yellow within the green."[10] If yellow is all that we really need to develop mental capacities, then every classroom in the country had better be painted yellow before another week passes.

Most mysterious of all, peridot is "transmitting the ray-waves of a still unseen planet."[11] If the planet has never been seen, how was this interesting information discovered? One never ceases to marvel at the mystic's propensity to discern things that neither the microscope nor the telescope can bring into focus, and that no human being other than himself has ever observed. Of course, people who hallucinate can do this sort of thing but their particular fantasies are not usually recorded in books or taken seriously by others.

The colors of peridot are unusual among gem materials. Just as lay persons are most likely to identify any red stone as a ruby, and any blue stone as a sapphire, so they are also most likely to ask the wearer of a faceted peridot, "What stone is that?" It is often given as a birthstone for either August or September, depending on which birthstone list you prefer. Some people feel very much drawn to its lively, tart color.

---

1. Anderson, 55. 2. Richardson & Huett, 105. 3. Gurudas, 91, 139. 4. Harold, 174. 5. Kunz, 67, 133. 6. Gurudas, 91. 7. Stein, 216. 8. Gurudas, 139. 9. Parkinson, 154. 10. Chocron, 72. 11. Bravo, 223.

PETRIFIED WOOD (Silicon Dioxide)

Petrified wood is stone, not wood. The original wood structure is retained, but all its cellulose has been replaced by silica, which means some kind of chalcedony or opal. With considerable inaccuracy, a crystal mystic says that petrified wood hardens over time into "several types of minerals" described as agate, opal, jasper, and silica—which are really all the same mineral. He further says that petrified wood can improve the human body's "assimilation" of silica and silicon—which are never assimilated into the body at all.[1]

Others suppose that petrified wood may be used "to recall past incarnations," presumably because of its great age, although other kinds of stone are just as old if not older.[2] The practice of recalling past incarnations means sitting quietly with a piece of stone and waiting for some mental imagery to suggest a scene, which is then attributed to a past life. It is as easy as rolling off a (petrified) log.

The most interesting way to meditate on petrified wood is to reconstruct in imagination the whole life cycle of the original tree, the animals and plants that inhabited the land around it, the possible cause of its demise, and the conditions under which it was buried. Considerable real knowledge is required for this exercise. Fantasies come cheap, but real knowledge demands some investment of time and attention to preliminary reading of serious texts. In thus opening the way to genuine curiosity about past ages of the earth, petrified wood may be a true knowledge stone.

---

1. Gurudas, 140. 2. Cunningham, 125.

PREHNITE (Calcium Aluminum Hydroxyl Silicate)

Prehnite is classified as a minor gemstone. First brought to Europe from Africa in 1774 by a Dutchman, Colonel van Prehn, it is usually found in translucent botryoidal (grapelike) crusts of tiny crystals, pale leaf-green, limeade green, grayish green, or white. An aggregate of prehnite crystals shows a fascinating surface that, when viewed under magnification, can resemble the ropy wrinkle lines of pahoehoe lava, or an eroded "badlands" landscape as seen from a space satellite.

Prehnite can be cut, faceted, or polished as a cabochon gem, made interesting by its unusual range of colors, which are unlike any of the colors of more familiar stones. Nevertheless, the rough prehnite is even more interesting. In a strong light, its surface glitters like diamonds, and its green translucence looks as inviting as a deep rock pool on a hot day. This is a fine meditation stone. It is good for a collection to include at least one piece of prehnite rough. Prehnite gems tend to be translucent rather than transparent. The polished material has a lovely soft, velvety appearance, almost pearly in some instances.

PUMICE (Glass)

Pumice is the rock that floats on water—the solidified froth formed on the surface of viscous lava or blown violently into the air during eruptions. Light and spongy, pumice is a natural spun glass whose numerous gas pockets and vacancies give it a texture that is more air than stone. Crushed pumice provides grit for cleaning products and dentifrices.

The floating ability of pumice is said to symbolize an ability to "rise above" one's troubles, so pumice is used in rituals for getting rid of problems.[1] Pumice also symbolizes the dualism of nature. When it falls in the form of gritty ash on human habitations near a volcanic eruption, it is a most tenacious type of dirt. Yet its most common appearance among us is as a cleanser.

1. Cunningham, 127.

PYRITE (Iron Sulfide)

Pyrite is "fool's gold," the commonest of all sulfides. It is named from the Greek word for fire, because it will produce sparks when struck by iron.[1] Pyrite crystals often form perfect cubes of a bright, shiny metallic gold color, looking as if they had been artificially shaped. The ancient Chinese earth symbol, a golden cube, may have been derived from pyrite. Mexican Indians used to make pyrite mirrors for divination.[2] Such mirrors are still used by crystal mystics to "awaken psychic impulses."[3] In gold-rush days, pyrite mingled with quartz rocks frequently fooled uninformed prospectors into believing that they had struck gold; hence its nickname.

Pyrite is a major cause of acid rain. When coal containing pyrite is burned, sulfuric acid is formed through oxidation. Stone used for building must be free of pyrite because, in weathering, pyrite would release corrosive iron sulfates that discolor and destroy the stone.[4]

Pyrite is sometimes cut as a gemstone and marketed under the misleading name of marcasite. True marcasite is a different mineral with the same constituents, an iron disulfide. True marcasite is not really suitable for jewelry because it is less stable than pyrite. It can slowly decompose in air, becoming coated with a white powder of iron sulfate.[5] Even more misleading is the popular application of the name "marcasite" to jewelry made with faceted bits of silvery hematite, otherwise known as black diamond. This material is not even the same color as marcasite or pyrite. Sometimes, the imitation is imitated by yet another substitute, cut steel, and still sold under the name of marcasite. In short, if you buy any jewelry labeled "marcasite," what you really get is anybody's guess.

1. Sinkankas, *M. A.,* 305. 2. Kunz, 99. 3. Cunningham, 169. 4. Medenbach & Wilk, 46. 5. Schumann, 162.

QUARTZ (Silicon Dioxide)

Clear quartz, the most popular of all New Age stones, is "rock crystal," sometimes misleadingly shortened to plain "crystal." One mystical source claims that clear quartz is the only truly transparent stone. All other "nonquartz gemstones" have a "restricted transparency quotient."[1] This is not true, but it demonstrates the exaggerated quality of quartz fanaticism.

Quartz is also pink (rose quartz),

gray-brown (smoky quartz), white (milky quartz), yellow (citrine), purple (amethyst), and green (aventurine), and often contains inclusions of other variously colored minerals such as chromite, crocidolite (tigereye), and rutile. Twelve percent of the earth's crust is quartz, which is silica, the same mineral as opal and all of the large chalcedony family.

Aside from the recognized variations, certain crystal mystics distinguish sixteen different kinds of quartz crystals: devic, attunement, energy, healing, archetype, library, numerological, transmitting, modulatory, vision, toning or singing, surgery, abominological [sic], and open-ended or generalized crystals, also energy rods and power rods.[2] How these are to be differentiated from one another remains a mystery.

In addition, many mystics refer to a seventeenth variety, the generator crystal, usually identifiable by its large size. Generator crystals "open the ethers to the material plane" and "magnify and intensify thoughts up to 1,000 times."[3] Generator crystals are said to have provided all the electrical power, communications, heat, light, and transportation for whole cities in the dear dead days of Atlantis and Lemuria. This notion encourages mystics to say that quartz "conducts electricity and magnetism"—although it does neither—and that in the future, quartz will be developed "as a major and safe source for lighting and heating fuel."[4] In 1983, a crystal mystic predicted "in the next few years" the invention of something called an electrinium battery, whose major component would be ground quartz (that is, sand).[5] So far, the invention has not materialized.

Alas, quartz is not as talented

anymore as it must have been in Atlantis. The largest quartz crystal at present on record is twenty feet long, a "generator" if there ever was one, but it has never emitted a single ampere of electric current or shown the slightest sign of mental activity.

Quartz was the origin of the word *crystal,* Greek for "ice," because the ancients thought it was unmeltable ice. Derived from this was the folk belief that thirst could be quenched by holding a quartz crystal in the mouth. Saint Gregory the Great might have been better enlightened by God, but he was not; he wrote that water is turned "by strength of cold" into nonmelting crystalline quartz.[6] The chemist Johann Kunckel insisted in *Ars Vitria* (1689) that quartz is nothing but "coagulated ice."[7] Even Linnaeus, as late as 1777, still believed that quartz is fossil ice.[8]

Priests and priestesses in the ancient world used to "draw down fire from heaven" to light altar fires by focusing sunlight through quartz crystals. The biblical sons of Aaron became sacrificial victims similarly consumed on the altar by "fire from the Lord" (Leviticus 10:2). Quartz-focused sunlight was also used for cautery of wounds. Pliny recommended for this purpose "a ball of crystal, acted on by the sun." Roman ladies carried quartz crystal balls, not only for medicinal purposes, but also to cool their hands in warm weather.[9]

The old tradition of focusing sunlight through quartz leads some modern mystics to declare that quartz "energy" comes from the sun. But others say, "Quartz crystals are not energized by the Sun. . . . It is the Moon which stimulates the energy field of a quartz crystal."[10] To make a quartz "elixir," some recommend placing the crystal-bearing water in sunlight; others insist that it must be exposed to moonlight. Both claim that drinking such water will cause "subtle" improvements in one's health—usually so subtle as to seem indiscernible.[11]

A cult that arose in northern New York State about 1900 practiced a somewhat less innocuous use of quartz to improve health. Members believed in eating quantities of "vital ore" (quartz sand) to combat sore eyes, hemorrhoids, dizziness, sore throat, and indigestion.[12] They probably had considerable indigestion to deal with.

American Indian shamans used quartz crystals as divining and hunting charms, believing that they were inhabited by spirits, who had to be fed periodically by rubbing the crystals with deer's blood. Mexican Indians believed that the indwelling spirits were souls of the dead. Crystal mystics the world over have always claimed to establish communication with the spirits in stones, and quartz has always been a favorite stone. A book published in 1908, *Practical Psychomancy and Crystal Gazing,* set forth a basic theory, now embraced by nearly all mystics, that the molecular structure of quartz somehow enables it to bring out "the latent faculty of astral vision."[13]

"Molecular structure" is a term that crystal mystics love to use, though few of them seem to understand what it means. One actually believes that molecular structure can be perceived with the naked eye. The reader is invited to look at this molecular structure while contemplating the crystal in hand, to notice how geometrically exact are the crystal's molecular arrangements.[14] Such observation would need a keen eye indeed! Another says, "The

passage of ions through the molecular structure makes them a valuable aid in clearing and neutralizing negative conditions in the aura of people. . . . When laid on the body the Crystal Quartz decrystallizes the knots which block the flow of energy."[15] Another claims that by reason of its molecular structure, quartz is a "bio-magnetic resonator" with "facets that breathe as you breathe air." Quartz crystals can be "pre-programmed to react in certain ways that measure and fix the understanding of the stars in the circuits of time and space. . . . They pre-program a creation at its earliest point."[16] This is pseudoscientific nonlanguage, doubletalk.

Some mystics do not seem to know what quartz's vital "molecular structure" is made of. One says, "The clear quarts [*sic*] crystals are composed of seven basic elements," when in fact there are only two. The mythical unspecified seven will "produce a field of healing negative ions, while clearing the atmosphere around them of positive ions."[17] Crystal mystics really don't seem to care if some of their statements are meaningless, as long as they are pleased with the sound of them.

The aberrant hollow-faced type of crystal known as skeletal quartz has been given a newly coined name in mystical parlance. Such crystals are "elestials." It is said that "their source is beyond time itself and their origin is the celestial realm." Their particular virtue or function is not easy to ascertain from the description: "These crystals stabilize brain wave frequencies and neutralize erratic confused thought forms." And yet, contrariwise, "If one is confused or emotionally imbalanced these crystals will amplify and magnify those feelings."[18]

According to some, quartz is indiscriminate in its beneficence. "From all forms of natural rock quartz flows a continual stream of electromagnetic energy, which is released into the atmosphere to benefit all life forms." On the other hand, the "electromagnetic energy" may come from elsewhere and be moderated in some way by quartz, which produces only "a natural harmony between mankind and the electromagnetic energies which continually flow through the ethers. These in turn aid the formation of the positive and negative ions."[19]

Technological uses of quartz are frequently cited as evidence of the stone's wondrous powers. Its use in electronic equipment is regarded as particularly significant. Mystics tend to overlook the fact that natural quartz is not suitable for such use because its crystals are not sufficiently uniform and are generally internally twinned. Despite the abundance of natural quartz, then, manufacturers of electronic equipment ignore it in favor of the synthetic quartz that is produced in vast quantities for the purpose.[20]

The mystics' ideas of technological uses for quartz sound weird and wonderful, having little to do with any of its real functions. For instance, it is said that quartz crystals were used to levitate huge blocks of stone for the building of Solomon's temple. Likewise, the stones of the Great Pyramid were moved by "mental energy" directed through "quartz-like" crystals.[21] Quartz is said to be something like a computer's memory bank, containing whole histories of civilizations and scientific information. To recall one's dreams from a quartz crystal, one has only to charge it to "record all dream activity" and put it

under the pillow. In the morning, take it in hand and request an instant replay.[22]

Most of the esoteric functions of quartz crystals are not defined at all, despite rivers of verbiage purporting to define them. A sampling follows:

"Clear quartz crystal energy enters the L-field (the spaces between atoms and energy of the aura bodies) . . . to transmit changes to the cell-source blueprint of regeneration."[23] "The DNA grid structure of crystals is contained within the spiral molecular energy patterns in relationship to the specific angular configuration."[24] It is said that the pointed termination of a quartz crystal makes a connection between the crystal's assortment of atomic particles and an unnamed "universal source of infinite energy."[25] "Interdimensional scientists work in close conjunction with the various levels and orders of Crystalline Intelligence. Many of the more advanced crystal growing devices function, in part, as an attraction module—a specifically designed energy field that serves as an antenna-attracting unit for receiving the desired influences of a particular universal Intelligence-pattern."[26] Finally, quartz causes "man" to remember that "he, too, is part of a total number of crystals which are formed in the same manner with the same similar shape."[27] This seems to indicate that "man" is hexagonal and prismatic.

Quartz crystals are undeniably beautiful and inspiring, but when inspiration goes completely off the rails and attempts to present fantasy in the guise of fact, no progress can be made in either realm. Meditation with nature's beautiful crystals should produce clarity, not confusion. There is nothing but confusion in statements to the effect that every quartz crystal generates negative ions, to create a "harmonious, uplifting atmosphere around it," or that quartz crystals are formed "from the elements silicon and water" (water is not an element), or in the measuring of a nonexistent "field," concluding that a half-inch quartz crystal "will project a field of around three feet."[28] Such statements are nonsense. Being an admirable mineral in many ways, quartz deserves better attention than this.

For many centuries, quartz passed for diamond more often than not, when the average European never saw a diamond and readily gave the name to almost any colorless stone. Consequently, a strange superstition about diamonds had its real origin in an ancient method of dealing with quartz. The superstition said that before a diamond could be cut, it had to be "softened" by immersion in goat's blood. This softening by immersion was actually one of the world's oldest gemstone treatments, used at least fifteen hundred years ago—on quartz, not diamond. It produced "iris" or "rainbow" quartz by heating the stone, then plunging it suddenly into liquid (water, blood, wine, or dye) to produce internal cracks that would refract light in rainbow colors.[29] Cracked quartz is still used today as a medium for dye, to make imitations of various colored stones. In addition, quartz with internal cracks is still appreciated by collectors for its colorful responses to changing angles of light.

1. Baer & Baer, *C. C.*, 201. 2. Baer & Baer, *W. L.*, 54–59. 3. Raphaell, *C. E.*, 59. 4. Stein, 146. 5. Burbutis, 7. 6. Fernie, 201. 7. Medenbach & Wilk, 76. 8. Dake et al., 82, 110. 9. Weinstein, 178, 181.

10. Harold, 18. 11. Cunningham, 90. 12. Wodiska, 237. 13. Kunz, 214, 255. 14. Raphaell, *C. E.*, 24. 15. Chocron, 35. 16. Rea, 71–74, 80. 17. Burbutis, 1, 5. 18. Raphaell, *C. H.*, 129, 135. 19. Harold, 49, 92. 20. Medenbach & Wilk, 76. 21. Gurudas, 6, 17. 22. Harold, 56–57. 23. Stein, 145. 24. Baer & Baer, *W. L.*, 38. 25. Raphaell, *C. E.*, 3. 26. Baer & Baer, *C. C.*, 370. 27. Richardson et al., 64. 28. Silbey, 7, 8, 13. 29. Nassau, *G. E.*, 130, 158.

RHODOCHROSITE (Manganese Carbonate)

Rhodochrosite is found in many delicious shades of pink: strawberry, raspberry, watermelon, or cotton-candy pink, striped with peach, cream, or milky white. Some specimens even resemble rare beef—an altogether edible-looking mineral.

Another name for rhodochrosite is Inca rose, after the belief among Andean Indians that the blood of their ancient Inca rulers was turned to stone in this form.[1]

Like other pink stones, rhodochrosite is mystically connected with love. It is said to bring acceptance and forgiveness, as well as relief from various physical troubles such as liver disease, ulcers, asthma, palsy, constipation, and congestion.[2] One mystic declares that rhodochrosite is a good conductor of "energy" because it has "a high copper content."[3] Rhodochrosite does not contain copper, although it may have traces of calcium, iron, magnesium, or zinc.[4]

A mystic who spells it "rhodocrocite" says that it can restore poor eyesight. It also "vibrates" the consciousness, raising it into a condition of spiritual knowing, which can be channeled into the material body when the crystal is worn "in the semi-precious state."[5] The reader's only problem is to decide what might constitute a semi-precious state. Another mystic says that rhodochrosite "cleanses" the subconscious mind and "detoxifies" the kidneys.[6] All this, from a mere touch of the stone! Still another mystic says that (nonmagnetic) rhodochrosite will "immediately magnetize and hold any force field whether it be of another person or persons, or a particular area."[7] It also "knits together rends and tears in the etheric fibre" and "quickly seals the aura."[8]

These might seem unduly ponderous notions of a modest mineral, chiefly admirable for its range of pretty, rosy colors. A whole rose garden could be carved of rhodochrosite blossoms and enjoyed without any mystical overtones at all. Though it is too soft for jewelry (3.5 to 4 on the Mohs scale), rhodochrosite makes decorative boxes, bookends, lamps, ashtrays, and figurines. Perhaps because such imaginative works can be fashioned of rhodochrosite, some mystics call it a stone of creative thinking. One such "expert" attributes the creativity to manganese, and states absurdly that "rhodochrosite consists entirely of manganese."[9] If this were so, it would be elemental manganese and not rhodochrosite.

In some localities, rhodochrosite is found not in its usual massive form but in splendid transparent cherry red crystals. These rarities are prized by collectors as much as the finest rubies. Whether they encourage creative thinking or not, such objects do stimulate aesthetic pleasure.

1. Medenbach & Wilk, 100. 2. Stein, 225. 3. Chocron, 66. 4. *Audubon Society Field Guide*, 435. 5. Raphaell, *C. E.*, 120, 157, 163. 6. Parkinson, 241. 7. Lorusso & Glick, 74. 8. Rea, 324. 9. Uyldert, 69.

RHODONITE
(Manganese Silicate)

Another of the pinkish-purplish-red minerals typically produced by manganese, rhodonite also includes dark streaks caused by manganese oxides. Rhodonite is harder than rhodochrosite, and may be faceted as a gemstone.

Crystal mystics seem unable to invent credible new powers for rhodonite. It is said to promote balance, and to shut down the psychic centers.[1] Alternatively, it protects the lungs, and can "keep emphysema stirred to the point that it would not harden or dry into the cells." Naively assuming that, for some unaccountable reason, the chemical composition of rhodonite has never been ascertained, one source says that rhodonite "would be good for chemists to look into."[2]

Another source says that water into which rhodonite has been dipped can "strengthen" the inner ear, but it is not clear whether the water should be drunk, bathed in, or poured into the ear. Since rhodonite is associated with sound, at least according to this view, it is recommended that the stone be stored in a vacuum.[3] Not many households have facilities for creating or maintaining a vacuum, so it is not likely that many rhodonite specimens will be stored in the recommended way. Nevertheless, even when exposed to air, pieces of rhodonite will cheer the heart with their warm color, and will invite contemplation.

1. Cunningham, 128. 2. Richardson et al., 131–132. 3. Gurudas, 150.

ROSE QUARTZ (Silicon Dioxide)

Though it rarely forms visible crystals but nearly always occurs in chunky masses, rose quartz is perhaps the most beloved New Age stone. It is constantly associated with love, tenderness, sweetness, comfort, nurture, peace, and joy. It soothes heart pain, warms and eases those in distress, and brings contentment to the aged—as well as smoothing out their wrinkles.[1] All this is extrapolated from nothing more than the mineral's gentle shell pink color, which apparently reminds nearly everyone of maternal qualities and a sense of security such as might be experienced by an infant at its mother's breast and remembered subconsciously in adulthood.

Rose quartz, one mystic says, will put you in the "pink" of health.[2] Another says it is a mild cardiac stimulant and diuretic; it also vibrates to keep one's "polarities in rotation."[3] Another assures us that rose quartz was used to "restructure the heart in Atlantis when the thymus was no longer the dominant gland."[4]

Such assertions are absurd enough, but there is no doubt that rose quartz is one of nature's prettiest products. Its pink translucence can be found in generous quantities, so anyone may own a piece. Pleasant to contemplate, its soft color seems almost too tender for such a hard stone. One almost expects it to feel soft and giving to the touch—though, of course, it does not. Especially pretty are the transparent rose quartz crystals, which occur only rarely. Since other types of quartz so readily form large crystals, this relative scarcity of macrocrystalline rose quartz is a geological mystery.

---

1. Stein, 224. 2. Rea, 329. 3. Bravo, 139. 4. Gurudas, 174.

RUBY (Corundum: Aluminum Oxide)

Ruby is the red gem variety of corundum. All other colors of gem corundum are called sapphire—even the pink. "Corundum" is from Sanskrit *kuruvinda*, "ruby."[1] According to Hindu legend, red corundum was created from the colorless diamond of a maharani (queen) when she was stabbed to death by a jealous courtier. Her blood stained the stone and all others like it.[2]

One of the early myths about ruby was that its intense red color could store heat, so that a ruby placed in cold water could bring the water to a boil.[3] Of course this was a fiction, despite one mystic's claim that under "modern testing," rubies have been found to give off heat.[4] No proof for this statement is cited—perhaps for the good reason that none is possible. Another mystic says that ruby held in the left hand gives off "short, intense bursts of stored heat and red energy," which are apparently not felt if the stone is held in the right hand.[5] It hardly matters, since the effect is wholly subjective. Try testing it with a blindfold.

Another favorite centuries-old myth was that rubies can give off their own light, instead of simply refracting and reflecting light that strikes them. It was said that Pegu, king of southern Burma, lighted his whole city with rubies that flared as brightly as torches.[6] The Christian writer Epiphanius declared that a "carbuncle" (ruby) could not be stolen, because its indomitable glow would shine even through the thief's clothing.[7] The fabulous ruby on top of the Temple of the Holy Grail was said to shine in the dark like a beacon. Despite all such myths, rubies will not glow in the dark unless they are exposed to ultraviolet radiation ("black light")—for they do fluoresce a bright, characteristic red.

Star rubies, with their six-rayed moving lights, were regarded as love stones in Europe where six was the traditional number of Venus.[8] Primitive people often regard star stones with awe. They say that any stone with moving lights (actually, moving reflections) is the residence of a spirit.

Many myths surrounded the mining and marketing of rubies, as will happen with any mineral generally considered valuable. Rubies are found in many parts of the world, although one crystal mystic erroneously believes that true rubies come only from Ceylon, Burma, and Thailand; all others are spinels.[9] In many of the places where rubies were mined and sold, it was believed that they had to ripen like fruit into a rich red color. Pale ones were those that had been taken from the mine too soon, before they were ripe.[10]

Sometimes miners would steal rubies by inserting them into a cut made on the leg or arm, covered by a bandage. Perhaps it was this practice that engendered the Burmese belief that a ruby will confer invulnerability on its owner, provided it is inserted into the flesh and made a part of the body.[11]

The ruby's blood red gave rise to all kinds of healing lore associated with blood, the heart, body heat, energy, or elan vital. Ruby was said to be ruled by Mars, the red planet.[12] It would ward off plague, banish foolish thoughts, and make the wearer prudent.[13] It would guarantee marital happiness, cure toothaches, and guard against poison and the plots of enemies.[14] Rubbed on the face, it would preserve the freshness of youth.[15] Touched to the corners of a

house, garden, or vineyard, it would preserve the area from storms and worms.[16] In the thirteenth century, the Hebrew *Book of Wings* said that a ruby carved with the figure of a dragon would guarantee health, wealth, and happiness.[17] Rubies were to be worn on the left, "female" side of the body, which was associated with the heart's blood.[18]

Modern prescriptions are like the old ones. Ruby "worn as a broach [*sic*]" helps circulation and the free flow of blood, as well as "stabilizing" the eyes.[19] Ruby cures leukemia, plague, and "immune system problems."[20] Ruby "does have an affect [*sic*] on the heart in that it is a cleansing vibration for the blood."[21] It heals "cancers and blood diseases."[22] One mystic recommends ruby for blood, menstruation, birth, anemia, leukemia, AIDS, cancer, hemorrhage, and liver trouble.[23] Another says it can be used to establish telepathic communication with nature spirits. One can talk to them through the gemstone as if it were a mental microphone.[24] And, of course, it is a fairly safe bet that your brain will answer, because that is what brains do.

Beyond that, if you are fortunate enough to possess a good ruby, it may be sufficient to enjoy its warm color—for it is one of the reddest of all red stones—and remember the romance of its long, checkered history. The price of a virtuous woman, says the Bible, is far above rubies (Proverbs 31:10), but rubies have been able to buy nearly everything else. Even if your ruby won't cure leukemia, it may bring you joy.

1. Sinkankas, *M. A.*, 323. 2. Stern, 40. 3. Kunz, 101–102. 4. Bravo, 133. 5. Stein, 190. 6. Anderson, 74. 7. Rouse, 16. 8.

Thomson, 59. 9. Hodges, 21. 10. Stern, 40. 11. Kunz, 103. 12. Cunningham, 129. 13. Fernie, 2. 14. Thomson, 47–48. 15. Rutland, 164. 16. Fernie, 142. 17. Anderson, 147; Kunz, 133. 18. Rutland, 164. 19. Richardson et al., 107. 20. Parkinson, 135. 21. Bravo, 134. 22. Alper, 1/26–4. 23. Stein, 190. 24. Gurudas, 14.

RUTILE (Titanium Oxide)

Natural crystals of rutile are opaque, reddish brown to black, with a metallic luster. Rutile also occurs as shiny, elongated, needlelike or hairlike crystals included in other minerals, such as clear quartz. Rutilated quartz has been nicknamed such things as maiden hair, Venus hair stone, Cupid's arrows, or sagenite. Miscalling the rutile inclusions "natural needles of metallic fiber," one crystal mystic claims that they magnify and electrify the quartz energy and "detoxify" people addicted to drugs or cigarettes. Smoky quartz with rutile inclusions will encourage "strange dreams" and also balance the "etheric body centers," which seem to be perpetually out of balance.[1]

Rutilated quartz is common, and pretty, and inexpensive, all of which help to make it a popular New Age stone. It has been credited with many wonderful effects. It can quell fears and ease depression, and it even "helps reverse aging."[2] The ubiquitous extenuating word "helps" naturally implies that something else does the actual work of reversing aging—but what this something else might be, no one has any notion in this world.

Rutile is the mineral that is added to synthetic ruby and sapphire (corundum) during crystal growth in order to create star stones. The effect is produced by .1–.3 percent of rutile in the melt. Asterism is the result of tiny crystals of aluminum titanate, aligned

in sheets at 60 degrees to each other throughout the material.[3]

Rutile has been synthesized in clear transparent crystals, to be cut and marketed as diamond substitutes. This synthetic material was popular in the 1940s and 1950s but has now been replaced by more satisfactory products. Brilliant-cut synthetic rutile has more fire than diamonds, owing to its very high dispersion, but the background color is always a bit yellowish, and the hardness is only moderate. Rutile gems were sold under such names as: Astryl, Capra, Diamothyst, Lusterite, Meredith, Rutania, Sapphirized titania, Star-tania, Tania-59, Titania Midnight stone, Ultimate, and Gava, Java, Johannes, Kenya, Kima, Kimberlite, Rainbow, Sierra, Tirum, Titan, or Zaba gem.[4] The synthetic process provided large, attractive gems at a reasonable cost, although the rutile was more expensive than more recent diamond substitutes like cubic zirconia.

Natural or synthetic, rutile is most assuredly *not* what a prominent crystal mystic says it is: "Rutile is clear rock crystal in which golden or reddish hairlike needles of titanium are present." Rutile is not rock crystal, clear or otherwise. What is being described here is rutilated quartz, and the "golden or reddish hairlike needles" are not titanium; they are rutile. The same source also claims that modern French doctors prescribe rutile (or rutilated quartz?) necklaces for bronchitis.[5] It seems unlikely that medical schools in France would sanction this prescription.

Rutilated "Venus hair stone" is an excellent gem for meditation on feminist themes, however. One can readily imagine the rutile needles to be hairs from the head of the Goddess. They are especially beautiful in sunlight. Nature seems to have sealed them into clear crystals just as old-world lovers used to wear each other's hairs sealed in lockets. To carry such a natural symbol of the Goddess can represent devotion to, and concern for, the welfare of our common Mother, Earth.

---

1. Stein, 179–180, 268. 2. Parkinson, 241. 3. O'Donoghue, *G. M. G.,* 117. 4. Nassau, *G. M. M.,* 213–214. 5. Uyldert, 105.

SAPPHIRE (Corundum: Aluminum Oxide)

Not only blue, but also white, green, violet, yellow, brown, orange, and pink gem corundum is called sapphire. Only the red has a special name, ruby. The word "sapphire" came from Persian *saffir,* Arabic *safir,* Greek *sapphiros,* meaning "beloved of Saturn."[1] Sapphire was the English translation of the biblical *sappur,* the substance of God's throne (Ezekiel 1:26). Jewish tradition said that the tablets of the law that God gave Moses were also made of sapphire. However, the biblical term really meant lapis lazuli. Ancient civilizations around the Mediterranean probably were not aware of corundum sapphire, but they did apply the word to lapis lazuli.[2]

According to Saint Jerome, the sapphire stone gains the goodwill of princes, liberates the captive, counteracts sorcery and enemy plots, and "actually assuages the wrath of God himself." Epiphanius said that powdered sapphire in milk will cure ulcers. Several authorities recommended sapphire to heal boils "with a single touch," sweeten the blood, stop fluxes, and heal sore eyes.[3] The inventory of Charles V included an oval sapphire from the Orient—probably this one was corundum—for curing eye troubles with its touch. Bartolomeus wrote that sapphires could work great wonders when in the hands of witches. Star sapphires were regarded as especially powerful and were known as Stones of Destiny.[4]

In the Orient, sapphires were thought so potent against poison that they could instantly kill venomous creatures. Persians claimed that sapphires were made of the last drops of *amrita,* the elixir of immortality, sometimes called the life-giving milk of the Goddess.[5] When Sir Richard Burton traveled in the East, he gained special attentions by allowing the natives to look at his star sapphire, because they believed that one look at such a stone would bring them good fortune.[6] Among Moslems, it was said that the magical and mysterious seal of Solomon was a sapphire.

Both churchmen and witches in medieval Europe believed that sapphire could confer powers of prophecy on its wearer.[7] Sapphire was advertised also as a charm against plague, poison, sorcery, smallpox, headache, and eye troubles. It was a love gift, able to turn pale if the lover was unfaithful.

In the twelfth century, Pope Innocent III ordered that all bishops' rings should contain this stone, which would enable churchmen to resist "inharmonious influences."[8] It was done, in obedience to the papal command, and Pope Gregory XV decreed sapphire rings for cardinals. Nevertheless, the orders seem to have been carried out with considerable dishonesty. Dr. Fernie visited a display of old ecclesiastical rings in the Victoria and Albert Museum and reported that "these finger jewels, though sacerdotal, were made most commonly in their day from some base metal, bronze, or brass-gilt, and not of gold. They are thick, clumsy, block-shaped, hump-backed Rings, furnished in several instances with mock Sapphires, of pretentious blue paste; or even simply of opaque glass. The shabby, pretentious grandeur of these adornments, associated of old with Cardinals, and other high dignitaries of the opulent Romish Church, is surprising."[9]

It is still being said in mystical circles that star sapphires attract love, and ordinary ones heal the eyes, stop nosebleeds, and keep their owners out of prison.[10] But, worn by "intemperate Taureans" (the new version of the unfaithful lover), sapphires will grow dull.[11]

Sapphire heals Alzheimer's disease, multiple sclerosis, dementia, fevers, burns, swellings, and inflammations. It also "stabilizes" the heart rate.[12] It treats depression, hyperactivity, and stress; "cleanses the aura"; and facilitates astral projection, psychokinesis, channeling, telepathy, and clairvoyance.[13]

Sapphire is said to have been used by Lemurians as a regulator of their higher and lower chakric forces, and also by Atlanteans to adjust the assimilation of proteins by the abdominal and intestinal "accords." A sapphire elixir, consisting of seven drops of water in which a star sapphire has lain, is recommended as a daily dose when one is fasting for one week each month, living on nothing but a daily quart of mango or papaya juice.[14] Wearers of sapphire are cautioned that the position of the stone on the body is of prime importance. As a ring, it sends out healing, but as a "heart stone or pendant," it draws destructive force to its wearer.[15]

Now sapphire is a lovely stone, which does not deserve to be mocked with concepts as silly as these. Moreover, as every modern lapidary knows, today's synthetic sapphire is just as lovely as any natural stone, and just as durable, and not at all like the old churchmen's "pretentious blue paste." In fact the twentieth-century achievement of synthetic corundum has not only greatly benefited the jewelry industry but contributed to many technological advances as well. It seems amazing that, when people may buy a good synthetic stone that nothing but a microscope and a highly trained eye can distinguish from nature's product, they will still insist on having a natural stone for more than a hundred times the price. But then, scales of value have never been reasonable and in the world of gemstones may be seen at their most erratic.

Colorless synthetic sapphire has been sold as a diamond substitute under such names as Brillite, Crown Jewels, Diamondette, Diamonflame, Emperor-lite, Gemette, Ledo Frozen Fire, Mr. Diamond, Thrilliant, Vega gem, Vesta gem, Walderite, and Zircolite.[16] Sapphire is not as "fiery" as diamond, but it is suitably hard and durable. The colored synthetic stones may be more satisfactory than white ones trying to masquerade as diamonds, for the colors are fine, clear, and bright, rivaling the best of the natural products at a mere fraction of the cost. Even the rare flame-colored sapphire called padparadschah ("lotus flower") is now readily available in synthetic form. And it is still a sapphire, despite the crystal mystic who insists on calling it "king topaz.[17]

1. Weinstein, 60. 2. Kunz, 104; Smith, 436.
3. Fernie, 96, 103–104, 110; Desautels,
G. K., 24. 4. Kunz, 105–107, 388. 5. Stern,
49. 6. Kunz, 106. 7. Rutland, 164.
8. Thomson, 58–59. 9. Fernie, 98–99.
10. Cunningham, 132. 11. Harold, 170.
12. Stein, 251. 13. Parkinson, 164–165.
14. Gurudas, 155, 162. 15. Richardson et
al., 111. 16. Nassau, *G. M. M.,* 210.
17. Uyldert, 116.

SARD (Silicon Dioxide)

According to a New Age source, the sard stone "came from a greater depth beneath the earth's crust than chalcedony, and subsequent earth-changes have caused this stone to vanish from the planet's surface."[1]

Not to worry; the sard stone has not vanished, and it *is* the same stone as chalcedony. Nothing has been lost but its old name. The reddish-brown chalcedony that used to be called sard is now called carnelian. Sometimes the term *sard* is used to describe chalcedony that has been artificially dyed a carnelian color.[2] There is no need to postulate improbable earth movements and the inexplicable disappearance of a whole class of minerals just to explain a small case of word obsolescence.

Nowadays, the term *sard* may be used also to describe a carnelian that is a little darker brown and a little more opaque than the usual carnelian color.[3]

1. Richardson et al., 27. 2. Schumann, 126.
3. Arem, 159.

SARDONYX (Silicon Dioxide)

Sardonyx is one of the layered forms of chalcedony, combining brownish red (sard) with black and/or white onyx.

According to the ninth-century bishop of Mainz, Hrabanus Maurus, the biblical sardonyx on the breastplate of the high priest showed the classic three colors of the Virgin-Mother-Crone trinity of the Goddess: white, red, and black. Sardonyx was a magic stone said to strengthen the intellect of its owner. "Worn often and consistently it eliminated stupidity."[1] It was also said to dispel tumors.[2]

The New Age sardonyx gives off an "antiseptic" vibration, protecting its owner from infections.[3] It "works well with the vertebrae, the thyroid, and the larynx," and also "balances the metabolism," which in New Age thought is always becoming unbalanced.[4] Sardonyx also cures cancer of the bone because it alleviates "cell disturbances" within the bone marrow. But the healers add the usual disclaimer: it will not work unless there is "conscious acceptance on the part of the one to be healed."[5] In other words, if the healing fails, it is the fault of the patient and not of the treatment.

In the real world, sardonyx has been a popular material for the cutting of cameos. A white layer can be carved into the desired figure, contrasting with the underlying darker background. Through the centuries, expert lapidaries have evolved many imaginative ways of using layered stones, sardonyx among them.

1. Anderson, 116, 135. 2. Fernie, 354.
3. Harold, 174. 4. Parkinson, 145.
5. Richardson & Huett, 113.

SCAPOLITE (Complex Sodium-Calcium Aluminosilicate)

Scapolite is not a single mineral but a series, ranging from marialite, the sodium-rich end member, to meionite, the calcium-rich end member. An intermediate form is called mizzonite. To make the nomenclature even more confusing, scapolite is sometimes called wernerite, after the German geologist A. G. Werner (1750–1817). Its formula is as complex and variable as its names, including assorted quantities of chlorine, potassium, carbonate, and sulfate; the many different forms that scapolite can take reflect this complexity. When it occurs in transparent crystals, it can serve as a gemstone. Specimens can be yellow, white, pink, violet, or grayish white, and may show chatoyant (cat's eye) varieties.

Scapolite is a good choice to represent a person of multiple interests, one who "wears many hats" and switches from one role to another fairly often. Different forms of scapolite could even symbolize different roles, as designated according to one's own taste. The many personalities of this mineral series can reflect different personalities one can identify within one's self, and pieces from the collection may be carried or worn accordingly. Gem scapolite can represent a person who, like an actor, readily puts on a different-colored character and later sheds it again.

Exposure to X rays or radium turns yellow scapolite an amethystine purple; later, the new color disappears. Naturally purple scapolite does not fade, however.[1]

---

1. Nassau, *G. E.*, 161.

SELENITE (Gypsum: Hydrous Calcium Sulfate)

Selenite is the transparent crystalline form of gypsum, which also appears in massive form as alabaster, as the fibrous "satin spar," or as the sand-filled rosettes known as desert roses. Gypsum is often used in plaster and cement. Selenite is a soft, fragile, splintery mineral, easily chipped and marred on the surface of the crystal, although specimens carefully preserved can be water-clear and shiny. Nevertheless, selenite is so soft (2 on the Mohs scale) that tiny dust particles in the air are enough to scratch and becloud its surface.

Because *selenite* means "moonstone"—even though selenite and moonstone are not the same, not even related—the mystics sometimes attribute various kinds of moon magic to this stone. It is often claimed that "ancient magicians" placed records of their knowledge into selenite crystals, which can replay the stored information directly into the modern mind. One mystic insists that selenite crystals can be used for telepathic communication because they record information, perhaps like mineral telephone-answering machines. Moreover, a selenite crystal will automatically record the details of a theft committed in its presence, so that the crystal can be "tuned into" later, to discover the criminal.[1] But the crystal's evidence probably would not stand up in court.

It is also said that the calcium content of selenite will heal broken bones and cure calcium-deficiency diseases like osteoporosis.[2] Oddly enough, this claim is not made for the same mineral under its other name, gypsum. What's in a name?

Selenite specimens come in a variety of shapes. The transparent material has a silvery quality that does evoke moonlight. Sometimes, selenite forms natural wands: long, smooth crystals that may be either straight or curved. The famous Cave of Swords in Mexico features selenite crystals up to five feet in length.

---

1. Raphaell, *C. E.*, 152. 2. Stein, 259.

SHATTUCKITE (Copper Hydroxyl Silicate)

Shattuckite is a rare mineral found at the Shattuck Mine in Bisbee, Arizona. It is perhaps the rarity of this mineral that inspires the crystal mystic to credit it with truly astonishing powers, apparently secure in the confidence that few people will have an opportunity to check these claims. Therefore it is flatly stated (without a scrap of proof being offered) that shattuckite directly affects human genes, causing "increased cell division in each generation." Water into which shattuckite has been dipped has a powerful "impact" on the genetic code, and should be of interest to "those involved in genetic engineering research."[1] So far, however, researchers have shown a notable lack of interest in this mineral, not having any reason to believe in these alleged effects.

Even though devoid of any noticeable "impact" on the genes, shattuckite is prized by collectors for its rarity and its pretty sky blue color. It is one of Nature's mineral blossoms, an attractive surprise among her more ordinary rocks. Surely it needs no further recommendation than that in order to be appreciated.

---

1. Gurudas, 158.

SIDERITE (Iron Carbonate)

Siderite occurs in many shades of brown, from very pale to very dark, and in numerous forms: rhombohedral or saddle-shaped crystals, botryoidal, compact, granular or fibrous masses, occasionally in prismatic or scalenohedral (triangle-sided) shapes. It is not generally considered a handsome or decorative mineral, but it has been used as a magic one. The ancient Orphic poem *Lithica* describes the divinatory sphere of the Trojan soothsayer Helenus as a heavy, dark globe of siderite. The wizard treated his globe as a newborn infant, and made offerings to it until it took on a personality and became "a living soul."[1] Stones can be—and are—treated in much the same way today.

Another name for siderite is chalybite, from an ancient Greco-Roman term for iron or steel, derived from the Chalybes, an early tribe of northeastern Asia Minor noted as ironworkers. Possibly the legend of Helenus could be traced ultimately to the practices of Chalybean shaman-smiths.

In at least one place in the world, siderite has been found with crusts of tiny, sharp crystals showing a remarkable iridescence. That place is the Campbell Shaft in Bisbee, Arizona. Iridescent siderite from Bisbee is prized by collectors as a unique form. In some specimens, iron is replaced by manganese in varying proportions. At the other end of the series is manganese carbonate, rhodochrosite.

---

1. Kunz, 178.

SILVER (Element)

The ancients revered silver as the metal of the Moon Goddess, whose influence was protective. Even in patriarchal societies, it was said that silver bells and silver bullets repel or destroy evil spirits. Those who wear silver jewelry to bed—that is, during moon time—will have oracular dreams.[1] Women were told to pray not to the Christian God but to their own deity, the moon, turning a silver coin meanwhile. Even in biblical tradition, silver was considered an oracular metal sent from the moon. Joseph's silver cup of prophecy was an ancient symbol of the moon as a source of the waters of enlightenment (Genesis 44:5).

"Silver" comes from Old English *seolfor*. The silver mines of Joachimsthal in Bohemia were so rich that a mint was established there, to manufacture silver coins called *Joachimsthaler*. This was abbreviated to *thaler*, which became the English "dollar."[2] Silver was the common "dollar" medium of exchange, especially among the gypsies, whose injunction to "cross my palm with silver" at the start of a fortune-telling session is now a byword. Even today it is sometimes stipulated that silver be used "at the start of psychotherapy." It is also said that silver should be exposed to moonlight to arouse its powers.[3]

Medieval alchemists believed that they could make silver out of "a clear white quicksilver and a clean white sulfur," just as they believed that they could make gold out of the same combination, with yellow sulfur. They also believed in the medicinal properties of silver. They thought it would create "good blood," taking away putrid flesh or "evil scabbiness" from festering wounds.[4]

Metallic silver was prescribed in the nineteenth century for joint pains, hoarseness, and "irritative congestion of the windpipe," which could mean asthma, croup, bronchitis, cancer, or a simple sore-throat cold. *Animal Simples* stated in 1899 that epileptic fits would be prevented by wearing a silver ring made from a coin collected at a church communion, or else from nine coins donated by persons of the opposite sex to that of the sufferer.[5] The latter appears to be the pagan magic; the former, the Christianized version.

Lama Sing remarks in his incomparably impenetrable style that silver "improves somewhat the isolative quality and moves its primary range of influence to the second-third endocrinal center. . . . Is often denoted at the throat center and at the heart center. Affects somewhat the flow, the blood flow through the aortic, the valves."[6]

Today, when silver jewelry is commonplace and nearly every home possesses some kind of silverware, crystal mystics must be cautious in claiming too many occult powers for this metal. Sometimes it is stipulated that certain shapes made of silver have talismanic value, shapes such as pentacles, crescent moons, stars, or crosses. Silver is always an appreciated gift for rites of passage: christenings, weddings, birthdays, and anniversaries. Many people still remember its archaic associations with the moon.

---

1. Cunningham, 170. 2. Shaub, 162.
3. Gurudas, 159. 4. Medenbach & Wilk, 11.
5. Fernie, 403, 406. 6. *Gems, Stones and Metals*, 21.

SMITHSONITE (Zinc Carbonate)

Smithsonite was named after James Smithson (1765–1829), the founder of the Smithsonian Institution in Washington, D.C. It is an allochromatic mineral, which means that it can assume many different colors according to its content of other trace elements; that is, its own color is not its diagnostic. With traces of cadmium, smithsonite can be yellow;

with cobalt or manganese, pink or violet; with iron hydroxides, brown; with copper impurities, blue or green. Copper-bearing smithsonite approximates the color range of turquoise and is used as a turquoise imitation.

Smithsonite commonly occurs in mammillary (breastlike) or botryoidal (grapelike) masses, sometimes with brilliant color and an interesting silky surface. This mineral rewards study under magnification. Smithsonite is sometimes confused with hemimorphite, which can assume similar appearances and colors.[1]

An old name for smithsonite was bonamite, which has now lapsed from use but may be occasionally encountered.

---

1. Schumann, 198.

SMOKY QUARTZ
(Silicon Dioxide)

Smoky quartz is known as cairngorm or morion in Scotland, where it was a sacred stone from the time of the Druids. The royal Scottish scepter was tipped with a sphere of smoky quartz. Another such sphere, now in the British Museum, is reputed to have been the famous "shew stone" of Dr. Dee, astrologer, wizard, and court diviner to Queen Elizabeth I.[1]

The attractive gray-brown tints of smoky quartz are created by irradiation of quartz that contains tiny traces of aluminum (less than twenty parts per million). It makes no difference whether the material is exposed to natural earth radioactivity for a long time or to laboratory X rays or gamma rays for a short time; the result is the same. Conversely, when smoky quartz is heated to about 400 degrees Celsius, electrons displaced by the radiation can move back to their original positions, and the crystals become clear again. Their color can be changed back and forth, indefinitely, by alternate irradiation and heating.

Apparently unable to grasp this information, a crystal mystic presents instead a bizarre kindergarten notion that the quartz gets "suntanned" because it lies in rocks within twenty feet of the surface, where sunlight can reach it (actually, sunlight does not penetrate the ground at all), and if the tanned quartz is kept out of the sun, it will clear up in about ten million years.[2] If this person imagines that the sun's tanning rays can get through twenty feet of rock, few places are left where anything could be kept out of the sun, except perhaps in the deepest caves.

Another mystic says that smoky quartz has a high frequency vibration that removes "negative patterns" and "auric debris," although what sort of debris might exist in an aura must remain forever unexplained.[3] Smoky quartz is said to have an "impact" on the abdomen, kidneys, pancreas, and sexual organs, and to "augment" the adrenals.[4] The curative powers of this stone are described as limitless, "because it emits an ultrasonic frequency that creates tremendous healing."[5] Nevertheless, despite our abundance of highly sophisticated instruments for detecting ultrasonic frequencies, not one piece of smoky quartz has ever been caught in the act of emitting anything of the kind.

New Age fantasies aside, smoky quartz is a nice gem. Its strangely luminous gray-brown tinge is unmistakable, different from nearly all other mineral colors. Some people feel that the darker color lends smoky quartz more character than clear quartz, and therefore prefer it as a personal talisman. The range of available shades is wide, all the way from a slight, weak tea–colored off-white to a deep mink brown or almost black, and every level in between. Smoky quartz can be carved, faceted, polished en cabochon, or shaped into attractive ornaments. Some people claim to detect a difference between the color qualities of naturally and artificially irradiated smoky quartz, but every gemologist knows that they cannot be told apart, even by testing with instruments.[6]

1. Kunz, 181, 183, 190. 2. Rea, 328.
3. Raphaell, *C. E.,* 91. 4. Gurudas, 144.
5. Chocron, 40. 6. O'Donoghue, *G. M. G.,*
63.

SODALITE (Sodium Aluminum Chlorine Silicate)

Sodalite was not recognized by the ancients. Some crystal mystics even today seem unable to distinguish it from lapis lazuli, although its appearance is quite different—a darker, duller shade of blue—and its chemical composition is obviously not the same. Some who do recognize sodalite claim that it will heal diabetes, wounds, infections, headaches, high blood pressure, and sinus trouble.[1]

Still, there is little agreement. One writer says that sodalite cannot be considered useful for meditation or reflection, because it is "too dense."[2] Another says, "It is a fine meditation stone, and . . . . promotes wisdom."[3] One says that sodalite is "still in a process of evolution" and can only function on a low level; another says that it performs the fairly sophisticated feat of dispelling guilt, fear, and inner turmoil.[4]

While the mystics argue, others

may simply enjoy this handsome opaque navy blue stone, often spotted with white calcite and other inclusions, which makes interesting cabochons and ornamental pieces, and has about it a pleasant solidity and weight. Sodalite is tough, easy to cut, durable, and a favorite with lapidary hobbyists. Fortunately, it is also plentiful and fairly inexpensive. Strings of sodalite beads are very pretty, and readily available.

1. Stein, 250. 2. Chocron, 78.
3. Cunningham, 135. 4. Chocron,
78; Cunningham, 135.

SPHALERITE (Zinc Sulfide)

Sphalerite was named from Greek *sphaleros,* "deceiver," because its bright metallic luster and heavy weight made early miners think that it might contain useful iron, and they were disappointed. Its alternate name, blende, came from German *blendet und betrügt,* "that which blinds and deceives."[1] It was not until 1734 that sphalerite was found useful after all, as the principal source of zinc.

Sphalerite crystals can range through the reddish brown shades to nearly black and are sometimes found colorless, yellow, or pink. Crystals have a brilliant surface luster that can rival diamonds, but sphalerite has not anything like a diamond's hardness; it is only 3.5 to 4 on the Mohs scale. Nonetheless, sphalerite is sometimes faceted as a cabinet specimen for collectors.

Crystal mystics have not discovered sphalerite, so the stone remains as yet unburdened by nonsense and open to any impression that one may choose to consider when using it as an aid to meditation.

Black sphalerite has a special name. It is known as marmatite, after the locality Marmato, in Italy.[2]

---

1. Medenbach & Wilk, 30. 2. Arem, 176.

SPINEL (Magnesium Aluminum Oxide)

One of history's classic hoaxes is the famous Black Prince's ruby in the British crown, found to be not a ruby at all but a red spinel, valued by gemologists in the 1940s at about twenty dollars.[1] In India, where the name of spinel means "pomegranate," it was common practice to substitute the cheaper spinel for the more expensive ruby.[2] Much the same stories were told of both. Likewise, Camillus Leonardus wrote in 1502 that both spinel and ruby will cure liver diseases and prevent damage from thunderstorms and worms.[3] Certain New Age mystics seem unsure about the difference between the two stones and think *spinel* refers to a star ruby.[4]

One writer, doubly or triply confused, classifies spinel (along with zircon and topaz) as corundum, that is, aluminum oxide, then goes on to say that spinel "consists of crystallized pipe-clay and magnesium oxide (thus there is *no* aluminum in it."[5] It is odd, to say the least, that such a statement could be so decidedly expressed, and even italicized; for both corundum and spinel contain aluminum, and zircon and topaz cannot be classified with either.

It is said that spinel is " a powerful general cleanser," to be used during "detoxification," which means either fasting or taking an enema, or both. The writer warns that "sometimes nausea might develop."[6] Alternatively, spinel "works on the underside" of the solar plexus, and should be worn hanging on the chest, "about six inches down from the will center."[7] Before measuring, it is necessary to ascertain where the will center is. Alas, no guidelines are given. One can only guess.

Like diamond and fluorite, spinel can form perfect octahedrons. It also occurs in aggregates. Since 1920 there have been synthetic spinels; they can be made in many different colors to imitate other gemstones and often show better luster than the stones they are designed to imitate. Synthesis of spinel was discovered by accident during the addition of magnesium oxide to aluminum oxide in an effort to create better synthetic sapphires. The most common use of synthetic spinel today is to imitate aquamarine, for the synthetic material easily takes a pretty, soft aquamarine blue. It also appears in chrysoberyl yellow, morganite pink, sapphire blue, and diamond white. With fine clarity and a hardness of 8 on the Mohs scale, a synthetic spinel is no inconsiderable gem, and no apologies need be made for it. For every purpose that one might care to envision, it will do.

Nevertheless, synthetic spinel has received many fanciful names implying that it is a variety of some other stone: Aquagem, Emerada, Berylite, Perigem, Hope Sapphire, Brazilian emerald. Colorless synthetic spinel is used as a diamond substitute under such names as Alumag, Corundolite, Jourado diamond, Lustergem, Magalux, Radient, Strongite, and Wesselton Simulated Diamond.[8] For a long time, red spinel has been misleadingly called balas ruby. Such names are more or less acceptable in the gem trade, where their real meanings are known and only the uninitiated are fooled by the habit of labeling a stone with the name of some other stone. Of course, to fool the uninitiated is the whole idea.

Natural spinel is really a group of related minerals in which zinc, iron, or manganese substitute in various proportions for magnesium. Some of the other group members are gahnite, galaxite, hercynite, picotite, and the dark-colored ceylonite or pleonaste. Colors range from dark blues, greens, and reds to black. Lodestone (magnetite) is also a member of the spinel group. Strong magnetism appears in synthetic lithium-iron spinel, which is chemically similar to lodestone.[9]

1. Stern, 68. 2. Wodiska, 89. 3. Spencer, 161. 4. Harold, 181. 5. Uyldert, 112, 116. 6. Gurudas, 161. 7. Richardson et al., 132. 8. Nassau, *G. M. M.*, 211, 248. 9. Webster, 403.

STAUROLITE (Iron Aluminum Hydroxyl Silicate)

Staurolite is the mineral that forms the famous Fairy Crosses, or *piedra della croce* as the Italians say. Twinned intergrown crystals cross each other either at a sixty-degree angle, forming an *X,* or at a ninety-degree angle, forming a Greek cross. Staurolite twins have been used as talismans and good-luck charms for many centuries. According to one version of their legend, these cross stones were formed from the tears shed by the fairies when they learned of Christ's crucifixion.[1] In another version it is said that the fairies were not grieving for Christ but for themselves, foreseeing the downfall of their own ancient religion along with the conquest of their shrines by their Christian enemies. Alternatively, from the Christian viewpoint,

staurolite twins were interpreted as nature's reference to Christian symbolism, and were worn like amuletic crucifixes as protection charms.

Well-formed natural staurolite crosses with nearly perfect four-way symmetry are very rare. Of all the hundreds of thousands of lucky-charm Fairy Crosses that have been sold, a majority are fakes. The shape is easily carved in feldspar or some ordinary rock, so craftsmen have been supplying souvenir shops with imitation staurolite for many decades.

There is a blue cobalt-containing staurolite found in Africa. It has a different name: lusakite, from Lusaka, Zambia. A rare zinc-containing staurolite displays a color change from yellowish green in daylight to reddish brown in incandescent light.[2]

1. Kunz, 271. 2. Arem, 180.

STIBNITE (Antimony Sulfide)

Stibnite—not to be confused with stilbite—is the major ore of antimony. It is named from the Greek word for antimony, *stibium,* "that which marks," so called because it was used in ancient times as an eyebrow pencil.[1] The chemical symbol for antimony is still Sb, from the old name. Confusingly, the late Greek *antimonium* means "flower," referring to the ore, stibnite, not to elemental antimony.[2] Stibnite forms flowerlike radiating sprays of long, thin, silver gray acicular (needlelike) crystals. Japanese stibnite is especially famous for museum-quality groupings of crystals up to twenty inches long.[3]

Stibnite was used in the refining of gold and in the manufacture of *vitrium antimonii,* a glassy compound used as a

Agate (butterfly)   Courtesy of John Rudowski

Aquamarine

Amethyst

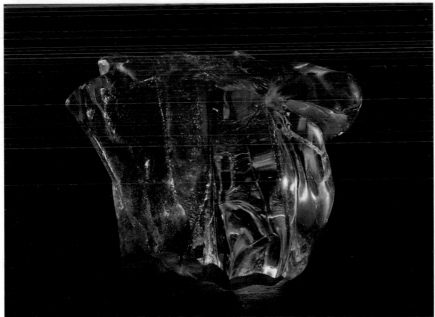

Amber   Courtesy of Schiffer Lapidary

Aventurine

Azurite

Atacamite

Benitoite in matrix.

Chalcanthite (home grown)

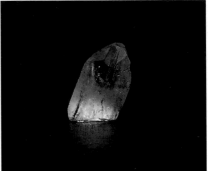

Brazilianite

Bloodstone

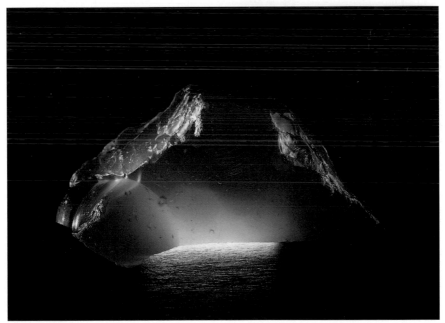

Carnelian

Chrysoprase

Cinnabar

Charoite

Chrysocolla

Courtesy of Schiffer Lapidary

Citrine

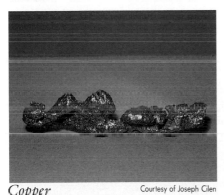

Copper   Courtesy of Joseph Cilen

Coral   Courtesy of Schiffer Lapidary

Crocoite

Dolomite

Emerald

Dioptase

Desert rose (barite)

Fluorite

Fire agate   Courtesy of Schiffer Lapidary

Garnet (hessonite)

Fire opal   Courtesy of Allan W. Eckert

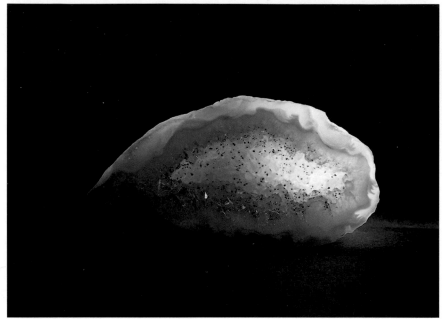

Geode

Hematite

Halite

Goldstone

Jade　　　　Courtesy of John Rudowski

Kaemmererite

Hiddenite　　　Courtesy of Allan W. Eckert

Jasper　　　　Courtesy of Schiffer Lapidary

Lepidolite (with tourmaline crystals)

Malachite

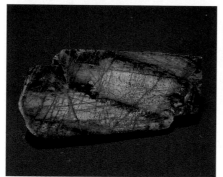

Labradorite

Lapis lazuli

Orpiment

Peridot

Opal

Paste

Rhodonite

Rose quartz

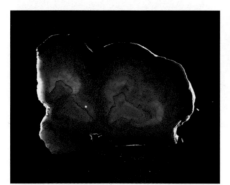

Rhodochrosite   Courtesy of John Rudowski

Prehnite

Smithsonite

Shattuckite

Ruby

Sodalite

Sugilite

Tanzanite   Courtesy of Joseph Cilen

Sulfur

Stichtite   Courtesy of Joseph Cilen

Tigereye

Thulite   Courtesy of Joseph Cllen

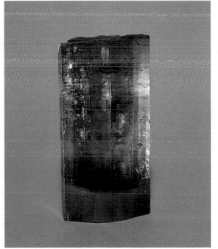

Tourmaline

Turquoise   Courtesy of Schiffer Lapidary

Zincite

Wulfenite

Willemite

Variscite

laxative and purgative. Nowadays, stibnite crystal clusters are appreciated by collectors.

1. Sinkankas, *M. A.,* 284. 2. Medenbach & Wilk, 42. 3. Sinkankas, *M. A.,* 305.

STICHTITE (Hydrous Magnesium Chromium Carbonate)

Stichtite was named after Robert Carl Sticht, an American mineralogist who became general manager of the Mt. Lyell Mining Company and figured prominently in the development of mining in Tasmania. The mineral has a characteristic greasy feel and a range of colors from bright rose-pink through magenta to gentle lavender or grayish purple. Although stichtite cannot be faceted, its attractive colors make it suitable material for cabochons, as well as a good collector's item.[1]

Stichtite is a decomposition product of chrome-bearing serpentine, a mineral group that includes chrysotile asbestos, antigorite, and lizardite.[2] Most members of this group have greenish colors. Sometimes, green serpentine, black chromite, and purple-pink stichtite are handsomely combined in a single specimen. Because stichtite is quite soft, it benefits by this combination with somewhat harder minerals.

1. Arem, 181. 2. Schumann, 202.

STILBITE (Hydrous Sodium Calcium Aluminum Silicate)

Stilbite is the "wheat-sheaf stone," so named because of its common habit of forming aggregates that swell at the ends and pinch in the middle, very like bound sheaves of wheat. Slender sheaves can resemble bow ties; large clusters can resemble heads of cauliflower. The name of stilbite comes from Greek *stilbein,* "to glitter."[1] It is also called desmine, from Greek *desme,* "a bundle."

Stilbite is a member of the zeolite group of tectosilicates (framework silicates), which are popular among collectors. Other common zeolites are heulandite, chabazite, analcime, natrolite, and mesolite. Zeolite minerals contain water in microscopic channels within their framework; but the water can be driven off by gentle heating of the crystals without causing a collapse of their structure. These minerals tend toward white or pale colors. Stilbite specimens, however, may range from pale yellowish or grayish shades through some dark reddish browns. Stilbite often forms handsome groupings with other minerals, yielding specimens that show several different kinds and colors of crystals in the same piece. Many collectors prize such combinations more than uniform samples of a single mineral, considering a variety of texture and shape especially interesting to the eye.

1. Sinkankas, *M. A.,* 467.

SUGILITE (Potassium Sodium Iron Lithium Silicate)

Sugilite is a newcomer in the world of New Age stones, and a practically overnight success, thanks to a great deal of publicity and promotion. It was first discovered in Japan in 1944 and named after the Japanese petrologist Kenichi Sugi. Later finds were made in India and in Africa at the Wessels mine in the Kalahari Desert near Hotazel, where the material was tentatively named wesselsite. An American jewelry designer bought a large quantity of this material and introduced it under the name Royal Lavulite at the Tucson Mineral Show in 1981. The next year, sugilite made another debut under the auspices of a California company who gave it the trademarked name Royal Azel, derived from its place of origin (Hot-azel). The "royal" referred to the mineral's rich magenta-purple color. "Lavulite" was supposed to suggest "lavender," but this name has been largely discontinued because it is too easily confused with lazurite, lazulite, and lava.

The complexity of nomenclature has dreadfully confused at least one crystal mystic, who calls the mineral either Royal Lazel or Luvulite, claiming that it can cure any disease, including cancer. "Luvulite is the chalis [sic] into which the holy grail is poured."[1] (Most of us thought the chalice was the grail itself, but never mind.) The same writer also says, "Luvulite is the male aspect of the purple ray as it ushers the intuitive knowing into the intellect."[2] Evidently this does not succeed, however, in teaching the intellect how to spell.

The mystics explain that there are good reasons why sugilite has been found so recently. One claims that "the discovery of the planet Pluto in our solar system in 1930 caused the discovery of Sugilite,"[3] although it may be difficult to understand how the two events might be connected. Another says that up to the present, "the human race has not been ready for the deep purple ray" that emanates from sugilite.[4] We don't know what this deep purple ray is going to do for us, or in what manner we suddenly became ready for it; but here it undeniably is, and even small bits of it are being sold for very high prices.

One mystic rather tentatively suggests that sugilite "seems to facilitate psychic awareness when worn or carried."[5] Another prescribes it for autism, dyslexia, epilepsy, difficulties of vision or physical coordination, and "any malfunction of the motor nerve response."[6] Another says the stone will "cleanse toxic blood conditions" when pieces of it are placed on the groin, under the arms, along the collarbones, and over the liver and spleen.[7]

Sugilite has much to recommend it: beautiful color, firm texture, acceptable hardness (6.5–7.5), interesting bands and patterns in the opaque stones. Like most overnight stars, it will probably outlive the first flush of excessive popularity and find a more modest place in the mineral hierarchy as time goes on.

---

1. Raphaell, C. E., 122, 125. 2. Raphaell, C. H., 36. 3. Bravo, 262. 4. Raphaell, C. E., 121. 5. Cunningham, 138. 6. Gurudas, 151. 7. Raphaell, C. E., 124.

SULFUR (Element)

It is hard to believe that burning sulfur (brimstone) was used for centuries as a fuel and for purification of sickrooms, hospitals, charnel houses, or plague spots. Burning sulfur stinks, and it produces poisonous sulfur dioxide gas. Nonetheless, Homer's term for sulfur was "dispeller of the plague." Greeks called it *theion*, the god-given. A more accurate translation would be Goddess-given, for sulfur was sacred to Athene. *Brimstone* (sulfur) came from her alternate name, Brimo. The medieval alchemical symbol for sulfur was the same as Athene's sign. When alchemists tried to combine mercury and sulfur to make gold, this was called the marriage of Hermes

(Mercury) and Athene. Sulfur was not known to be an element until this was demonstrated in 1777 by Antoine Lavoisier.[1]

The original purificatory use of sulfur was based on the theory that evil spirits (such as the spirits of disease) would be repelled by its bad smell. Some remnants of this theory were still extant in the early twentieth century, when it was thought that ill-smelling asafetida bags hung around children's necks would protect them from colds and flu. Sometimes popular charms called for the wearing of chunks of sulfur in a red bag around the neck.[2] If the theory worked, it could have been by keeping other people—and their germs—at more than arm's length.

Because of the ancient association between the idea of sulfur and the idea of evil spirits, by the beginning of the Christian era the two were connected in popular notions about hell. Typically, hell was a place of fire and brimstone, that is, of heat and stench. Now it seemed that instead of being repelled by burning sulfur, demons had furnished their underworld home with it. Myths do not demand consistency. Since the early church had diabolized all forms of the pagan Goddess, nearly all her symbols and attributes reappeared at times in a new context of hellishness.

Native sulfur does not look very hellish. It is a bright, sunny yellow, varying somewhat in shade from lemon or butter color to a warm honey gold. Sulfur crystals are beautiful but fragile. They conduct heat so poorly that even the warmth of a hand can cause cracking or crumbling. Also, they may give off a faintly unpleasant odor, because small amounts of sulfur dioxide gas are generated by normal oxidation. Nevertheless, they are prized by collectors and provide a note of cheery, brilliant color among specimens of more sober hues.

---

1. Medenbach & Wilk, 20. 2. Cunningham, 139.

TANZANITE (Calcium Aluminum Hydroxyl Silicate)

The blue-violet gemstone tanzanite is now widely known, thanks to an intensive publicity campaign conducted by its promoters, Tiffany and Company, after its discovery in Tanzania in 1967. Advertised as an alternative to blue sapphire, tanzanite soon became almost as expensive as sapphire, though its brittleness and its inferior hardness (6 to 7 on the Mohs scale) make it unsuitable for heavy wear, as in a ring.

Tanzanite is a variety of zoisite. It can provide both transparent and chatoyant (cat's eye) stones. It is strongly pleochroic; that is, it can look blue when viewed from one direction, and violet or grayish blue when viewed from another.

What is not often mentioned about tanzanite is the fact that when mined, it is usually an unattractive brownish or yellowish material, requiring artificial heat treatment to suppress the yellow tones and bring out the blue.[1] This is done by heating the stone to about 800 to 900 degrees Fahrenheit.

Like any expensive gem, tanzanite is imitated. "There are glass imitations on the market; also doublets of glass with a tanzanite crown, or of two colorless synthetic spinels glued together with tanzanite-colored glue."[2]

It is recommended that tanzanite jewelry never be cleaned with the ultrasonic cleaners now commonly used by jewelers. It has low resistance to ultrasound and can be irreparably damaged by such treatment.

Despite its disadvantages, tanzanite is said to have "potent" healing abilities, in that it "strengthens the male genitals or the female cervix" and magically increases fertility.[3] However, most owners of tanzanite are satisfied simply to call it pretty.

1. Nassau, *G. M. M.*, 282. 2. Schumann, 160. 3. Parkinson, 244.

TEKTITE (Glass)

Tektites are the black or brownish, scarred and fused nodules of glassy material that, like moldavite, have been called outer-space stones. They have no trace of crystal structure. They are glass, but the temperatures required to melt them are about two hundred degrees higher than the temperature needed to fuse Pyrex glass.[1]

It is still not clear whether tektites originated as molten material from meteorites, or as terrestrial rock melted by the meteorites' impact. Their name comes from the Greek word for "molten." Some have varietal names. Tektites from Texas are bediasites; those from Borneo, billitonites; those from Australia, australites. Moldavite from Czechoslovakia is also considered a type of tektite.

Naturally, crystal mystics interpret the tektites as visitors from deep space, either devic spirits or messages of some kind. In fact they are very interesting-looking objects, suggesting all manner of imaginative ideas. The typical black tektite somewhat resembles a prune, and one may easily envision its pits and wrinkles as the result of encounters with particles of space dust. For some unaccountable reason, one writer describes as "brown tektites" the small obsidian nodules

nicknamed Apache tears, although their origin is unequivocally earthly and their appearance quite unlike that of a tektite.[2]

To hold a tektite in the hand is exciting, if one also holds the thought that it may have traveled to this particular place through extraterrestrial or even extragalactic space.

1. Sinkankas, *G. N. A.*, 492. 2. Uyldert, 106.

THULITE (Calcium Aluminum Hydroxyl Silicate)

Thulite is a manganese-bearing variety of zoisite, having only recently won acceptance as a gemstone. It commonly occurs in masses, colored pale candy pink to raspberry red. It was named for Thule, the old title of Scandinavia, where it was first found.

Thulite has been drawn into public awareness by its more heavily promoted sister minerals, the blue-violet gem tanzanite and the green ruby-bearing zoisite that is sometimes polished as an ornamental stone. The zoisite family covers an interesting range of colors. The green massive variety often includes black streaks of hornblende as well as splashes of deep red ruby (corundum), making attractive contrasts.

Thulite now serves as a lapidary material. Its dense sugary masses can be cut and polished for cabochons. Despite its close relationship to tanzanite (being chemically the same), it bears little resemblance to the latter, but on the basis of superficial appearance it may be confused with other pink minerals.

TIGEREYE (Silicon Dioxide, with Inclusions)

Tigereye is a silkily chatoyant stone with shimmering streaks of golden yellow to brown, which switch around according to the angle of the light, like the colors in watered silk. In some specimens, the predominant color is not golden but a dark gray-blue, in which case the material is called hawkeye.

This mineral is made of quartz enclosing many slender fibers of crocidolite, a variety of riebeckite, a sodium iron silicate. Riebeckite belongs to the same amphibole group that includes hornblende and the tremolite—actinolite series in which nephrite jade and asbestos are found. One crystal mystic falsely describes tigereye as a "fibrous form of massive quartz."[1]

On the basis of its name alone, apparently, tigereye is credited with the ability to improve the eyes and to augment one's powers of insight. It can give one "the power to see God in all material forms."[2] Meditating on a tigereye stone in sunlight is supposed to "enable one to look into both the past and the future."[3] Tigereye also aids the "absorption of silicon" into the body, one writer insists, although the body has no use for silicon and does not absorb it at all.[4] In fact, the body cannot absorb anything that is not soluble in water, and silicon is most definitely not soluble in water at ordinary temperatures.

It is also said that tigereye "transmits . . . the brown ray from an undiscovered source."[5] Not only the source is undiscovered, but so too is the brown ray, which has never been seen or heard of outside of this mystic's statement.

Nonsense aside, however, tigereye is a fascinating quartz variety and would probably cost enormous sums of money if it were not so fortuitously common. Polished as cabochons and pendants, it makes handsome jewelry. One can watch the sliding lights just beneath its surface for long stretches of time without wearying of the phenomenon, for it is another of Mother Nature's endlessly inventive aesthetic creations. It makes highly attractive crystal artifacts, such as spheres, eggs, beads, and tumble-polished shapes. It delights children as well as adults, and at least one piece of it is found in even the smallest and most modest mineral collection.

Polished tigereye is a wonderful symbol of cyclic reality, the alteration of light and dark in the world of nature and of time: day/night, summer/winter, seedtime/harvest, life/death, and so on. Like the famous Chinese yang-and-yin symbol, it shows darkness contained in the light, and light contained in the darkness. As one turns the stone to different angles, the bright stripes become dark, and the darker stripes mysteriously brighten, like watered silk, but in an even more complex and interesting way. Tigereye is so fascinating in its variability that, if it were rare, it might be more costly than the finest gems. Fortunately, it is common enough; but that should not be taken as a reason to undervalue its charm or its symbolic effectiveness.

1. Stein, 209. 2. Raphaell, C. H., 193.
3. Cunningham, 141. 4. Gurudas, 177.
5. Bravo, 229.

TIN (Element)

Elemental tin is not found in nature. Tin occurs in the form of ores, chiefly cassiterite (tin oxide), from which it must be smelted. One of the important economic reasons for the Roman invasion of Britain during Julius Caesar's time was that Bronze Age Rome was constantly hungry for tin to make its bronze, and Britain had rich tin mines. Tin was sacred to Rome's chief god, Jupiter, while copper—the other constituent of bronze—was sacred to the Goddess. Like lead, the metal of Saturn, tin was often used for divinatory procedures, such as melting a small amount and throwing it into cold water to take omens from the solidified shapes.

Among the Cornish, whose ancestors mined the local tin for well over two thousand years, it was said that a piece of tin placed in a tankful of ants, on a certain night of the moon's cycle, would turn into pure silver before morning.[1] The difficulty was that no one seemed to know which was the right night. The probable origin of this myth was an ancient poetic metaphor of the riches to be earned by selling tin to the military legions from empires in the south, which were sometimes described as *myrmidons,* or "ants."

Of course, tin was credited with other magic powers too. It was claimed that a disc of tin fastened to the forehead would cure headaches; fastened to the chest, it would cure tuberculosis. Powdered tin was fed to those who suffered from tapeworms and other intestinal parasites, although at least one doctor described the agonies endured by animals to whom this remedy was administered and advised against using it on humans.[2]

Tin is rarely mentioned by today's crystal mystics, who dislike the connotations suggested by its universal use in the tin can and other cheap

modern conveniences. Of course, the tin can is really an iron alloy with a tin coating thinner than paper, used only to discourage rusting of the metal beneath.

---

1. Cunningham, 172. 2. Fernie, 455–456.

TOPAZ (Aluminum Hydroxyl-Fluorine Silicate)

Topaz was named for the fabled Red Sea island Topasos, or Topazin, meaning "to seek," now identified with the island of St. John. But the original "topaz" from this island was probably peridot.[1]

Gem topaz can be greenish, like peridot, or it can be transparent white, or pale blue, or the golden-to-sherry warm yellow known as imperial topaz. It can also be turned a rosy pink by heating. People tend to think of topaz as typically yellow, but most topaz is colorless. Topaz is hard (8 on the Mohs scale) but has perfect cleavage across the crystals, which means that it readily separates into sharp slices. This tendency to cleave might account for the apocryphal story that the emperor Maximilian was strong enough to break topazes in his fingers.[2]

Saint Hildegard of Bingen claimed to cure "dimness of vision" by lightly touching the eyeball with topaz moistened in wine. A fifteenth-century Roman doctor claimed to cure the plague with a topaz that had belonged to two popes.[3] Precious stones were often touted as plague cures, because the persistence of the plague could be accounted for when the cure lay beyond the means of common people. Topaz was especially associated with the wealthy. A topaz engraved with a falcon was a popular charm to attract the goodwill of rich patrons.[4]

Topaz was often recommended as a "cooling" stone. Unlike ruby, which could bring cool water to a boil, topaz could instantly cool boiling water, according to Adamus Lonicerus in the seventeenth century. Therefore, it was also believed that topaz could cool the passions of the flesh, and extinguish "the carnal desire of lechery."[5] Like ruby, however, the topaz could make its own light. Even in the twentieth century, Dr. Fernie imagined that this stone "possesses a gift of inner radiance which can dispel darkness, just as the Carbuncle does." He also thought the topaz could stop bleeding, prevent baldness, and "through its fluorides" promote the health of teeth and bones.[6]

Topaz was prescribed, and in some circles is still prescribed, for a mind-boggling number of ailments. It treats adenoids, cough, croup, deafness, goiter, mumps, pancreatitis, obesity, quinsy, tonsillitis, whooping cough, hemorrhage, gout, poor circulation, calcium deficiency, tension headaches, insomnia, depression, lunacy, nightmares, arthritis, and "negative magic." It reverses the aging process.[7] It is even called a cure for death![8]

The "electrifying nature" of topaz "magnetizes our whole being," according to one mystic.[9] Topaz also "causes the cells within the head to be released," a remark that evokes a very strange mental picture.[10]

Topaz is called an electrical coagulant, stimulating blood, liver, kidneys, urinary tract, spleen, pancreas, eyes, and appetite.[11] It draws warmth and love. It prevents accidents and fires.[12] Associating gems on the basis of color, but seemingly ignorant of their composition, one writer states that "citrine and amber are a lower

vibration of topaz."[13] Another declares that topaz "becomes strongly electric" upon the approach of a thunderstorm.[14] Of course it does no such thing; nor does any other gemstone.

Colorless topaz is one of the classic imitators of diamond, although it has less fire and looks generally less lively than a diamond. The crown jewels of Portugal boasted the so-called Braganza diamond of 1680 carats—until the royal gem was tested and found to be a topaz. Very large gems are sometimes cut from topaz. In the Smithsonian Institution, Washington, D.C., there are faceted blue topazes of several thousand carats.[15] Nature has been known to produce single crystals of topaz weighing more than two hundred pounds.

---

1. Stern, 58. 2. Fernie, 168. 3. Kunz, 389. 4. Anderson, 147. 5. Medenbach & Wilk, 198. 6. Fernie, 3, 163, 355. 7. Parkinson, 194; Cunningham, 141; Bravo, 226. 8. Stein, 278; Wodiska, 237. 9. Chocron, 62. 10. Richardson et al., 118. 11. Stein, 204–205. 12. Cunningham, 141. 13. Bravo, 83. 14. Uyldert, 119. 15. Schumann, 102.

TOURMALINE (Complex Borosilicate)

Tourmaline is pyroelectric: warmed, it develops a static charge that draws dust and other lightweight particles to its surface. Its original Sinhalese name, *turamali*, or "colored stone," meant also an attracter of ashes.[1] The Dutch called tourmaline *aschentrekker*, "ash-drawer," using it to draw ashes out of pipes. A Dutch legend said that some children found tourmaline pieces discarded by lapidaries and discovered that these pieces would attract ashes when the sun had warmed them.[2]

No other gemstone is so complex. Tourmaline varieties are dravite (brown, orange), uvite (dark brown, green), schorl (black, blue), buergerite (iridescent dark brown), elbaite and liddicoatite (multicolored), chromdravite (dark green), ferridravite (brown, green), and tsilaisite (yellow, brown). Tourmaline has over a hundred colors. Some popular names for color varieties are: rubellite (pink, red), indicolite (blue), siberite (violet), verdelite (green), achroite (colorless), and watermelon, the variety with a pink core surrounded by a skin of white and an outer covering of green. Colors can change abruptly at different levels in the same crystal. Most gem tourmaline is elbaite, named for its discovery on the isle of Elba. Crystals are typically long, three-sided in cross-section, and heavily striated lengthwise. These striations have inspired a crystal mystic to talk about the highly charged electrical current moving swiftly along the striations of a tourmaline crystal.[3]

But don't worry; there is no such current. You can handle tourmaline without risking a shock. Despite its pyroelectric and piezoelectric properties, tourmaline is a nonconductor and will not transmit electric current. Mystics don't seem to know the difference between static charge and current flowing through a medium. To them, any kind of electricity may be indistinguishable from every other kind. Iron-rich tourmalines, such as schorl, usually lack even pyroelectric abilities.

There are no long-standing mystical or magical traditions concerning tourmaline in Europe, because it was unknown to Europeans until Dutch traders brought some stones from the East in 1703. When first recognized in eighteenth-century Western literature, tourmaline was declared a stone of the Muses, inspiring and enriching the mind.[4] It was characterized as a lucky charm for artists, writers, and actors.[5] By Victorian times, it had become a popular gemstone.[6]

Nowadays this complex and variable mineral has aroused some crystal mystics to some of their highest flights of fancy, sometimes literally leaving the earth behind. It is claimed that tourmaline was not originally indigenous to this planet but was materialized here by "higher life forms." It is still being created as magic wands in secret "alchemical laboratories deep in the Andes in South America," whence it is dematerialized, transported, and rematerialized into the rocks of the mines.[7] One writer, perhaps unduly influenced by *Star Trek,* declares that blue tourmaline transmits "a multi-ray from the yet undiscovered planet named Vulcan."[8] Another declares that this ray is a "blue ray of peace," good at curing chronic sore throats, speech impediments, and thyroid problems.[9] Another states (erroneously) that tourmaline was "once called the 'Christ Stone'" because of its "etheric" abilities.[10]

Watermelon tourmaline is particularly admired. It is "used for healing projections working directly with the devic builders of form on the inner planes. This presents a picture of an element that is able to work with the unification of matter before it becomes matter. The watermelon variety has the ability to aid in altering cellular structure."[11] It also balances metabolism and acts as "a general harmonizer."[12]

Green tourmaline "has the quality of calming and balancing the brain and nerve fluids," the ductless gland system, and the immune system.[13] Black tourmaline "grounds and deflects" that perennial New Age bugaboo, negativity. It also treats *both* diarrhea and constipation.[14] The influence of tourmaline on the intestinal tract is said to be so powerful that it must be employed with caution. Some mystics claim that black tourmaline causes constipation, green causes "a churning effect," yellow causes "smooth flowing." Moreover, no tourmaline of any color whatsoever should be worn "on the body."[15] Wearing tourmaline can "lead to over-stimulation of the bowels."[16]

Tourmaline reduces fever and high blood pressure, combats colds and flu, calms the nerves, cures exhaustion, and "balances the rational and creative mind."[17] Tourmaline influences the nervous system "because of its tremendous electrical nature."[18] Tourmaline not only protects one against "negativity" and "the earth's radiation," it also treats cancer.[19] How unfortunate it is that the medical profession has not yet discovered this panacea!

Even the mystical imagination is uncomfortably strained by the common occurrence of tourmalinated quartz—that is, quartz containing inclusions of many small tourmaline crystals, usually schorl. Tourmalinated quartz is often tumbled or polished as a gemstone, but the task of combining the alleged magical properties of both these miracle minerals into a single expression seems to defeat the mystics' powers. Therefore, this particular mineral entity is generally ignored.

Although tourmaline is often faceted and set into jewelry, it is more interesting in its natural crystal forms, because they are so different from the forms of other gem crystals. Once cut, tourmaline is just another transparent colored stone. But left in its natural shape, it is a unique individual with an unmistakable style all its own. The Europeans who first looked at tourmaline and decided to call it a talisman of creativity may have been close to the mark, after all. It is a stone that dares to be different. Those who find this idea inspiring may find that the tourmaline will become a special favorite.

1. Fisher, 89. 2. Wodiska, 166. 3. Raphaell, *C. E.*, 126. 4. Stern, 55. 5. Thomson, 53. 6. Medenbach & Wilk, 182. 7. Raphaell, *C. E.*, 127–129. 8. Bravo, 56. 9. Raphaell, *C. H.*, 187–188. 10. Rea, 331. 11. Lorusso & Glick, 84. 12. Stein, 228. 13. Chocron, 71; Parkinson, 187. 14. Stein, 181. 15. Richardson et al., 121–122. 16. Harold, 175. 17. Stein, 229. 18. Chocron, 64. 19. Gurudas, 165–166.

TURQUOISE (Hydrous Copper Aluminum Phosphate)

Turquoise means "Turkish stone." The Turks called it *fayruz,* the lucky stone. The Tibetans called it *gyu,* the same as Chinese *yu,* "jade." Apache Indians called it *duklij,* meaning either a green or a blue stone; like the ancient Greeks, they did not distinguish these colors from each other.[1] Turquoise was the primary holy stone of the tribes of the southwestern United States. Every Navajo Indian used to carry a personal turquoise. It was believed that turquoise thrown into a river would bring rain.[2] Pieces were set in door lintels to guard against evil spirits. Powdered turquoise was mixed with corn meal as a thank offering to the gods. Because of its spiritual value, many Indian tribes used turquoise as a common medium of exchange.[3]

Hindus believed that it is very lucky to look at a turquoise immediately after looking at a new moon. In Persia, this belief was slightly altered: it is very lucky to see the reflection of the new moon in a turquoise. After the advent of Islam, people began to say that the luck came from seeing the reflection of the new moon either in the eyes of a friend or in a copy of the Koran.[4]

Middle Eastern tradition insisted that the turquoise would guard against accidents, specifically those caused by falling.[5] Turquoise was used as a horse amulet, to prevent horses or their riders from falling down. Europeans copied the tradition to some extent, allowing that, while a fall might occur, a wearer of turquoise would never suffer any broken limbs. Emperor Charles V's court jester made a famous joke on the subject: "If you should happen to fall from a high tower whilst you were wearing a turquoise on your finger, the turquoise would remain unbroken."[6]

Arabians thought the turquoise would warn of approaching danger by changing color. It is true that the color of some turquoise is easily disturbed by heat, sunlight, moisture, dryness, oil, perspiration, or simply by washing the hands while wearing a turquoise ring.[7] The basic color is variable, also. Turquoise may be any shade between blue and green, the blue contributed by the copper content and the green by traces of ferric iron.[8]

Dr. Fernie thought the phosphates in turquoise might serve to "confer fresh brain-powers."[9] But if exposing the skin to some kind of phosphate were all that is needed for development of a powerful brain, then surely our most intelligent individuals would be those who routinely handle fertilizers.

Turquoise occurs in cryptocrystalline nodules, not in obvious crystals. To the lasting regret of mineralogists, a misguided Virginia copper miner found the world's first known fully crystallized turquoise and burned it away by trying to smelt copper from it.[10]

The New Age also has been careless in its treatment of turquoise. Among some of the more careless statements, it is said that something very like turquoise "exists now in the physical planet Venus," and that turquoise is most useful to "older souls" who experienced it in previous incarnations in Atlantis.[11] Lama Sing says that turquoise is "most widely known" (to whom? one wonders) for its ability to "affect somewhat drosses and to stimulate vibronic forces which can eliminate drosses which occlude or block the duet [sic] or bursa function, somewhat increasing lacteal flow, and to an extent eliminating some dioxide saturation in muscle tissue."[12]

Or again, it is said that turquoise is a profound master healer and will "relieve excessive mucous [sic] in the body."[13] It also attracts new friends and lovers, money, and happiness; guards against accidents, poison, violence, migraines, snakes, and all diseases.[14] Moreover, it "carries knowledge and wisdom of all the ages."[15] It is unfortunate that the people who write such things have not seen fit to provide themselves with a little more knowledge of turquoise.

Turquoise is very widely imitated. Plastics and ceramics can be made to resemble turquoise. Howlite, a white porcelain-like mineral often showing dark veins, is easily dyed turquoise blue and sold to unsuspecting buyers as turquoise. Turquoise is imitated by stained ivory, calcite, marble, glass, porcelain, polystyrene resins, and pressed turquoise powder. "Bone turquoise" is not turquoise at all. It consists of fossil teeth or bones colored blue with vivianite. Its proper name is odontolite ("tooth stone"). "Viennese turquoise" is a false name for aluminum phosphate colored by copper oleate and pressed. Another turquoiselike mixture known as Neolith is copper phosphate and bayerite.[16]

Even natural turquoise is extensively cosmetized. Nowadays, nearly all turquoise is "color-stabilized" by impregnation with wax, plastic, or sodium silicate, often with dye added to enhance the color.[17] Because some specimens begin to lose color when they are taken from the mine and exposed to light, dealers keep them embedded in moist soil until they are sold. Other specimens may look solid but will soon begin to craze, crack, and fall to pieces. The buyer of turquoise needs to be blessed with a little luck and a lot of experience.

In addition to the outright imitations, two other minerals have been found that closely resemble turquoise and may be sold under the name turquoise. One is the zinc analog of turquoise, called faustite. The other is blue prosopite. This material is usually white or gray, but a blue variety has been discovered in Mexico that looks enough like turquoise to fool anyone but an expert with testing instruments.[18]

An ancient Egyptian name for turquoise was *majkat,* which early translations rendered "malachite." This may account for the dearth of reference to turquoise per se in Egyptian manuscripts, although the mineral was prized in Egypt. A very old turquoise mine at Serabit el Khadim was near

the temple of Hathor, called Goddess of Turquoise.[19] The stone was sacred to her, just as copper was sacred to her Cyprian counterpart, Aphrodite. Navajo Indians similarly revered the holy turquoise heart of Mother Earth. Zuni legend says the sky is blue because of light reflected from her divine Turquoise Mountain.

1. Webster, 80; Kunz, 113. 2. Axon, 129. 3. Sinkankas, *G. N. A.,* 208. 4. Kunz, 111, 345. 5. Wodiska, 237. 6. Kunz, 24, 109. 7. Smith, 439. 8. Stern, 61. 9. Fernie, 19. 10. Sinkankas, *G. N. A.,* 213. 11. Lorusso & Glick, 88. 12. *Gems, Stones and Metals,* 24. 13. Gurudas, 167, 192. 14. Cunningham, 143–144. 15. Bravo, 190. 16. O'Donoghue, *G. M. G.,* 183. 17. Nassau, *G. M. M.,* 284. 18. Arem, 152, 195. 19. Webster, 244–245.

ULEXITE (Hydrous Sodium Calcium Borate)

Ulexite is an interesting mineral that occurs in silky white "hairs," or slender fibers, typically in loose masses known as cotton balls. Fragments of ulexite are commonly sold at mineral shows under the name of "television stone." The material has earned this name because of its peculiar fiber-optic property; it transmits light along the length of the parallel fibers. Therefore, when a piece of ulexite is sliced across the grain and placed on a printed page, the printing underneath the stone appears clearly on its *upper* surface.

Ulexite is one of the evaporate minerals, like borax, and must be protected from moisture. Hot water will dissolve it. Although its silky chatoyancy has encouraged cutting of this material to imitate a cat's eye gem, such a vulnerable gem is doomed to a short life, even when protected under plastic in a triplet.[1] Ulexite spheres and other ornamental artifacts are soon

covered with whitish powder of
efflorescence.[2]

1. Nassau, *G. E.*, 76. 2. Sinkankas, *M. A.*,
384.

VANADINITE (Lead Chlorovanadate)

Vanadium and its ore, vanadinite, were
named by the Swedish chemist Nils
Sefström in 1830 in honor of the
Norse Goddess Freya, whose ancient
title was Vanadís, "Matriarch of the
Vanir."[1] In Norse mythology, the
Vanir were the old gods who preceded
the warlike patriarchal gods of Asgard,
Odin and his followers. The Vanir
were peace-loving agricultural deities
devoted to the principles of matriarchy
and to the Great Goddess, who
eventually became assimilated into the
new pantheon under the name of
Freya or Frigga.

Vanadinite is a warmly colored
mineral appearing in a variety of red,
red-orange, red-brown, and yellowish
shades, usually as crusts of small
hexagonal crystals. It is most
appreciated for its color, but it is also
rewarding to contemplate under
magnification that can reveal its
beauties of form.

Vanadinite also serves as a
secondary ore of lead.

1. Medenbach & Wilk, 144.

VARISCITE (Hydrous Aluminum Phosphate)

Variscite was named from Variscia, an
old term for the Vogtland district in
Germany, where the mineral was first
found. When variscite was discovered
in Utah, efforts were made to change
its name to Amatrice or Amatrix, for
"American matrix," but this term did

not catch on. A variety, however, is
still known as utahlite. Another
variety, in which iron substitutes for
the aluminum, is known as
strengite.[1]

Variscite is a fascinating mineral,
found in cryptocrystalline masses as a
rule, veined with other minerals such
as pale gray millisite or wardite,
developing concentric rings and "eyes"
in the same manner as malachite. The
basic colors of variscite are
yellow-greens through deeper greens to
blue-greens. Sometimes it is polished
and sold as a substitute for the more
expensive turquoise, which it may
resemble. But variscite has its own
kind of beauty and should not
masquerade as something else. Good
pieces, showing a rich variety of color
and pattern, are becoming rare and so
are all the more prized by their
fortunate owners.

1. Wodiska, 185; Sinkankas, *M. A.*, 409.

WAVELLITE (Hydrous Aluminum Phosphate)

Wavellite is one of the interesting
minerals that form natural
mandalas—that is, radiant circles—in
aggregates of needlelike crystals
springing outward from a common
center. These radiant clusters can occur
as flat, circular crusts or as
three-dimensional spheres and
hemispheres. Flat masses of wavellite
can cover matrix rock like a garment
printed with intricately overlapping
starburst patterns.

The colors of this mineral are
usually subdued, from off-white
through greens and browns. Radiating
crystals shine with a silky sheen, and
can resemble wheels spinning around,
when tilted against a light source.
Perhaps this resemblance gives

wavellite a connotation of travel, or of symbolic karmic wheels.

The mineral is named after its English discoverer, William Wavell, who died in 1829.

WILLEMITE (Zinc Silicate)

Named for King Willem I of the Netherlands (1772–1843), willemite has been found in large gem-quality crystals almost exclusively in the famous zinc mines of Franklin, New Jersey. Elsewhere it appears in crusts of microscopic crystals and in massive forms. Willemite may be colorless, yellow, reddish, or brown; but the characteristic color is yellow-green, with a spectacular chartreuse fluorescence under ultraviolet light. It is thought that trace amounts of manganese activate this fluorescence. Some specimens glow so vividly that their radiance is plainly seen even in broad daylight.

Transparent crystals of willemite, suitable for jewelry, are now very rare. Most collector's specimens are masses, but some are "gemmy" (containing small areas of transparency). Green willemite may be attractively marbled with black franklinite and white calcite, making handsome cabinet pieces. The much-admired "Christmas ore" combines brilliant green-fluorescent willemite with equally brilliant red-fluorescent calcite.

WITHERITE (Barium Carbonate)

Witherite is a relatively rare mineral named for the English mineralogist W. Withering (1741–1799). It is translucent, but dull in color, usually a pale yellowish gray or dirty white. It has interesting crystal forms, such as pseudohexagonal dipyramids and pseudohexagonal prisms. Held before a bright light, it displays fascinating wavelike surface markings and a strong internal glow, as if it would like to turn transparent if nature had not decreed otherwise.

Witherite is heavy because of its barium content. It is sometimes used as an ore of barium, although it seldom occurs in sufficient quantity to make mining worthwhile.

WULFENITE (Lead Molybdate)

Wulfenite has been nicknamed the butterscotch stone, because it appears typically in shiny tabular (flattened) crystals of a bright orange-yellow or honey-brown color, resembling butterscotch candies or caramels. Its name perpetuates that of an Austrian mineralogist, Franz Xavier von Wulfen (1728–1805), though butterscotch stone is a more descriptive and memorable designation. Being a compound of lead, wulfenite is heavy—seven times the weight of water. Despite its candylike appearance, it is most assuredly inedible.

Wulfenite is prized by collectors because its crystals make beautiful groupings and sometimes unexpected shapes; they are always rewarding to study under magnification. Wulfenite is too soft to serve as a gemstone, but a good specimen can be the "gem" of a collection. Famous and unusual specimens of wulfenite are fiery red crystals from the Red Cloud mine in Arizona, but the more familiar golden hues can provide handsome accents in any mineral display.

ZINCITE (Zinc Oxide)

Along with hematite, ruby, garnet, carnelian, and heliotrope jasper, zincite deserves to be called "bloodstone" because its deep red is very like the hue of blood. No significant quantity of zincite has been found anywhere in the world, however, except in one spot: the unique zinc deposits at Franklin, New Jersey. A few traces have been reported in Italy, Poland, Spain, and Australia, but these have been negligible. The Franklin mines produced astonishing numbers of minerals not to be found anywhere else, and zincite seems to be among them.

Large crystals of zincite are very rare, but a few have occurred, and some have been cut and faceted as gems.[1] Crusts of small crystals can resemble bloodstains on the underlying rocks. Zincite is not to be confused with commercial zinc oxide, which is created by oxidizing the vapors of boiling zinc metal, producing a brilliant white pigment often used in paints and glazes. Nature's zinc oxide is not white but red, perhaps owing to traces of manganese. This unusual mineral might well qualify as a symbolic blood of the earth and a reminder of the many mysteries as yet unsolved in ongoing human efforts to comprehend our home planet.

1. O'Donoghue, *E. M. G,* 93, 175.

ZIRCON (Zirconium Silicate)

Zircon is the radioactive gem. Many specimens contain radioactive thorium, uranium, or hafnium, which slowly destroys the crystal structure by bombardment with alpha particles. "High" zircon is still unaffected by radioactivity, whereas "low" zircon may have already become a metamict (decayed) mineral of dark, pitchy appearance and amorphous internal structure; and there are all stages in between. Heat treatment can sometimes restore low zircon to a crystalline state, but it will revert to its dark color. Gem-quality transparent zircon is obtained by heat treatment of the natural stones. Colorless zircon is called jargoon; flame-colored zircon is often called hyacinth. A dark reddish-brown variety known as cyrtolite is unequivocally radioactive.[1]

Some mystics say that zircon has no healing properties because it is "still evolving." Others insist that it treats the liver and stomach, stimulates dreams and astral projection, and acts as a wishing stone.[2] Alternatively, it "stimulates the appetite, aids digestion, and takes away sin."[3] Some say that its only effect is on the lungs, and zircon should be placed inside an iron lung "so that the outer light of the Universe could be transmitted through the stones onto the bare chest of the person within the lung."[4] An especially muddled source declares zircon "a gem of summer" and then lists it as a December birthstone.[5]

The black, amorphous low zircon might have been an element in the traditional zircon chastity test: someone who kisses a white zircon is revealed as unchaste if the stone turns black. Yellow zircon, however, attracts love and heightens sexuality. Red zircon heals injuries and soothes pain. Brown zircon—its usual natural color—is for "grounding."[6]

Colorless zircons served as cheaper substitutes for diamonds for many years, along with rhinestones (faceted quartz). Now zircons are valued as gems in their own right. Most of the zircon that is mined, however, is never converted into gems. Instead, it serves as an ore for zirconium, hafnium, and thorium. Because its crystals tend to look dull until they are cosmetically treated, natural zircon is not especially sought after. To be converted into a clear, sparkling gemstone, the naturally brown zircon is exposed to temperatures exceeding 1800 degrees Fahrenheit. The conversion is usually permanent, but if such heat-treated stones are exposed to radiation, they can revert to their original brown color. During the eighteenth and nineteenth centuries, colorless zircons were popularly termed Matara diamonds.[7] This name is still used occasionally.

1. Sinkankas, *M. A.*, 540. 2. Stein, 265. 3. Wodiska, 237. 4. Richardson et al., 127. 5. Parkinson, 220. 6. Cunningham, 145. 7. Webster, 153, 156.

Special for Knitters: How to Knit a Neck Pendant Crystal Pouch

Use your thinnest needles (size 1, or 0, or 00) and finest thread. Choose a pretty metallic, or silk, or crochet cotton, or embroidery floss, or even sewing thread. Another possibility is extra-fine braided nylon fishline, for a pouch that will never wear out.

Cast on 5 stitches.

Row 1 (wrong side)—Purl 1, * yarn over, purl 1; repeat from * .

Row 2—Knit across, working into the backs of all yarn-over loops so as to twist them and close up the holes.

Repeat these two rows twice more. The first increase row makes 9 stitches. The second increase row makes 17 stitches. The third increase row makes 33 stitches. Then work even in plain stockinette stitch (purl wrong side, knit right side) until the piece is long enough to cover your crystal, ending with a right-side row.

Eyelet row, wrong side—Purl 1, * yarn over, purl 2 together; repeat from * .

Next row—Knit, working into the fronts of all yarn-over loops so as to leave eyelet holes for threading a cord. Then knit 5 more rows (garter stitch) and bind off, leaving a long end to sew side seam. Sew down to the cast-on row, knot the two strands together, and fasten off on the inside.

For the cord, with matching thread and a small crochet hook, chain a length of about 24 inches, or enough to slip comfortably over the head. With a yarn needle, thread the cord through eyelet holes, center the pouch on the cord, and tie a loose half-square knot (slip knot) close to the pouch. Tie the extreme ends of the cord tightly together in a firm square knot (this will lie at the back of the neck). Insert crystal, and wear!

Variations: obviously, the number of stitches in this simple little bag can be increased at will, to accommodate larger stones that will not be worn around the neck. A fourth increase row worked like the others will make a total of 65 stitches; increases can be made more gradually by working only 4 or 8 or 12 increases evenly spaced every other row. Keep in mind that the total number of stitches must be a multiple of 4 plus one extra, so there will be an even number of eyelet holes.

To make a pouch for protection of a crystal sphere, egg, or other large piece, use *thick* yarn and small needles for maximum padding. Rug yarn, heavy cotton, or knitting worsted on size 1 or size 2 needles will make a protective "sweater" to keep your specimen safely pocketed during transportation or packing. Try out various types and weights of yarn, and have an assortment of the year's best-dressed stones!

Bibliography

Alper, Frank. *Exploring Atlantis*. 2 vols. Phoenix, AZ. Metaphysical Society, 1981.

Anderson, Frank J. *Riches of the Earth: Ornamental, Precious, and Semiprecious Stones*. New York: Windward, 1981.

Arem, Joel E. *Color Encyclopedia of Gemstones*. New York: Van Nostrand Reinhold, 1977.

Audubon Society Field Guide to North American Rocks and Minerals. New York: Knopf, 1978.

Axon, Gordon V. *The Wonderful World of Gems*. New York: Criterion Books, 1967.

Baer, Randall N., and Vicki V. Baer. *Windows of Light: Quartz Crystals and Self-Transformation*. New York: Harper and Row, 1984.

——. *The Crystal Connection: A Guidebook for Personal and Planetary Ascension*. New York: Harper & Row, 1987.

Bancroft, Peter. *The World's Finest Minerals and Crystals*. New York: Viking, 1973.

Bariand, Pierre. *World Treasury of Minerals in Color*. Geneva: Editions Minerva, 1976.

Bauer, Jaroslav. *A Field Guide in Color to Minerals, Rocks and Precious Stones*. London: Octopus Books, 1974.

Bell, Pat, and David Wright. *Rocks and Minerals*. New York: Macmillan, 1985.

Boegel, Hellmuth. *The Studio Handbook of Minerals*. New York: Viking, 1972.

Bonewitz, Ra. *Cosmic Crystals: Crystal Consciousness and the New Age*. Wellingborough, Northamptonshire: Turnstone Press, 1983.

Bravo, Brett. *Crystal Healing Secrets*. New York: Warner Books, 1988.

Brennan, Barbara Ann. *Hands of Light: A Guide to Healing Through the Human Energy Field*. New York: Bantam, 1987.

Bryant, Page. *Crystals and Their Use*. Albuquerque, NM: Sun Publishing, 1984.

Burbutis, Philip W. *Quartz Crystals for Healing and Meditation*. Tucson, AZ: Universarium Foundation, 1983.

Camp, John. *Magic, Myth and Medicine*. New York: Taplinger, 1974.

Chambers's Mineralogical Dictionary. New York: Chemical Publishing, 1945.

Chocron, Daya Sarai. *Healing with Crystals and Gemstones*. York Beach, ME: Weiser, 1986.

Clark, Andrew. *Rocks and Minerals*. New York: Exeter Books, 1984.

Court, Arthur, and Ian Campbell. *Minerals: Nature's Fabulous Jewels*. New York: Harry N. Abrams, 1974.

Cunningham, Scott. *Cunningham's Encyclopedia of Crystal, Gem and Metal Magic*. St. Paul, MN: Llewellyn, 1988.

Dake, H. C., Frank L. Fleener, and Ben Hur Wilson. *Quartz Family Minerals*. New York: McGraw-Hill, 1938.

de Camp, L. Sprague. *Lost Continents: The Atlantis Theme*. New York: Dover, 1970.

Deeson, A. F. L. *The Collector's Encyclopedia of Rocks and Minerals*. New York: Clarkson N. Potter, 1973.

De Michele, Vincenzo. *The World of Minerals*. New York: World Publishing, 1972.

Desautels, Paul E. *The Mineral Kingdom*. New York: Grosset & Dunlap, 1968.

———. *Rocks and Minerals*. New York: Grosset & Dunlap, 1974.

———. *The Gem Kingdom*. New York: Random House, n.d.

English, George Letchworth, and David E. Jenson. *Getting Acquainted with Minerals*. New York: McGraw-Hill, 1958.

Fernie, William T., M.D. *The Occult and Curative Powers of Precious Stones*. San Francisco: Harper & Row, 1973.

Fisher, P. J. *The Science of Gems*. New York: Scribner's, 1966.

Flammonde, Paris. *The Mystic Healers*. New York: Stein & Day, 1974.

Gait, Robert I. *Exploring Minerals and Crystals*. Toronto: McGraw-Hill Ryerson, 1972.

Galanopoulos, A. G., and Edward Bacon. *Atlantis: The Truth Behind the Legend*. New York: Bobbs-Merrill, 1969.

Gems, Stones, and Metals for Healing and Attunement: A Survey of Psychic Readings. Heritage Publications, 1977.

Gurudas (channeled through Kevin Ryerson). *Gem Elixirs and Vibrational Healing*. Boulder, CO: Cassandra Press, 1985.

Harold, Edmund. *Focus on Crystals*. New York: Ballantine Books, 1986.

Hay, John. *Kernels of Energy, Bones of Earth: The Rock in Chinese Art*. New York: China House Gallery, 1985.

Hodges, Doris M. *Healing Stones*. Perry, IO: Pyramid, 1961.

Holbrook, Stewart H. *The Golden Age of Quackery*. New York: Macmillan, 1959.

Holden, Alan, and Phylis Morrison. *Crystals and Crystal Growing*. Cambridge, MA: MIT Press, 1982.

Hurlbut, Cornelius S., Jr. *Minerals and Man*. New York: Random House, n.d.

Hutton, Helen. *Practical Gemstone Craft*. New York: Viking, 1972.

Jones, Robert W., Jr. *Nature's Hidden Rainbows: The Fluorescent Minerals of Franklin, New Jersey*. San Gabriel, CA: Ultra-Violet Products, 1964.

Kunz, George Frederick. *The Curious Lore of Precious Stones*. Philadelphia: Lippincott, 1913.

Lorusso, Julia, and Joel Glick. *Healing Stoned: The Therapeutic Use of Gems and Minerals*. Albuquerque, NM: Brotherhood of Life, 1985.

Lucas, Randolph, ed. *The Illustrated Encyclopedia of Minerals and Rocks*. London: Octopus Books, 1977.

Medenbach, Olaf, and Harry Wilk. *The Magic of Minerals*. Berlin: Springer-Verlag, 1985.

Metz, Rudolph. *Precious Stones and Other Crystals*. New York: Viking, 1965.

Nassau, Kurt. *Gems Made by Man*. Radnor, PA: Chilton, 1980.

———. *Gemstone Enhancement*. London: Butterworth's, 1984.

O'Donoghue, Michael. *A Guide to Man-Made Gemstones*. New York: Van Nostrand Reinhold, 1983.
———. *Quartz*. London: Butterworth's, 1987.
O'Donoghue, Michael, ed. *The Encyclopedia of Minerals and Gemstones*. New York: Crescent Books, 1983.
Parkinson, Cornelia M. *Gem Magic*. New York: Fawcett Columbine, 1988.
Pearl, Richard M. *1001 Questions Answered About the Mineral Kingdom*. New York: Dodd, Mead, 1960.
Pough, Frederick H. *A Field Guide to Rocks and Minerals*. Boston: Houghton Mifflin, 1960.
Randi, James. *Flim-Flam!* Buffalo, NY: Prometheus Books, 1982.
Raphaell, Katrina. *Crystal Enlightenment: The Transforming Properties of Crystals and Healing Stones*. New York: Aurora Press, 1985.
———. *Crystal Healing: The Therapeutic Application of Crystals and Stones*. New York: Aurora Press, 1987.
Rea, John D. *Patterns of the Whole. Vol. 1, Healing and Quartz Crystals*. Boulder, CO: Two Trees Publishing, 1986.
Rice, Patty C. *Amber: The Golden Gem of the Ages*. New York: Van Nostrand Reinhold, 1980.
Richardson, Wally, Jenny Richardson, and Leonora Huett. *The Spiritual Value of Gem Stones*. Marina del Rey, CA: DeVorss & Company, 1980.
Robinson, Lytle. *Edgar Cayce's Story of the Origin and Destiny of Man*. New York: Berkley Books, 1985.
Rogers, Cedric. *Rocks and Minerals*. London: Triune Books, 1973.
Rouse, John D. *Garnet*. London: Butterworth's, 1986.
Rutland, E. H. *An Introduction to the World's Gemstones*. New York: Doubleday, 1974.
Sanborn, William B. *Oddities of the Mineral World*. New York: Van Nostrand Reinhold, 1976.
Schumann, Walter. *Gemstones of the World*. New York: Sterling, 1977.
Scientific Properties and Occult Aspects of Twenty-two Gems, Stones, and Metals: A Comparative Study Based on the Edgar Cayce Readings. Virginia Beach, VA: A.R.E. Press, 1979.
Shaub, Benjamin M. *Treasures from the Earth: The World of Rocks and Minerals*. New York: Crown, 1975.
Shipley, Robert M. *Dictionary of Gems and Gemology*. Los Angeles: Gemological Institute of America, 1971.
Silbey, Uma. *The Complete Crystal Guidebook*. New York: Bantam, 1987.
Simon & Schuster's Guide to Gems and Precious Stones. New York: Simon & Schuster, 1986.
Simon & Schuster's Guide to Rocks and Minerals. New York: Simon & Schuster, 1977.
Sinkankas, John. *Gemstones of North America*. Princeton, NJ: D. Van Nostrand, 1959.
———. *Gemstones and Minerals: How and Where to Find Them*. Princeton, NJ: D. Van Nostrand, 1961.
———. *Mineralogy for Amateurs*. Princeton, NJ: D. Van Nostrand, 1964.
Smith, G. F. Herbert. *Gemstones*. New York: Pitman, 1958.
Sorrell, Charles A. *Rocks and Minerals*. New York: Golden Press, 1973.
Spence, Lewis. *The History of Atlantis*. New York: University Books, 1968.
Spencer, L. J. *A Key to Precious Stones*. New York: Emerson Books, 1959.

Stein, Diane. *The Women's Book of Healing*. St. Paul, MN: Llewellyn, 1987.

Stern, Max, and Company. *Gems: Facts, Fantasies, Superstitions, Legends*. New York: Max Stern and Company, 1946.

Tennissen, Anthony C. *Nature of Earth Materials*. Englewood Cliffs, NJ: Prentice-Hall, 1974.

Thomson, Horace L. *Legends of Gems*. Los Angeles: Graphic Press, 1937.

Uyldert, Mellie. *The Magic of Precious Stones*. Wellingborough, Northamptonshire: Turnstone Press, 1981.

Wade, Frank B. *A Text-Book of Precious Stones*. New York: Putnam's, 1918.

Webb, James. *The Harmonious Circle: The Lives and Works of G. I. Gurdjieff, P. D. Ouspensky, and Their Followers*. New York: Putnam's, 1980.

Webster, Robert. *Gems: Their Sources, Descriptions and Identification*. London: Butterworth's, 1983.

Weinstein, Michael. *The World of Jewel Stones*. New York: Sheridan House, 1958.

Whitlock, Herbert P. *The Story of the Gems*. New York: Emerson Books, 1963.

Wodiska, Julius. *A Book of Precious Stones*. New York: Putnam's, 1909.

Woolley, Alan, ed. *The Illustrated Encyclopedia of the Mineral Kingdom*. New York: Larousse, 1978.

Young, James Harvey. *The Medical Messiahs: A Social History of Health Quackery in Twentieth-Century America*. Princeton, NJ: Princeton University Press, 1967.

Zim, Herbert S., and Paul R. Shaffer. *Rocks and Minerals: A Guide to Familiar Minerals, Gems, Ores and Rocks*. New York: Golden Press, 1957.

Index

(Main entries appear in the index in all capital letters.)